D0394079

To Free a Family

To Free a Family

THE JOURNEY OF MARY WALKER

Sydney Nathans

Harvard University Press
Cambridge, Massachusetts
London, England
2012

Printed in the United States of America

Library of Congress Cataloging-in-Publication Data
Nathans, Sydney.
To free a family : the journey of Mary Walker / Sydney Nathans.
p. cm.
Includes bibliographical references and index.
ISBN 978-0-674-06212-2 (alk. paper)
1. Walker, Mary, d. 1872. 2. Walker, Mary, d. 1872—Family. 3. Fugitive slaves—Northeastern States—Biography. 4. Women slaves—North Carolina—Orange County—Biography. 5. African American women—Massachusetts—Cambridge—Biography. 6. Family reunions—Massachusetts—Cambridge—History—19th century. 7. Cambridge (Mass.)—Biography. 8. Orange County (N.C.)—Biography. I. Title.
E450.W322N37 2011
306.3′62092—dc23
[B] 2011023122

For

Judith, my light and my love

Bill and Lorna Chafe, friends of a lifetime

Mary Wolff, Ed Wolff, and Linda Cowan, who opened the way

Contents

To Free a Family

PROLOGUE

A Secret Striving

In September 1859, one of North Carolina's wealthiest women received an unsolicited letter. The carefully penned two-page letter to thirty-nine-year-old Mildred Cameron of Raleigh was written by a man she didn't know. He identified himself as J. P. Lesley, a professor of mining at the University of Pennsylvania. He wrote on behalf of "Mary Walker formerly in your family."

Mary Walker was Mildred Cameron's former slave.

> I have been lately touched to the heart with a case of heart breaking distress which you have it entirely in your power I find to cure. . . . I have come to know one Mary Walker formerly in your family, and I have seen how sick at heart she is about her mother and especially her two children.

Mary Walker had fled slavery eleven years before, alone.

> She has been herself in miserable health for some years and sometimes ready to die; but is now in her usual health, able to go about and do her daily work. . . . But with all this her heart is slowly breaking. She thinks of nothing but her children, and

> speaks of nothing else when she speaks of herself at all, which is very seldom. Her mother-heart yearns unspeakably after them.

The letter was an appeal—and an offer.

> She has saved a considerable sum of money to buy them, can command more from friends, and will sacrifice anything to see them once again and have their young lives renew the freshness of her own weary spirit. It is in this behalf that I address you,—to realize this hope of hers.

MARY WALKER WAS A fair-skinned fugitive slave woman who had escaped bondage in 1848, leaving her children and mother behind. Because of family ties, it was unusual for women to escape slavery, and exceptional for mothers to forsake their children. Mary Walker believed she had no choice—after a dispute with her owner, he had threatened to send her to the Deep South. Her options narrowed to *how* she would be separated from her family, rather than whether. For her and for thousands who fled, freedom came at a price: remorse at parting without a word, silence forced by the danger of disclosure, fear for her family's fate. One man, writing to the leader of the Underground Railroad in Philadelphia, gave voice to the pain felt by all who left family members in bondage. "My soul is vexed, my troubles inexpressible. I often feel as if I were willing to die. What is freedom to me, when I know that my wife is in slavery?"

Mary Walker's anxieties fueled an odyssey of a dozen years to recover her children. In the struggle to free her family, Mary Walker was not alone. The best-known of the women who escaped slavery knew no rest until they saw their relatives released. Like Mary Walker, Harriet Tubman, Harriet Jacobs, and Sojourner Truth each fled only when faced with an irrevocable change for the worse in their lives. Harriet Tubman sensed that her Maryland owner, mired in debt, would soon put her up for auction. Harriet Jacobs discovered that her North Carolina master planned to remove her children to a nearby plantation, where he could make them plantation slaves and punish her for refusing to become his concubine. Sojourner Truth, whose name in slavery was "Isabella," learned that the New York owner who'd promised her freedom meant to extend her bondage. Courage brought each woman to safety. But the fate of their families kept them in thrall. Harriet Tubman returned thirteen times to the eastern shore of Maryland to bring brothers, parents, and family friends to freedom. Harriet Jacobs escaped the snares of her owner, but remained for seven years in the cramped attic of her free black grandmother's home, until assured that her children were liberated. Sojourner Truth brought suit in a New York courthouse to reclaim the son sold to an Alabama planter. The triumphs of these women became the stuff of legend.

Mary Walker's experience was a more wrenching, more protracted, and probably more representative struggle than that of the trio of ex-slave women whose defiance made them heroines. A displaced person obliged to start a new life among strangers, Mary Walker had to learn whom to trust and how to survive. When she began the quest to reclaim her family, she turned to intermediaries, lest she reveal her location and risk recapture under the Fugitive Slave Law of 1850. Though many abolitionists renounced ransom or personal appeals to slaveholders as concessions to the crime of slavery, Mary Walker found friends who understood her anguish and who were willing to commit themselves to redeem her children. Together or separately, they ventured half a dozen attempts at liberation, from ransom to ruse to rescue.

To Free a Family is as much a story of the white couple who protected, employed, and assisted Mary Walker as it is of Mary Walker herself. Like many Northerners, Susan and Peter Lesley were sympathetic to the plight of the slave but reluctant to commit to an abolitionist crusade they saw as radical and divisive. First the Fugitive Slave Law of 1850, then Mary Walker and the cause of her children, transformed them. Their lives became intertwined with the public—as well as this very personal—struggle against slavery. Their deepening interracial friendship helped to offset the pain of endless waiting they all endured, waiting to see if word could be gotten to the slave-owners, or to Mary Walker's mother or children, that their mother was seeking their release.

Mary Walker's quest illuminates the secret strivings of thousands who sought to free family members still living behind the Cotton Curtain. For the refugees and those who helped them, theirs was a hidden epic of emancipation—the redemption of one family at a time—which paralleled the great social movement to end slavery altogether and preceded its ultimate triumph.

I WASN'T LOOKING FOR the letter about Mary Walker when I first came across it in a book entitled *The Black Family in Slavery and Freedom,* by the historian Herbert Gutman. What captivated me about Herbert Gutman's path-breaking book and equally about Alex Haley's *Roots,* both published in 1976, was the ingenuity of both authors in challenging the claim that slavery had destroyed African-American families. The two books led me to shift from work on nineteenth-century American political leaders to the social history of African Americans. I focused on enslaved people belonging to one family, the Cameron family of North Carolina. The state's wealthiest slave-holders, the Camerons had plantations in three states and owned a thousand workers. Using the vast collection of Cameron papers housed at the Southern Historical Collection at the University of North Carolina, and then oral interviews with descendants of their enslaved workers, I concentrated on the destiny of people sent from North Carolina to Alabama and Mississippi in the 1840s and 1850s. What was the impact of that forced western migration on black families? What happened to those people after Emancipation—and to their descendants in the twentieth century?

Yet I kept coming back to the 1859 letter, the most poignant document I'd ever read about a refugee from slavery. Who was J. P. Lesley, Professor of Mining, University of Pennsylvania—the author of the letter about Mary Walker? Where in the North did Mary Walker wind up? Did she ever get her children back? In Philadelphia, I went to the public library and discovered that it had the 1909 edition of the *Life and Letters of Peter and Susan Lesley,* two volumes containing more than a thousand pages of letters edited by the Lesleys' daughter Mary Lesley Ames. When I read the letters, I learned that Mary Walker had become an important part of the Lesleys' lives and had wound up in Cambridge, Massachusetts. In Cambridge, she had become the companion and caretaker of Susan Lesley's mother, Anne Jean Robbins Lyman. And yes, she had recovered her children. A "high-ranking official" with William Tecumseh Sherman's occupying army had found them in Raleigh in 1865; he had told them that their mother was living in Cambridge and that she wanted them to join her.

I put the story aside, but returned to it as I was ending a year of teaching and writing in Cambridge in 1989. During the month of May that year, I did nothing but research the story of Mary Walker—in census records, in manuscripts at Harvard's Houghton Library, in the deed records and wills of the Middlesex County Courthouse. The sources offered clues about what happened to Mary Walker, her children, and her grandchildren after 1865. The struggle to secure the freedom of her family had continued well after Emancipation, had entwined Mary Walker and the family of her antislavery friends for another generation, had brought the Walkers into possession of a famous Cambridge house, and finally had led to startling decisions by her descendants. A surprising cast of characters made cameo appearances—Ralph Waldo Emerson, Wendell Phillips, Lydia Maria Child,

Harriet Beecher Stowe, Frederick Douglass, Henry James, Henry Wadsworth Longfellow, even a future U.S. president. It became impossible to relinquish the story again.

A key question surfaced. Where were the rest of the letters of this family that had protected, employed, and spoken for Mary Walker? The trail led to Minnesota. Peter and Susan Lesley's daughter Mary—named to honor Mary Walker—had married in 1883 and the couple had moved to St. Paul. Her husband, Charles Ames, had gone on to found the West Publishing Company, and his family had become prominent in the civic and business life of the Twin Cities. I found that the Ames family was still listed in the Minneapolis–St. Paul telephone directory. So out went a letter to the Ames descendants, inquiring about whether there was a collection of papers that extended beyond those edited and published at the turn of the twentieth century. After some months came a response. There were indeed additional family papers in the Ames family home on Grand Avenue in St. Paul, but they were in trunks in an attic. A chance visit to Minneapolis–St. Paul in 1991 placed me within a block of the Minnesota State Archives. I disappeared into the archives for an hour, and discovered that the papers were out of the attic and being processed. A follow-up letter produced an invitation to come to their new digs at the home of family descendant Mary Wolff in Boulder, Colorado. Staying in the house, reading the papers in Mary and Ed Wolff's library almost around the clock, reporting at meals what I was learning, I found hundreds of letters and diary entries about Mary Walker. Perhaps the largest and richest collection of American family papers in private hands, the Ames Family Historical Collection in Boulder was a gold mine.

The Ames Family Historical Collection brought to life the intimate human relationship that emerged between an antislavery couple and a fugitive from slavery, even as they all defied a law that deemed Mary Walker and her protectors to be criminals. A sensitive and extraordinarily articulate pair, Susan and Peter Lesley were separated for months of the year by his fieldwork as a geologist, and so wrote frequent and detailed letters to each other. As the bond with Mary Walker deepened, as her trust in them became complete, the couple's letters focused ever more intently on what Mary Walker said and felt, on her desperate desire to recover her children, and on the Lesleys' decade-long efforts to help.

I supplemented the extraordinary Ames Family Collection in Boulder with three trips to Philadelphia to consult the J. Peter Lesley Papers housed at the library of the American Philosophical Society, where Peter Lesley served as secretary in the 1850s and 1860s, and with research in a dozen more manuscript collections of the Lesleys' antislavery friends. I returned to the Cameron Papers and related manuscripts at the Southern Historical Collection with a singular focus on Mary Walker. I immersed myself in social-history sources—city directories and city maps, birth and baptism and marriage records, even coroner's reports. For otherwise unattainable information about persons in this story, the digitized United States Manuscript Census, accessed through Ancestry.com, proved to be an extraordinary resource.

MARY WALKER WAS LITERATE and wrote many letters. But only three have thus far been found. Consequently, her story unfolds mostly through the accounts of her abolitionist friends, rather than in her own words. Sometimes the Lesleys or others in the family quoted her directly. Many other times they wrote observations about her, or reactions to what she was going through. A personal memoir or a large cache of her own letters would open a more transparent window onto Mary Walker's thoughts and would permit an unmediated rendering of her voice and vision. I have had to rely instead on accounts of her as seen through the lens of New Englanders of a different class and color, whose roles as her employers, protectors, and lifeline of hope for her family necessarily shaped their interactions. I try to provide enough of a portrait of Peter and Susan Lesley and of Mary Walker so that the reader can judge, without incessant asides from me, what their perspectives were, how roles shaped their relationships, and how they calibrated what they revealed and reported to each other. There were swings back and forth, between disclosure and withdrawal, openness and silence, confession and constraint. Nonetheless, by my lights, the relationship became one of deepening trust and candor. The reader must decide whether the evidence persuades.

AGAINST GREAT ODDS, MARY WALKER and the Lesleys, their allies and their descendants, strove to reunite Mary Walker and her children. Their struggle, their frustrations, and ultimately even their success revealed how long and how much it would take to free a family.

1 Reluctant Runaway

She was "a slender light coloured woman with dark straight hair and lightish eyes inclining to blue." They had their eyes on her from the first. When she arrived at a Philadelphia boardinghouse in June 1846, a block from Independence Hall, a waiter in the neighborhood took notice of her. Thin, her hair long and strikingly straight, she accompanied a seventy-year-old gentleman with white hair and two young women, his daughters, one unable to walk on her own. Mrs. Warden's place at Sansom and Seventh was known for hosting well-to-do visitors from the South. It was there that the woman was first seen by William Johnson, a twenty-six-year-old free black waiter who lived four blocks away from Mrs. Warden's, on Currant Alley. While running errands, the waiter repeatedly observed the twenty-eight-year-old woman. She was a "light colored woman, very light colored who could scarcely be distinguished from a white woman." He struck up her acquaintance. She "called herself Mary Walker."[1]

What he learned was that she'd been brought to Philadelphia from North Carolina by her owner to wait on his daughter, "who was sick." William Johnson and others had difficulty recalling the owner's name, Duncan Cameron. But they correctly learned that the man they mistakenly called "Judge Campbell" had once been a judge and had kept that title. The judge's family spent more than six weeks in the city in the summer of 1846. Johnson had "many opportunities of seeing . . . Mary Walker and Judge Campbell [Cameron] and his family" and encountered Mary Walker herself almost every day. From all the waiter saw and heard, the judge treated her as a free woman and "tried to create the impression that she was a free woman." William Johnson knew otherwise.[2]

The black waiter alerted others that an enslaved woman had been brought to Philadelphia. He made contact with a long-time black leader of the antislavery movement in the city, James McCrummill, who took Mary Walker under his watch. Born free in Virginia, James McCrummill had arrived in Philadelphia in his youth, had established himself as a barber with a largely white clientele, and had become a dentist as well. His activism coincided with the birth of the great antislavery movement of the 1830s. McCrummill had presided over Philadelphia's first interracial meetings; he had watched the building of the Antislavery Hall in 1838; he had cofounded the Philadelphia Vigilance Committee to help fugitive slaves find safety in Philadelphia or sanctuary farther north.[3]

In 1846, McCrummill responded cautiously to the news that an enslaved woman had been brought to town. Eight years before, he had witnessed the burning of the Antislavery Hall by a mob less than a week after its opening. Later the same year, the Pennsylvania legislature had disenfranchised the state's black voters. In 1842, rioters had attacked the homes of Philadelphia blacks high and low, with no police challenge. McCrummill's house was spared, but wealthy black comrade Robert Purvis, stunned by the rampage, was "convinced of our utter and complete nothingness in public estimation." Black unity dissipated, even on the one issue where all had once seemed to agree—namely, helping those in flight from slavery get away. With middle-class blacks fearful that aid to fugitives would invite further white attacks, the

Philadelphia Vigilance Committee had become dormant in 1842.[4] Slowly, with McCrummill's assistance, it had started to reconstitute itself in 1844.

So James McCrummill was guarded after hearing about Mary Walker from the young waiter who lived near her. In the summer of 1846, the free black dentist undertook simply to become acquainted with her. When the Camerons and Mary Walker returned to Philadelphia in the summer of 1847, McCrummill was on the waterfront to see them land "on the wharf at Dock street from the Baltimore Boat," at "which time they boarded in Sansom Street as before." He resumed his vigil. By then the dentist was aware, as were Mary Walker's other Philadelphia acquaintances, of a disfigurement that apparently did not disturb her owners—four or five of her upper front teeth were missing. At some point, McCrummill or a friend got close enough to Duncan Cameron to learn that the slave-owner had dropped the ruse of presenting Mary Walker as a free woman. Cameron simply announced, "This is my servant Mary who would not leave me because she is better off in her present situation than those free negroes of the North."[5]

There was another reason that McCrummill was deliberate. Usually when enslaved servants were brought to Philadelphia, they gave a sign if they wanted help. Mary Walker gave no outward sign. Still, observers seemed to wonder how long this woman would stay a slave in Philadelphia. "Mary was a very bright colored woman almost white with good straight hair same as a white woman," recalled black laborer Nicholas Boston, adding his opinion that she had "good features but rather lean." Free black dressmaker Annie E. Hall agreed: Mary Walker was a slim, delicate woman, a "very light person almost white."[6] Was she in fact utterly devoted to the family that owned her?

For his part, Duncan Cameron voiced complete confidence. The "Judge had brought her on to wait on them because he was not afraid she would run away."[7] He had good reason. Not only was Mary Walker a member of the most favored slave-family in his possession—but four hundred miles to the south, her children remained in bondage.

IN 1848, MARY WALKER WAS the mother of three children residing in Raleigh, North Carolina, the youngest age four and the oldest sixteen.[8] She was herself the fourth generation of her family to belong to the same line of slave-owners, going back to the middle of the eighteenth century. Her great-grandmother "Molly" and great-grandfather "Yellow Daniel"—so designated on a slave-inventory that gave only forenames—had been the property of Thomas Amis of the town of Halifax in eastern North Carolina. When Thomas Amis died in 1764, he bequeathed Molly and Daniel and three others to his eight-year-old daughter, Mary Amis. In 1776, at the age of twenty, Mary Amis married Richard Bennehan, a rising thirty-three-year-old merchant from the state's Piedmont region; she brought the family of Molly and Daniel with her to their new home in Hillsborough, North Carolina. In 1781, Molly gave birth to her third daughter—known as "Aggy"—who was destined to become Mary Walker's grandmother early in the next century. By the time Aggy was born, Richard Bennehan was rapidly on his way to becoming a planter as well as a merchant. In a short time, he had accumulated twelve hundred acres of land and forty enslaved people.[9]

The location of their plantation in the North Carolina Piedmont shaped the kind of slave-owners the Bennehans and their children became—and the kind of bondage that Molly, Daniel, and Mary Walker came to experience. Had Bennehan been to the manor born, reared to rule workers growing rice in the coastal region of South Carolina, or to preside over a sugar plantation in the Caribbean, or later to oversee cotton-growing land in the Southern interior, the prospect of windfall profits might have tempted him to push his laborers to the limit. But placed as his farm was in the red clay of the Piedmont, he grew wheat and tobacco, less profitable crops. His interest was to care for his laborers' health and welfare as if his livelihood depended on it—for indeed it did.[10]

Mary Walker's grandmother Aggy was born between the arrival of the slave-owners' daughter Rebecca Bennehan in 1778 and that of their son Thomas Amis Bennehan in 1782. Living amid a half-dozen black families, the Bennehan siblings grew up on the plantation that their parents called "Stagville," where they thought of the place and its people in familial terms—"our family, white and black." They might have come of age simply thinking of the plantation and its laborers as their rightful possessions, to manage as they saw fit. But their views of bondage were influenced by the ethos of postrevolutionary America, a time of debate about the morality of slavery. Thomas Bennehan was in the thick of those heated and heretical discussions in 1796, as an impressionable fourteen-year-old student at the recently founded University of North Carolina. So too was his cousin and classmate, Thomas G. Amis. Thomas Amis continued his soul-searching for another decade, sharing his deepening doubts about "this injured, unfortunate race" with his Bennehan cousin, his "one & only Bosom friend." The people they owned "are not brutes, they have sentiments." Like others of his generation, Amis espoused a remedy that fell short of liberation. "Exercise your power with mercy; with-hold the scourge 'till you reflect on their fate, 'till you think on their misfortunes." "Treat them as human beings, your interest will become theirs, the sweat shall drop unheeded from their brows & their toil shall not be bitter because they love him who shall enjoy its fruits."[11]

Thomas Bennehan and his sister Rebecca took to heart their cousin's exhortations about the treatment of their black family, especially when its members were ill. Rebecca Bennehan always found it "truly distressing to witness the sufferings of so many sick and afflicted fellow mortals." So too did her brother. Disappointed in love, Thomas Bennehan became a life-long bachelor—and devoted himself to plantation management and medical practice at Stagville. Only when his personal care proved insufficient for his sick workers did he relinquish them to trained physicians.[12]

BORN IN 1781, MARY WALKER'S grandmother Aggy might have lived an ordinary life as one of the Bennehans' enslaved workers, tilling the soil and starting her own family with a fellow bondsman. But in 1796, her life took a different turn. At the age of fourteen, she became pregnant. Though the father was never named, there seems a high chance he was a white man. She called the child, born in October 1796, Priscilla. It was a full name—not a diminutive, as "Aggy" was of Agnes. It was a European name—no black ancestor or known member of the slave-community possessed that name. Did the name Priscilla indicate that Aggy imagined a life for her daughter different from her own? All we know is that by 1804, her daughter was no longer called Priscilla but rather "Silla." In the same year, Aggy was fighting madness—the only member of the enslaved community in the eighteenth or nineteenth century ever to be designated insane.[13]

Whether sexual violence or dashed hopes or something else caused Aggy's "derangement," the result of her illness was that Mistress Rebecca took Aggy's eight-year-old daughter, Silla, under her wing as a young household servant. Trained as her mistress's personal helper, Silla was also taught to read, write—and sew. All female household servants were expected to stitch well enough to turn rough fabric bought for slave-clothing into completed shirts, frocks, and pants. Silla, however, became a highly skilled seamstress, who made and mended garments for the white family. When the mistress took sick, Silla looked closely after her; when Silla had a spell, her mistress rushed to the rescue. If seriously ill, as happened in 1816 and thereafter, Silla received sustained attention from the white family's personal physician.[14]

The marriage of Rebecca Bennehan to lawyer Duncan Cameron might well have changed the lives of Mary Walker's forebears for the worse. Duncan Cameron was an ambitious, hard-charging lawyer, the son of an Episcopalian minister in southside Virginia, who had come to the town of Hillsborough in the North Carolina Piedmont in 1799 to make his mark. Quickly his talents won him good cases and good clients; almost as quickly he set his sights on the most eligible young woman in the county. Rebecca Bennehan's long blonde hair, well-to-do merchant-planter father, and inheritance of twenty-five slaves led one bachelor to dub her the "girl with the golden fleece." Cameron won her hand and promise of marriage in 1803, besting a local rival. The defeated rival and fellow lawyer made some insinuating remarks—whether connected with the courtship or the courtroom is unclear. To the consternation of his bride and her family, Cameron accepted the challenge of a duel with his rival, went across the state line to Virginia, and there inflicted a wound which maimed and finally killed his nemesis.[15] Friend, foe, and family alike took note from that point on: challenge Duncan Cameron and there could be a high price to pay.

In fact, Duncan Cameron's marriage to Rebecca Bennehan brought the further elevation of the members of Molly and Daniel's enslaved family. Ruthless when crossed, Duncan Cameron preferred to achieve his will in a businesslike way rather than through coercion, and extended that approach to the enslaved workers who became his when he married Rebecca Bennehan. Reluctant at first to leave Hillsborough and his full-time law practice to oversee a plantation, he finally yielded to the preferences of his wife and father-in-law, who gave him three hundred acres of land to sweeten the shift. Cameron respected the sensibilities of his bride and his brother-in-law, and acknowledged their feelings when their people became unwell. Knowing his brother-in-law's mind, Cameron could "readily conjecture what his . . . sufferings are, amid so much sickness."[16] He understood that such emotional attachments, if mutual, had economic benefits.

Nonetheless in one dramatic gesture in 1809, Cameron signaled a different emphasis in dealing with his wife's people. To get the land cleared and prepared for the construction of a new plantation dwelling, he offered all enslaved laborers payments for working overtime. For every cord of wood they cut and delivered (a cord of wood was eight feet long, four feet wide, and four feet deep), they received credit at the country store owned by his father-in-law, Richard Bennehan. Over a period of two years, dozens of Cameron's workers exchanged cords of wood and hundreds of hours of labor for a bonanza of consumer goods—whiskey, hats, Dutch ovens, calico cloth, fish hooks, and locks. Cameron kept his eye out for the most able and willing workers. The store ledger confirmed that far and away the best man, who drove a horse and wagon and managed crews of fellow slaves, was the twenty-five-year-old Luke—the son of Molly and Daniel, and the uncle of thirteen-year-old Silla. Luke became what historian Michael Tadman has termed a "key slave" on the Cameron plantation: a trusted man for the plantation's tasks, a groomsman of horses, the man summoned to drive a wagon or a coach, the servant who accompanied Cameron on his still-active legal travels around the state, a courier between plantation quarters or to Raleigh or Hillsborough. Luke in turn was given a handmade "trim suit" for fall and a warm "great-coat" for winter—and his family received the protection of their white owner from harm or sale.[17]

IT WAS INTO THIS FAVORED family that Silla's daughter, Mary, was born on August 18, 1818. Later descriptions of her make it almost certain that her father was white. Some thirty years after her birth, a Philadelphian who knew both Mary Walker and Mary Walker's closest Philadelphia friend asserted that her father was Duncan Cameron himself.[18] Casting uncertainty on his claim is the fact that Mary's mother, Silla, remained the domestic servant and seamstress throughout the lifetime of Rebecca Cameron (who died in 1843) and stayed in the Cameron household until she herself died in 1864. It would have taken considerable tolerance on Rebecca's part for her to keep the servant and the child of an adulterous union in the household for almost a half-century. A much later source stated that Mary Walker's father was a man named Taylor. This could have been the physician William Taylor, called upon in 1816 and after to care for Silla during her intermittent illnesses. William Taylor lived in the vicinity of the newly cleared Cameron plantation. He and other doctors saw Silla more—and charged the Camerons more for treating her—than any other member of the household, black or white.[19]

Mary, like her mother, Silla, grew up as part of the "Big House" of her white owners and their enslaved household servants. Built between 1810 and 1823, imposing for its time and place in the Carolina Piedmont, Duncan Cameron's new home received the name "Fairntosh," after the ancestral manor of his Scottish forebears.[20] At Fairntosh, Silla continued to look after Rebecca Cameron, while it fell to Mary to be first the childhood playmate and then the servant of the younger girls in the Cameron family (there were six daughters), the last of whom—Mildred Cameron—was born in 1820. When the Camerons hired a Northern governess named Mary McLean Bryant to tutor their daughters, Mary was allowed to join them for lessons. It was from Miss Bryant, who had moved south from Ithaca, New York, that Mary learned the rudiments of reading and writing, and, from watching Miss Bryant and her white pupils, the manners of a lady. As she grew older, Mary accompanied the Cameron daughters to the small Episcopal chapel that Duncan Cameron built at Fairntosh in 1826, and later to city Episcopal churches as well. It's not clear where Mary and her mother lived. At the end of a row of Fairntosh outbuildings there were two cabins for house-servants, but they may have been for the Camerons' black cook and their black male attendants. More likely Mary and Silla lived near their kinsman Luke, who with his wife and daughters resided in a two-story dwelling about three hundred yards behind Fairntosh, separated from the main house by a shoulder-high brick wall.

The wall was a reminder of the separations that always ended the youthful intimacies of white and black playmates in slavery. For enslaved boys on plantations such as Fairntosh, assigned as childhood servants of their "Young Masters," the carefree role of playmate always gave way to the obedient role of slave. Young Master must be called "Sir"; he inherited the right to command and punish. For Mary, the divergence of her destiny from that of her young mistresses at Fairntosh came in a different way. At the age of fourteen she became pregnant. Sometime in 1832, Mary had her first child, a son she named Frank. There is no indication of who Frank's father was, or why Mary and Frank and her subsequent three children—born in the years 1837 to 1844—were given the surname "Walker." What is known is that two decades after his birth, Mary Walker's enslaved son was described as blue-eyed and "*freckeled*" and "so nearly white that with ninety five men in a hundred he will pass for a white man."[21]

The coming of children might have separated Mary Walker's life from that of the childless Cameron sisters in the 1830s. But a different kind of separation—a move away from the Fairntosh plantation—in fact intensified her ties with the young mistresses. The unforeseen consequences of the move also placed her on an ultimate collision course with Duncan Cameron.

AT LEAST THREE TIMES IN the 1810s and 1820s, frustration with the vagaries of plantation life plunged Duncan Cameron into a profound depression. Temperamentally a driven man, the lawyer-turned-planter recurrently found himself up against elements beyond his control—elements that he had himself set in motion. By the end of 1812, with the land for Fairntosh cleared by the overtime work of his enslaved laborers, bonuses stopped and store credits ended. Predictably, productivity slackened, and the need for more traditional inducements to slave-labor—punishment or the threat of punishment—returned. At the same time, alterations of the plantation landscape, intended as improvements, created an environment that bred disease. Cameron and his brother-in-law Thomas Bennehan owned low-lying property adjacent to the rivers that ran through their lands. In the mid-1810s, they ordered those lands cleared for planting, and had their laborers build dams and millponds to harness the river for gristmills to grind their wheat into flour. Both efforts created ditches and ponds where, especially in the rainy season, water backed up and mosquitoes thrived. Malaria became endemic on what black inhabitants soon called the "low grounds of sorrow." Weakened by malaria, plantation children and adults became vulnerable to more toxic diseases; epidemics of typhoid and diphtheria periodically swept through the black quarters, killing dozens at a time. After an epidemic in the late 1810s, a depressed Duncan Cameron, brooding on the possibility of his own death, wrote directives that his wife was instructed to follow if he died. He urged her to sell off most of the slaves—since almost half of them were unproductive or ungovernable—then move to higher ground, where she could have peace of mind and body.[22]

In what became a pattern, Cameron recovered his equilibrium and threw himself all the more vigorously into plantation improvements. He added mills, sought better wheat-grinding equipment, and bought new workers. Incorporating the approach of his wife and brother-in-law, Duncan Cameron purchased additional people in family groups. He acquired them from other slave-holders forced to sell but wanting to do so in good conscience. Such sellers drew comfort from knowing that their slave "families were not broken up"—not sold to "unfeeling Speculators"—but rather "would be purchased by a gentleman of such deserved reputation for good feelings." Cameron's calculation was that such families would work loyally in return for being kept together. It was an expectation that his slaves and their descendants understood fully.[23]

Nonetheless, the 1820s found Cameron again exasperated. In 1823, a friend reported him mired in "a most gloomy state of mind." A physician summoned in 1826 diagnosed him as suffering a "morbid sensibility of the brain." When a young nephew proposed to move to Mississippi to start a new plantation in 1828, Cameron sought to dissuade him from an occupation full of such "trouble & vexation."[24] Yet with hundreds of enslaved people and thousands of acres to manage, Cameron seemed to have no way to extricate himself from being a planter. Then an opportunity came that changed Duncan Cameron's life—and Mary Walker's life as well.

In late 1829, Duncan Cameron was asked by the directors of the State Bank of North Carolina to become its president, to help rescue an institution threatened with bankruptcy by the embezzlement of thousands of dollars by its long-time cashier. To his wife's astonishment, he immediately agreed and moved to Raleigh to take charge of the bank's affairs. A close friend thought the change saved him from becoming a "melancholy hypochondriac" and added years to his life. Cameron succeeded in stabilizing the bank and returned to Fairntosh in 1830, only to find himself again confronted by forces beyond his control. An epidemic broke out on his plantation; neither his repeated personal visits nor "the most devoted nursing with the best medical aid" could halt it. He again lapsed into depression and once more became "easily excited and as easily unstrung." Mercifully, in 1834 the call came a second time to take the helm of the State Bank. Cameron instantly accepted. In 1835 he built a magnificent mansion in Raleigh, and in 1836 he moved his wife, his six unmarried daughters, and a dozen house-servants to the new lot and mansion in Raleigh.[25]

Mary Walker; her mother, Silla; her son, Frank; and her uncle, Luke, all went with the Camerons to Raleigh. Groomed by her young mistresses to be the Cameron daughters' handmaiden, trained by her mother to be a skilled seamstress, eighteen-year-old Mary Walker seemed destined to serve and sew for the sisters as they made their way into the Raleigh social whirl and tested whether there were suitors audacious enough to court the daughters of one of North Carolina's wealthiest and most intimidating men.

Illness wrecked the family's hopes. In a four-year span, from 1837 to 1840, four of the six Cameron daughters came down with "consumption"—the nineteenth-century term for tuberculosis. Suddenly, Mary Walker's role shifted from handmaiden to caregiver. Low-level tuberculosis was likely rampant in the Fairntosh slave-quarters, for respiratory diseases readily took hold in victims weakened by malaria. But whites and blacks in the main household, on higher ground, were also exposed to the tuberculosis bacillus, because field hands deemed seriously ill were brought up to the "lot" at Fairntosh, and placed under close medical watch in the "kitchen." The kitchen was a two-story outbuilding where, with ill people upstairs, meals were prepared downstairs by black cooks and then brought to the white family in the main house fifty paces away. Far more than those who worked in the open air and slept in drafty rough-hewn cabins, blacks and whites at Fairntosh and afterward in the Raleigh mansion lived in poorly ventilated close quarters and were more likely to have latent tuberculosis that turned lethal. In the years 1837–1841, three black servants at Fairntosh and four at Raleigh died of consumption—more than from any other disease. All but one were women. During the same years, the four sick Cameron sisters went through the gruesome stages of the illness. By 1839, three had died.[26]

Twenty-two-year-old Anne Owen Cameron clung to life, and her desperate parents carried her to South Carolina and Florida in the winter of 1839, hopeful that the warmer climate would help her to survive. Mary Walker accompanied Anne Owen Cameron and her younger sister, twenty-year-old Mildred Coles Cameron, on their three-month trip. Anne had happy moments and encountered fellow travelers who conveyed good cheer and showed her every consideration. But she realized that her case was hopeless. In January 1840 she asked to return to Raleigh.[27]

Back home and approaching death, Anne Owen Cameron wanted

more than the ministrations of her grief-stricken family and the family's Episcopal minister. She knew through Mary Walker that there was a former bondsman regarded as a holy man in the black community. From Mary Walker, Anne Cameron had heard the story of Simeon, once enslaved on a nearby Piedmont plantation. He had "tried serving the Lord for many years. But the Lord hid his face. He met with nothing but cruelty from his fellow man and became profoundly discouraged that he could ever know God's grace." Chained one winter night, "sensing that he was about to freeze to death, he was ready to abandon God." But then "Simeon recalled that Christ too had been hung on a tree and that the Savior had bled and died for all. The remembrance shot a ray of gladness in Simeon's soul and sustained him through the night. The next morning he gave himself to Jesus and served him thereafter with all the strength he had." Simeon bought his freedom and moved about among the slaves, exhorting them at midnight prayer meetings, praying with the sick. Notwithstanding his enslavement and his suffering, "Simeon thanked his Maker for all He had done for him." Anne Owen Cameron wanted the holy man to pray for her soul. Mary Walker brought Simeon to Anne's bedside, and his fervor gave her soul ease.[28]

Simeon's gift of comfort, mediated through Mary Walker, brought an extraordinary bonus. A grateful Anne Owen Cameron begged "hard for Mary's freedom, and died with the promise of it." It was not unusual for consumption victims, in the final throes of protracted illness, to make a last request of family members. Certainly as the Camerons and close friends gathered at Anne's bedside in March 1840, the room palpable with gloom, there would have been every impulse to grant their daughter's dying wish.[29] Touched as Mary Walker may have been to learn of the family's pledge, she knew that it was a promise she would never redeem—not as long as her mother and children were in bondage.

No other Camerons died of tuberculosis, but all suffered its lingering repercussions. Brokenhearted, Rebecca Bennehan Cameron began to fail, and died in November 1843 at the age of sixty-five. Margaret Cameron, at thirty-two the older of the two surviving daughters, had a strong constitution and a generous temperament. She needed both. In the spring after their mother's death, her twenty-four-year-old sister, Mildred, developed baffling muscle spasms. Though Mildred had overcome her own early symptoms of consumption, the loss of her sisters and mother shadowed her psyche. She wondered why *she* was deemed worthy to live, absorbed as she was "with the things of this vain & unsatisfying world." Over the next eighteen months, Mildred's spasms worsened; gradually she lost mobility and appetite. No physician in Raleigh had an explanation for the symptoms; none was prepared to label hers a case of hysteria; no one had a remedy.[30] By the end of 1844, Mildred Cameron had become an invalid, and Mary Walker her full-time caregiver.

BY 1844, IT HAD BEEN eight years since Mary and her mother had moved from the manor at Fairntosh to the mansion in Raleigh. On the country plantation, mother and daughter had remained connected with their kin and friends—and with the traditions plantation people had adapted from their African and African-American heritage. Without a doubt, the most daring practice was the secret midnight prayer meeting. Reared in the black community before being taken in as a household servant by Rebecca Cameron in 1804, Silla had quietly sustained her traditional roots at Fairntosh, and continued to do so even after going to Raleigh. There, as Mary Walker later reported, her mother and other blacks from town stole away after dark for midnight meetings out in the country. Forbidden to meet for unsupervised "prayer & singing & reading the Bible," they arranged their gatherings "with the greatest care & secrecy" in "some lone hut, where one or two are stationed outside . . . to warn them if their voices rise too loud." Her mother knew that whites would find one hymn "especially obnoxious."

Our bondage it shall end
With our threescore years & ten
And to Canaan we'll return
By & bye, by & bye.
Jesus shall break the chain
And bear us to the throne
By & bye, by & bye.

If the guard discovered them they were thrown into prison, where, unless bailed out by their masters, they "received so many lashes." Nonetheless, pious slaves heartily joined in the meetings, becoming "sometimes so rapt into a religious ecstasy, that they even welcomed hard treatment & cruel overseers. 'If we suffer with Christ, shall we not also reign with him?'"[31]

It was a measure of the distance that had emerged between mother and daughter that Mary Walker declined to go to the midnight prayer meetings. She told her mother that she feared being caught and lashed. "I read the Bible all the more & prayed alone, but I was not ready to run the risk of stripes & imprisonment." Yet her mother knew that the reluctance ran deeper than fear. From childhood on, Mary Walker had spent as much time in the white household as in her own. The Cameron sisters had taken her in, first as a pet, then as their young servant. She had accompanied them to their lessons, gone with them to their Episcopal churches, mended their gowns, surely emptied their chamber pots, tended them in sickness, clothed them for burial. Her long association with the Cameron girls and their tutor had made Mary Walker, as much as an enslaved young woman could be, a cultivated person. When her daughter was born in 1837, she named the child after her grandmother and mother. But the name she gave the baby was "Agnes Priscilla"; the white family never abbreviated it to "Aggy." Her third child, Edward, who was born around 1840 and who died by 1848, also never had a diminutive. Her third son and last child, Bryant, born in 1844, she named not after a family forebear but after the governess from New York who had taught her as well as the Cameron girls. The name "Bryant" honored Mary McLean Bryant and all that she had contributed to Mary Walker's education.[32]

When Mary told her mother that she wasn't willing to go to those meetings for fear of reprisals—to herself and perhaps to her children—her mother bluntly, perhaps angrily, told her daughter that she had been lured away from the faith of her forebears. "That's your white folk's religion, Mary. Can't ye bear nothing for the Lord that's bot ye?"[33]

THE SEARCH FOR A REMEDY for Mildred Cameron's mysterious illness took the invalid, her sister, Margaret, and their father, Duncan, to Philadelphia. Starting in 1846, they went for three successive summers. Each time, Mary Walker accompanied them. In Philadelphia, they turned to physicians from the Jefferson College of Medicine, one of the country's best medical schools. They rented rooms—including a small back room for their servant—in a genteel boardinghouse close to the college and the heart of the city. Hope was high at first that doctors might find a cure. While physicians did their tests, Duncan Cameron kept up with commerce at the Philadelphia Merchants' Exchange and even took trips to New York City and Saratoga Springs. When not attending to the Camerons in their boardinghouse, Mary Walker ran errands in the city. Duncan Cameron had no fear that Mary Walker would leave them. Mary Walker reinforced that confidence. She told the Camerons she had "but little love for the north."[34]

In fact, Mary Walker was coming to know free people of color who, though not among "the *Elite* of our *People*" that a black Philadelphia author wrote about in 1841, were certainly among her own class of persons in service. William Johnson was a waiter at a nearby establishment who encountered Mary Walker daily. Dressmaker Annie Hall lived a few dwellings down from the waiter, on the same alley. James McCrummill was a barber and a dentist who made her acquaintance.

In 1846, Mary Walker's Philadelphia acquaintances could offer her friendship but no more. A Pennsylvania law, passed in 1788 and still on the books, allowed owners to bring enslaved people into the state for up to six months at a time without affecting their status. But events of the mid-1840s emboldened Northerners to defy slave-owners. The election of Tennessee slave-holder James K. Polk as president in 1844, the annexation of Texas as a slave-state in early 1845, Polk's incitement of war with Mexico soon thereafter, conflict beginning in 1846 over whether slavery should be allowed in California and the vast territory taken from Mexico—all fed into the Northern perception of a Southern conspiracy to extend bondage. In growing numbers, Northerners resolved to draw the line against the "Slave Power."[35] In early 1847, the Pennsylvania legislature passed a law that opened the way for any enslaved person, brought voluntarily into the state by a slave-owner, to claim his or her freedom.[36] There is no indication that Mary Walker's acquaintances urged her to act—they had to know she had children in bondage. Nonetheless they surely conveyed to her, on her return to Philadelphia in mid-1847, that the way to legal freedom was open, should she elect to take it.

By the summer of 1848, when Mary Walker and her owners made their third trip to Philadelphia for Mildred Cameron's treatment, the mood in the family had decidedly shifted. Though physician Hugh Hodge believed that his patient was making headway, her progress was erratic. Each easing of her symptoms was followed by returning spasms. The city's weather became oppressive; temperatures of ninety to ninety-six degrees kept Duncan Cameron and his daughters sheltered in the boardinghouse all day long; nausea compounded Mildred Cameron's ailments. Even her physicians seemed to be at wit's end. They did not "think it necessary that she should continue longer under their personal observation." Duncan Cameron had never seen his daughter "as depressed in spirits since the appearance of her affliction as she has been of late—and *that* makes us sad." "We endeavor to seem cheerful," he wrote home. But in fact Duncan Cameron was edging again toward depression. By late 1848, a close friend found "the old commanding figure gone." Distracted, unable to concentrate, Cameron would resign from the bank presidency at the end of the year.[37]

It was in this atmosphere of rising tension, in the summer of 1848, that Mary Walker and Duncan Cameron clashed.

ON THE FIRST OF JULY, after a suffocating month of June in Philadelphia, Duncan Cameron decided to take his daughters to the small seaside resort of Cape May, New Jersey, half a day's ferry-ride away. They had all gone to Cape May for a brief stay the previous summer. Mildred Cameron's physician thought the trip would do her good and would enable them all to escape the heat and confinement of the city. Mary Walker went with them. They arrived on July fourth for what turned out to be a month-long stay. By the end of their time on Cape May, Mary Walker confided a secret to Nicholas Boston, a free black friend and summer laborer on the Cape: when the Camerons got back to Philadelphia, "she resolved to leave" her owner.[38]

What had transpired between the slave-owner and Mary Walker in July 1848 is not known. All that is recorded is her friend's statement of the outcome. "Mary told me before she left Judge Campbell [Cameron] that ~~they~~ he threatened to send her to his farm in Alabama and because of that she resolved to leave him knowing that as she was brought here she was free by the law."

It is possible that Mary Walker's awareness of the law of 1847, along with the heightened assertiveness of her free black friends in Philadelphia, led her to say something that gave offense to Duncan

Cameron—a remark that sounded like an assertion that she *could,* after all, claim her freedom. Two years later, when the Cameron sisters again brought an enslaved servant north, they took care to select a young woman known for her submissiveness and relayed regular reminders of her mother at home. Nonetheless, as the sisters reported it, four months in Philadelphia made that young servant into "a person wholly devoid of principle or feeling." They couldn't wait to be "rid of her."[39]

But there may have been a different cause of the conflict between Mary Walker and Duncan Cameron. Some years after Mary Walker's black confidant of 1848 learned that the owner had "threatened to send her to his farm in Alabama," a white New Englander recounted a different version of what happened. The later acquaintance described Mary Walker as a runaway slave from "Raleigh NC [who] had a husband who was sold to go South. She left several children in Raleigh, preferring to leave them rather than submit to the fate which she saw impending over herself from a young & reckless master."[40]

Questions abound. What "farm in Alabama"? What "husband"? What "young & reckless master"? Was exile—or sexual submission—the "fate which she saw impending over herself"?

BEGINNING IN NOVEMBER 1844, there *was* a Cameron plantation in the Deep South. It was the brainchild not of Duncan Cameron but of his thirty-six-year-old son, Paul Cameron. A decade earlier, against the hopes of his father and father-in-law that he practice law, Paul Cameron had dropped a short-lived legal career to become a full-time planter. When his father became president of the State Bank of North Carolina and moved to Raleigh in 1835, the son eagerly took over the management of Fairntosh and other slave-quarters, assuming the supervision of hundreds of workers and their families. Within a few years he encountered the same frustrations that had beset his father—illnesses and epidemics that took the lives of his laborers; harvests that fell short because of droughts or floods; workers who disappointed his expectations. By 1840, the son's way out was not to leave the plantation but to expand it—to buy land in the Deep South and send slaves there, where his workers could produce a far more profitable crop than the grains and tobacco of the Piedmont.[41]

The son envisioned that cotton and a cotton-growing plantation would allow him, even as an absentee owner still dwelling at Fairntosh, to show his mettle, and to prove himself more than the dutiful custodian of his father's and grandfather's fortunes. After a year of discussion, Paul Cameron persuaded his reluctant father to go along with his plan. In the fall of 1844, he sent 114 men, women, and children—most in family groups—on their way to western Alabama, and then raced ahead of them by coach and steamboat to find land for them to work. With his father's funds, he purchased a 1,600-acre tract just below Greensboro, Alabama, not far from the home of his wife's uncle. The uncle had found and recommended the purchase of a $20,000 plantation about ten miles from his own. It was already in cultivation and provided with slave-cabins, and the uncle advised Paul Cameron to snap it up: "Had I your means and labor I would take it d—d quick. It is worth the price he asked in weighed gold."[42]

It proved anything but. The topsoil in what was known as the "Black Belt" of Alabama, so named for the color of the soil and of the people forced to work it, was rich but shallow. The harvests of the first owner had depleted the land's nutrients. Paul Cameron felt betrayed—"not only a dupe but a *victim.*" Imagining himself enslaved, he fantasized revenge, ready "to enter a room *naked* armed with a two edged sword to meet a foe from whom I could only escape by victory." Duncan Cameron, determined to preserve family comity, demanded that his son repress such sentiments.[43] Paul Cameron complied, but seethed for a second chance to start a profitable plantation—this one on virgin land that his workers would be the first to clear and cultivate. Duncan Cameron proved reluctant to spend still more money and send still more workers west. But by January 1848, his persistent son had won his consent. Paul Cameron let it be known to potential sellers in Louisiana and Mississippi—and to one or two highly trusted slaves—that he sought another place and planned another exodus of workers.[44]

Duncan Cameron or his daughters may have let slip to Mary Walker that the son planned another forced removal of enslaved people from North Carolina to the Deep South. Possibly someone in the Cameron black family may have learned of the plan and passed the news on to Mary Walker's mother, who periodically wrote to her daughter in Philadelphia.[45] Either way, Mary Walker may have feared that among those Paul Cameron might conscript would be the unnamed man she considered to be her "husband." Alarmed, she could well have spoken to Duncan Cameron in a way that the slave-owner—already agitated by his daughter's illness and his son's entreaties—felt to be a demand. Something like that chain of events may have been transmuted into the stories of 1848 and later on: that Mary Walker had escaped to avoid banishment to the Deep South, the fate of her "husband," and the designs of a "young & reckless master."

Exactly what transpired between Mary Walker and Duncan Cameron in July 1848 remains uncertain. But it is clear that during that turbulent Philadelphia summer, words passed between slave and owner, words that Duncan Cameron regarded as the gravest sin of a slave, short of flight or resistance: *impudence.* For her insubordination, he threatened that Mary Walker would be sent away.[46] Duncan Cameron was not a man known to make threats idly. No matter what happened, she would lose her children.

Faced with the choice of exile or escape, Mary Walker chose refuge in Philadelphia. On August 8, 1848, the day before the Camerons departed for North Carolina, their thirty-year-old servant disappeared.[47]

2 Sanctuary

When Mary Walker left the Camerons in early August 1848, her friends in Philadelphia did not divulge where she had gone. But they knew and she knew the place where most fugitives first went to get help.

At 31 North Fifth Street, five blocks north of the Camerons' lodging house at the corner of Washington Street and Independence Square, was the office of Philadelphia's leading antislavery newspaper, the *Pennsylvania Freeman.* The weekly paper was edited by Quaker James Miller McKim and was the voice of abolitionism in the state. The editor's assistant in the office, who held the title of clerk, was William Still, a free person of color in his mid-twenties. William Still's mother had escaped bondage before his birth, and had begun a new life with her husband in New Jersey. Still had come to Philadelphia in the 1840s, married, and hired on as a clerk in the office of the *Freeman* in 1846. His job for the paper was to gather information, solicit new subscribers, and collect payment from delinquents. But his larger role, which would be formalized in December 1852 when he became the head of the reconstituted Philadelphia Vigilance Committee, was to find safe havens for escaping slaves. William Johnson and James McCrummill would have known to take Mary Walker to the office of the *Pennsylvania Freeman.*

In the *Freeman,* Mary Walker's helpers had read about a well-reported case: an enslaved woman had claimed freedom in New York City, but then, alone and depressed among strangers, had returned herself to bondage. They intended no such fate for Mary Walker. Dentist James McCrummill arranged for her to receive false teeth to replace the upper front teeth she was missing.[1] She was taken to the neighborhood where William Still lived with his wife, Letitia, a dressmaker; their home was on one of the city's many "Washington Streets," this particular Washington consisting of a single block in an area populated by people of color.[2] Mary Walker was entrusted to a couple who lived just across the street from the Stills, a carpenter named James Fells and his wife, Eliza. On his way to considerable success in his trade, the thirty-two-year-old Fells, along with his wife, was a prominent member of the nearby Union Baptist Church, whose minister, David Scott, also lived in their building at 11 Washington Street. All three were active contributors to the black American Baptist Missionary Association, as was fellow Baptist James McCrummill.[3]

Whether Mary Walker lived for a time with James Fells or the Stills is not known. But dressmaker Letitia Still likely helped her find work as a seamstress, and all four neighbors were undoubtedly sensitive to the fact that though Mary Walker had claimed her freedom, she had lost her family. Either James or Eliza Fells had been enslaved in Virginia before being manumitted by an owner; they had either chosen or been required to leave the state and their relatives there.[4] William Still, born free in New Jersey, knew that his once-enslaved mother had escaped from bondage with her two daughters, but only after a failed first attempt convinced her that she could not succeed unless she left her two young sons behind.[5] Both couples were listed in census records as "mulatto." When William Still in 1853 started a secret journal about fugitive slaves who came through Philadelphia, he singled out those with the blood of both races in their veins, especially the literate and skilled women who had fled despite eating "the white bread of slavery."

The impetus to leave was almost always the imminent danger of separation or sale.[6] Mary Walker's Washington Street friends understood what she was going through.

Mary Walker left the Camerons at a moment when both abolitionism and black self-assurance—battered in the late 1830s—were resurgent in Philadelphia. Six weeks after her escape, three major black abolitionists came to speak at rallies in the city's predominantly black neighborhoods. Frederick Douglass, Henry Highland Garnett, and Martin Delaney arrived on a concerted mission to raise consciousness, to challenge laggards, and to drum up support for Douglass's recently founded antislavery newspaper, the *North Star,* published in Rochester, New York. They fanned out to every hall and black congregation open to them, including the Shiloh Baptist Church and little Wesley Methodist Church, blocks from the Washington Street homes of James Fells and William Still. Even if Mary Walker attended none of the meetings, the speeches were the talk of the city, and William Still would have brought back to Washington Street reports of what the *Pennsylvania Freeman* called the extraordinary "antislavery revival" in the city.[7]

Antislavery momentum was at work not only in Philadelphia, but throughout the North, so much so that the abolitionist *Pennsylvania Freeman* had to caution its readers to beware of undue optimism. Debate over slavery, once suppressed by both political parties and avoided by most political leaders, had moved to the center of national politics. Forcing the issue was the status of slavery in territories taken from a defeated Mexico. Both major parties in 1848 had nominated presidential candidates who seemed at best ambiguous and at worst supportive of slavery in the new lands. A consequence was a movement to create a new party dedicated to stopping slavery's expansion. On August 9, a convention of a thousand persons had descended on Buffalo, New York, to see if they could agree on a platform and leaders to take their cause to the country. Despite the number and diversity of those at the three-day gathering, the Free Soil Party was born and its candidates were chosen—none other than former President and Andrew Jackson protégé Martin Van Buren as the party's presidential nominee, and presidential son and grandson Charles Francis Adams as its vice-presidential candidate. To the editor of the *Pennsylvania Freeman*, James McKim, the good news was that existing parties were fracturing and silence was ending over the slavery question. The flaw was that the Free Soil Party was committed only to stopping the expansion of slavery. For editor McKim, the victory in November 1848 of the Whig presidential candidate—Mexican War general Zachary Taylor, a Louisiana slave-holder—only confirmed the need to continue the moral crusade to change the country.[8]

Nonetheless, it was a heady time for people of color, for abolitionists, and for Mary Walker. She and others who had left slavery had good reason to feel secure in Philadelphia. Whether brought into the state voluntarily or arriving in the city after flight from the South, they could believe themselves shielded from slave-catchers by the 1847 law, which had propelled Pennsylvania to the forefront of states protecting those escaping slavery from recapture. Indeed, in 1848 and 1849 Philadelphia became the destination for two of the boldest escapes from bondage on record. The light-complexioned slave Ellen Craft shortened her hair and traveled by train and steamboat from Georgia to Pennsylvania disguised as an ailing white planter, accompanied by a dark-skinned slave—her husband—who successfully pretended to be her servant.[9] Even more audacious was the dispatch from Richmond to Philadelphia of Henry Brown, a two-hundred-pound man who had himself packaged in a crate—three feet long, two and a half feet deep, and two feet wide—that was nailed shut and sent by steamship to dockside Philadelphia, via express mail. Though stevedores ignored the painted instructions that said "THIS SIDE UP, WITH CARE," and forced the fugitive to travel upside down for hours, Brown arrived alive, and was delivered to the office of the *Pennsylvania Freeman*. Editor

McKim tried to suppress the stories of Brown and the Crafts, lest slave-owners be on guard against those means of flight. His warning failed. William Lloyd Garrison trumpeted the Crafts' bold deception in the *Liberator*, and Henry "Box" Brown was soon regaling antislavery audiences in New England with the tale of his daring escape.[10]

For Mary Walker, Philadelphia was more than a safe haven. It was also a place where her work as a skilled seamstress became known to a young man starting out as a merchant in Philadelphia. Some months after her arrival, James Lesley, Jr., agreed to have Mary Walker reside in his household shop at Sixth Avenue and High Street—soon to be renamed Market Street—and to use it as a base to sew shirts for him and to do outwork for others.[11] The chain of connection between Mary Walker and twenty-six-year-old James Lesley, Jr., can only be conjectured. Most likely she was introduced to him by his domestic servant, a free woman of color named Sarah Elbert. Sarah Elbert had grown up in Chambersburg, Pennsylvania, where she and her mother had served as the domestics for James Lesley, Sr., and his wife, Ellen.[12] The senior James Lesley abhorred "slavery in his inmost soul" but declined to join an abolitionist society. His bolder son subscribed to the major abolitionist weeklies, and whether they were welcome or not, he passed on copies of the *Liberator* and the *National Anti-Slavery Standard* to his cautious father and conservative uncle.[13] When "Jimmy"—as he was known to members of his family—decided to strike out on his own in Philadelphia, Sarah Elbert went with him to look after his dwelling at 243 High Street, which doubled as his home and his shop. Thirty-year-old Sarah Elbert already had a relative in the city. Her aunt lived at 8 Raspberry Alley, two blocks over from the 10 Currant Alley lodging of waiter William Johnson—Mary Walker's first black acquaintance in Philadelphia.[14] Ever on the lookout for his North Carolina friend, the peripatetic waiter may have spoken with Sarah Elbert's nearby aunt about Mary Walker's skill as a seamstress, and then she with her niece.

Mary Walker's Philadelphia

Morris St.
Coates St.
Schuylkill River
Vine St.
Logan Square
Noble St.
Callowhill St.
13th St.
12th St.
9th St.
8th St.
Cherry St.
Race St.
Franklin Square
Filbert St.
(Market St.)
Arch St.
6th St.
Pennsylvania Freeman Office
Broad St.
High St.
Zane St.
4th St.
3rd St.
Front St.
Sansom St.
Chestnut St.
Locust St.
Walnut St.
Independence Square
Pine St.
21st St.
Rittenhouse Square
Spruce St.
Washington Square
Cedar St.
15th St.
7th St.
Delaware River
Windmill Island
19th St.
17th St.
Lombard St.
Shippen St.
11th St.
13th St.
Prime St.
Catherine St.
Carpenter St.
Federal St.
10th St.
County Prison
Broad St.
7th St.
6th St.
5th St.
4th St.
Front St.
9th St.
8th St.
Wharton St.
Dickenson St.
0 1/4 1/2 mile

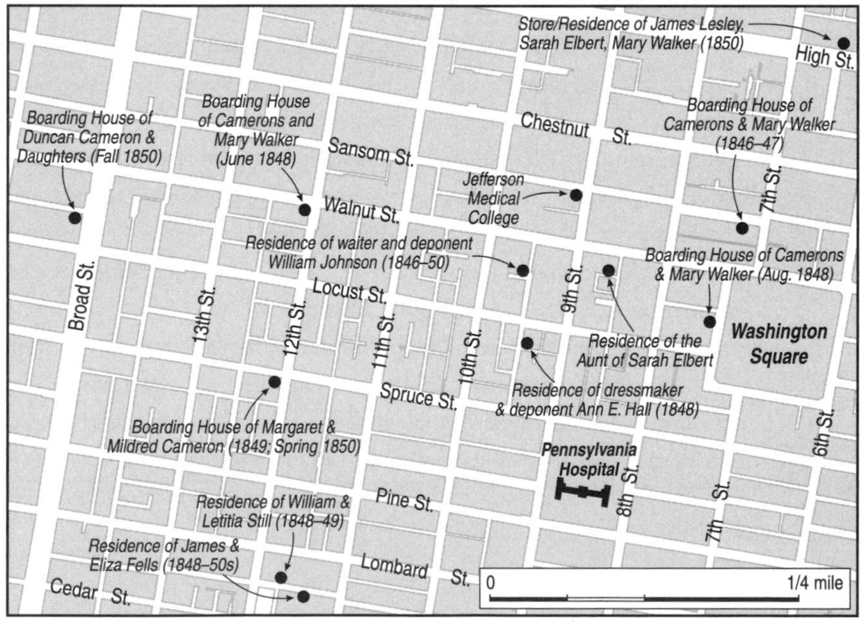

However they made contact, Mary Walker and Sarah Elbert became each other's closest friends in the city, and both were in Jimmy Lesley's employ by 1850.

EIGHTEEN-FIFTY, HOWEVER, PROVED to be a year of reversals for Mary Walker, for Philadelphia's people of color, and for abolitionists everywhere. The dispute over the fate of slavery in the territories acquired in the Mexican War had simmered in Congress since 1846, when Pennsylvania Democrat David Wilmot first introduced a proviso to bar bondage from the conquered lands. Southerners, whose soldiers and officers had helped to win the Mexican War, demanded the right to bring their slaves into the surrendered territory. Dividing along sectional lines, a House majority had voted for the ban and the Senate had rejected it; by 1850 the impasse was in its fourth year. The festering territorial controversy magnified other issues for the South, foremost of which was the refusal of Northerners and Northern legislatures to help with the recapture of escaped slaves. The personal-liberty laws galled Southern leaders, as did the celebrated escapes of William and Ellen Craft and Henry "Box" Brown. When the *Pennsylvania Freeman* forecast a tenfold increase in the flight of fugitives from the South, it wildly exaggerated.[15] But so long as slaves could flee to a Pennsylvania where sheriffs, jailors, judges, and citizens were barred from aiding their capture or return, the specter of hemorrhaging existed. To some Southerners, the only true safety was in secession. Others, for the moment less extreme, called for a decisive remedy.

That sweeping remedy was proposed in mid-January 1850, by Virginia senator James Mason. He introduced a bill designed to override all Northern personal-liberty laws. It provided that a fugitive slave could be arrested by a master or his agent anywhere in the country. The person could be taken before any official—a judge, a clerk of courts, a local commissioner, a federal marshal, or even one of the country's forty thousand postmasters. If by affidavit or oral testimony the owner could show that the arrested person had escaped from a slave-state, the official was obliged immediately to authorize the owner or agent to take his property back to bondage. Anyone who interfered—harassing the owner or his agent, obstructing the officials, aiding an escape—would be fined a thousand dollars.[16] From January on, Mary Walker, her employer James Lesley, and her friends in the city could follow the unfolding nine-month debate over the bill in the pages of the *Pennsylvania Freeman.* The Virginian's proposal received an enormous boost on March 7, 1850, when the North's legendary "Defender of the Constitution," Senator Daniel Webster of Massachusetts, gave his full support to a more stringent fugitive-slave law. Momentum for change in Washington was matched in Pennsylvania by a call for the complete repeal of the state's personal-liberty law of 1847. Designed to soothe Southerners and demonstrate Northern good faith, repeal won endorsement from the Judiciary Committee of Pennsylvania's House of Representatives, but fell short of approval.[17] All sides expected the proposal to come up again.

The failure in Pennsylvania and elsewhere in the North to revoke state personal-liberty laws intensified the pressure in Washington for a new national measure. On June 6, 1850, the ominous provisions of the "Slave-Catching Bill" were headlined in the *Pennsylvania Freeman:* "FREEMEN UNPROTECTED"—"JURY TRIAL DENIED." There was no need to read the fine print of the evolving bill, yet the fine print was even more startling. Any person who aided or concealed a fugitive was not only "to forfeit a thousand dollars for the benefit of" the slave-owner, but was "to be imprisoned for the term of twelve months." "And in no trial or hearing under this act shall the testimony of such fugitive be admitted in evidence."[18]

Ironically, President Zachary Taylor, the Louisiana slave-holder and victorious general of the Mexican War, opposed the Southern-led effort to jam through slavery in the territories and a volatile new law on fugitive slaves. Then, unexpectedly, Taylor fell ill after attending a blistering Fourth-of-July ceremony at the unfinished Washington Monument. The president died on July 9, 1850. His successor, New York Whig Millard Fillmore, gave his full backing to the proposed new fugitive-slave law, and reinforced his support by naming the bill's most prominent Northern advocate, Daniel Webster, as his secretary of state. Stunned, the *Pennsylvania Freeman* reported passage of the "Fugitive Slave Bill" by the U.S. Senate on September 5. "It may seem incredible to those who have not measured the proslavery depravity of our American Government, that such an act could find one Senator bold enough to insult the justice and humanity of the world by advocating it; yet it passed by a vote of 27 to 12," with both Pennsylvania senators in favor. Two weeks later the bill won passage in the House of Representatives and, signed by the president, became law.[19]

For Mary Walker and for her Philadelphia friends, the first reports of "Recent Kidnapping Cases" came quickly, though initially from afar. Attempted arrests of fugitive slaves were reported in mid-September from New York City and Providence, Rhode Island, where Henry "Box" Brown was the target. By September 30, there were "kidnappers in Harrisburg." On October 1, a hundred and fifty persons of color from Pittsburgh and Allegheny County left for Canada, "armed and organized." On October 9, the "Man-Hunt" reached Philadelphia. Slave-catchers attempted the early-morning arrest of an alleged fugitive slave in Germantown. Alert friends warned the man, neighbors raised "the cry of kidnappers," and their prey got away. But the incident decisively awakened black Philadelphians "to the atrocity of the kidnapping law, and their own peril under it." On October 14, a "very large meeting of colored citizens" crowded into the Wesley Church at Lombard and Sixth, where William Still served as the evening meeting's secretary. The meeting resolved "to resist this law at any costs and at all hazards." Unanimously members of the overflowing crowd pledged never to "refuse aid and shelter, and succor to any brother or sister who has escaped from the prison-house of Southern bondage."[20]

FOR MARY WALKER, THE UNFOLDING events of 1850 would have been unsettling under any circumstances. What made them alarming, then terrifying, was that the Camerons had come back to Philadelphia. Duncan Cameron's two daughters, Margaret and Mildred Cameron, returned to the city by themselves in November 1849, to seek treatment again for Mildred Cameron's incapacitating spasms. On their visit the year before, the two sisters had come to trust physician Hugh Lenox Hodge of the Jefferson College of Medicine, who had found ways to mitigate—although not cure—the spasms that had rendered Mildred Cameron an invalid, bedridden or confined to a couch much of the time. Hodge's treatment lengthened the intervals between attacks and created opportunities for the patient to ride in a carriage or even walk on occasion.[21] The two North Carolinians lodged at a boardinghouse near the corner of Spruce Avenue and Twelfth Street—a block and a half from the Currant Alley address of Mary Walker's friend William Johnson, and two and a half blocks from the home of James Fells on Washington Street. There can be little doubt that Mary Walker knew that the Cameron sisters were in Philadelphia. She also had to know that their father was only intermittently with them during the first half of 1850. Duncan Cameron still suffered from the effects of the nervous breakdown he had experienced at the end of 1848. Cameron came to visit his daughters in May and again in June. On his third visit, in August 1850, he felt well enough to stay, and moved their lodgings four blocks west to a quieter and smaller boardinghouse set back from the street, at Broad and Brighton.[22]

From the Cameron sisters alone, Mary Walker likely anticipated no danger. Both sisters were by temperament calm and forbearing, made the more so by the need to avoid any turbulence that might aggravate Mildred Cameron's condition. When the new servant they had brought with them from North Carolina to Philadelphia became insubordinate by May 1850, presumably under the influence of free blacks in the city, they kept their resentment hidden from her, and left it to their father to take her away and inflict suitable punishment.[23] Revealingly, when Mildred Cameron's pet canary flew out of their room at Spruce and Twelfth, she simply left the window open in the hope that her pet would voluntarily return to its cage, which it did. Duncan Cameron was another matter. His daughter-in-law registered his return to vigor in late 1849 by observing his treatment of the servants. "He has until the last three days been here, there and every where himself, and I had to keep *things straight* I tell you. He did more whipping in two or three days than he has done in eighteen months I am sure."[24]

Duncan Cameron's letters from Philadelphia in the summer and fall of 1850 made no mention of Mary Walker or of the Fugitive Slave Law that took effect in late September. He clearly was preoccupied with his invalid daughter's condition, which worsened soon after his arrival. Despite Mildred's reluctance to leave her Philadelphia physician, Duncan Cameron saw little improvement, and became impatient for them all to return to Raleigh before winter set in. In mid-October, however, her spasms suddenly shifted from her arm and chest to her throat, silencing her for a week. The unhappy trio remained in Philadelphia well into November.[25] Nothing in his letters home indicated that lawyer Duncan Cameron decided during that time to go after his former slave. Yet two of Mary Walker's friends claimed that in early November, he attempted to do so.[26]

If Duncan Cameron did try to reclaim his former slave, he was too late. By early November 1850, Mary Walker had left Philadelphia.

THOUGH IT WAS STILL POSSIBLE that Pennsylvania's 1847 Personal Liberty Law might have offered protection to Mary Walker, who had been taken voluntarily to the state by her owner, it was just as likely that the Fugitive Slave Law would supersede all state laws. With the

Camerons back in Philadelphia, Mary Walker believed she was in imminent danger. "For her own safety," she had to find "a more secure home."[27]

But security where, and with whom? Mary Walker's employer, James Lesley, pooled funds with two Philadelphia relatives and bought her a train ticket to Boston, the home of the nation's most outspoken and determined abolitionists. In response to the Fugitive Slave Law, black and white antislavery leaders had publicly pledged that no fugitive from bondage would ever be captured in their city. There was another reason for sending Mary Walker to Boston. James Lesley had a thirty-one-year-old cousin, a recently married minister, who lived on the outskirts of the city in Milton, Massachusetts. It was to Peter Lesley and his wife, Susan, that James Lesley directed Mary Walker.

Jimmy Lesley guessed that of all the members of his family, his cousin Peter would be prepared to take in a fugitive from bondage. Peter Lesley had not joined an antislavery organization or spoken at an antislavery rally or even given a sermon against slavery. Nonetheless, the cousin knew that since 1848, the young minister had stood up to every authority in his life. If any Northerner seemed ready to scorn the re-enslaving law of 1850, it was his cousin Peter.

MARY WALKER WAS DISPATCHED TO the household of a man who had learned some things about self-emancipation. Peter Lesley's father, as a young man of seventeen, had been obliged by family circumstances to take up woodworking and had become the head of the household. Successful at his trade and then in business, he wanted for his sons what he never had for himself. As they came of age, he sent them to preparatory schools for a classical education. At home, he made every meal a lesson, where they were to state what they had observed each day, or, when words fell short, to sketch what they had seen with pen and paper. Born in 1819, Peter proved as able and spirited as his brothers, but was frail and nearsighted. Compelled to wear thick glasses from the age of seven, he strove to overcome his physical limits by sheer will. The father, a devout Presbyterian, saw a special destiny for his sensitive and studious namesake. First there would be college in Philadelphia, then Princeton Theological Seminary, finally the ministry. The devoted son embraced the father's vision of his life's work.[28] He was miscast.

As he came of age, Peter Lesley wrestled with tensions between inquiry and piety, clashing tenets instilled in his upbringing. At nineteen, he confided doubts to his father. "Will my faith never be stronger? I have been very cold and dead to my God." Whether it was apprehension about his future or exhaustion from his schoolwork, Peter neared collapse as he finished his studies at the University of Pennsylvania in 1838. Over six feet tall but weighing scarcely more than a hundred pounds, the son, in his gauntness, shocked a family friend who encountered him walking with his father down a Philadelphia street. The friend, Alexander Dallas Bache, was a professor of chemistry at the university and a leader of the elite Franklin Institute, which included distinguished scientists of the city. Bache immediately suggested to the father that his son needed time away from books, and thought that outdoor work would restore his health and spirits. With the father's consent, Bache arranged for the young man to hire on as an assistant to geologist Henry P. Rogers, a fellow member of the Franklin Institute, then in the midst of conducting the first geological survey of Pennsylvania.[29]

Peter Lesley loved the work. Though he was deadly afraid of the dark, a few descents down mine shafts and tunnels to take rock and coal samples convinced him that he was perfectly safe. The fastidious twenty-year-old laughed at how readily he took to being "a dirty geologist" and even found sublimity in the subterranean. "You can scarcely imagine, how beauty and deformity, sweetness and filth, sterility and mud, are strangely mixed in this singular place"—"it is truly my home." Skill at observing the landscape and precision in rendering it in topographical maps won the quick confidence of Henry Rogers, who turned over arrangements and plans to his young assistant. Peter Lesley thrilled at both scientific discovery and the latitude he was given—at being "neither hampered nor pushed nor blamed."[30]

Nonetheless, to Princeton Theological Seminary he dutifully went in 1841, where for three years he immersed himself in its prevailing Calvinist theology. Enormous effort—hours, sometimes days of imagining sermons—brought disappointment. "I have tried prayerfully to know my own powers," he wrote his father, "and they are small."[31] At least he felt stimulated by lively discussions of biblical passages. At his clerical examination in 1843, however, he learned that his personal opinions were of no interest whatsoever to the committee on ordination. Creedal correctness was what the clerics were looking for. What was sought was "*Yes!* and *No!*" Unless he submitted, ordination would be denied, his studies wasted, his future shipwrecked. Yield he did, but with a feeling of abasement that he later likened to "theological circumcision."

His license painfully achieved, he took time off for a year-long trip to Europe to encounter the great religious thinkers of the day, then returned to undertake missionary work among the German-speaking "Pennsylvania Dutch" of the western part of the state. For a year he became a *colporteur*—an itinerant missionary who delivered religious tracts to country folk and preached at isolated churches that lacked regular ministers. His effort at practical Christianity went well—if six sermons a week constituted "well"—but proved exhausting. When scientist Henry Rogers again offered him the chance to undertake geological work, his protégé seized the chance. This time, Rogers summoned Lesley to Boston, there to translate the rough notes of fieldwork into sophisticated topographical maps, maps that then would be incorporated into the finished geological survey of Pennsylvania.[32] In December 1846, twenty-seven-year-old Peter Lesley moved to Boston. It was a choice that changed his life.

In Boston he encountered a world of spiritual and theological ferment. Through Henry Rogers's good offices, Peter Lesley took lodging at the residence of Rogers's friend George Hillard, a brilliant young lawyer and literary scholar, a friend and law partner of Charles Sumner. The drawing room in the dwelling of George and Susan Hillard at 62 Pinckney Street in Boston was a salon for freethinkers, where people of all creeds met and challenged each other. His father worried that he was being drawn away from the "simplicity of the Gospel" by the cold intellectualism of Boston. The son reassured him that the challenges offered "an opportunity given me by the Lord to increase in Wisdom."[33] But that wisdom was relentlessly moving Peter Lesley away from orthodox religion.

As he worked to conclude the topographical map that Henry Rogers had commissioned—painstaking labor that left his eyes blurred and his head throbbing—Peter Lesley fantasized about his future. The ideal would be a country church in New England, close to Boston. As if by miracle, a week after he finished Rogers's map in June 1847, a pulpit opened up in Milton, just six miles from Boston. He became the interim minister of Milton's small Congregational church, and there, no longer identifying faith with dogma, he preached a liberated "practical godliness." In September 1847, a pleased Henry Rogers asked him to do more map work for the geological survey, allowing science to supplement his small clergyman's salary. In December 1847, the Milton congregation invited him to become its full-time minister.[34] He considered himself blessed.

Bliss was short-lived. Peter Lesley had received a license to preach from the Presbyterian Association of Philadelphia in 1843. But his changed views placed him well outside the Presbyterian fold. He decided to seek release in good standing from the Presbyterians, to clear the way for ordination as a Congregational minister. But when he arrived in Philadelphia in May 1848 to arrange the release, he discovered that an orthodox Massachusetts bishop had written a letter accusing him of *heresy.* When he refused to recant his beliefs, the Philadelphia synod withdrew his license, and gave its reason in a word: *"heterodoxy."* He returned to Milton and tendered his resignation. His church refused to accept it, and encouraged him instead to seek ordination from the most liberal Congregational Association in Massachusetts, that of Boston. Though wary, he met with thirteen Congregational clergymen in June and again in December 1848, stated what had transpired in Philadelphia, and requested that they examine him on his religious views. Summarily they refused.[35]

Ostracized, the young minister felt pursued "like a hunted slave."[36] Ministerial friends turned away from him, fearful that "the flagellation which they were sure to receive should prove beyond their endurance." Against the advice of family and parishioners, he decided to confront the authorities who sought to subjugate him, less (he claimed) on his own behalf than on behalf of all young clergymen tyrannized by "unworthy masters." In a tract of fifty-eight pages, published in May 1849 with an additional seventy pages of appended sermons, he erupted with words long "shut up and burning in my spirit." The clerical leaders who had rejected him exercised a "despotic power." He "denounced," "arraigned," and three times "censured" them as "arbitrary," "unlawful," and "notorious" keepers of a "spiritual aristocracy." He defied "the imperious men who rule your councils." Determined to "stand up for the rights of the helpless," the outcast vowed never to "preach as a minister what I will not practice as a man."[37]

When James Lesley read Peter's scathing address in the summer of 1849, he joked that his cousin had surely forfeited all "benefit of clergy."[38] A year later, when the Fugitive Slave Law made Philadelphia treacherous for Mary Walker, the cousin had no doubt that Peter Lesley was ready to preach and practice abolitionism.

INDEED, FROM HIS FIRST MONTHS in Boston, the man to whom Mary Walker would be sent had found himself drawn to the abolitionists of the city, and they to him. In Boston, abolitionist friends arranged for him to supply pulpits and give sermons around the city. He soon made acquaintance with Wendell Phillips, who was as legendary for his personal openheartedness and camaraderie as he was for his blistering denunciations of slavery, slave-holders, and Northerners whose silence sustained bondage in America. "I esteem him highly," Peter told his father. "We are to be dear friends one day." Early in 1848, Phillips gave the visiting Philadelphian a pile of books on antislavery. "I am sifting and writing on the whole abolition subject." By the end of the year, as Lesley came to grief with Boston's clerical hierarchy, Phillips intervened to get him lecturing opportunities and arranged for him to borrow books from a radical Unitarian minister and fellow abolitionist, Theodore Parker. In the besieged minister—who vowed "never to conceal my views, nor consent to an injustice"—Phillips and Parker saw a soul mate.[39]

Yet attracted as he was to these Bostonians and their ideas, Peter Lesley held back from committing himself to their cause and the stridency that accompanied it. His ideal antislavery leader was William Wilberforce, the saintly and successful British crusader against the African slave-trade. What he admired in Wilberforce was a model of reform that American abolitionists, chastened by resistance, had long since abandoned. To Lesley, Wilberforce blended a temper that was meek with a passion for what was right, acted boldly on behalf of the slave yet pursued abolition with love on his lips—"a strange and beautiful sight."[40] In Boston he found instead "enthusiastic, partisan souls, who can see no faults in friends, nor virtues in enemies." In combat, "these men, or the more excitable among them, bait each other like dogs and bulls, to the shame of all their honors, and the origin of personal feuds of the most bitter and personal kinds." Peter Lesley admitted that the "general result is however probably attained, and will prove good."[41] Good results notwithstanding, he drew the line at abolitionist denunciation. Wendell Phillips understood that many who abhorred slavery nonetheless shied from damning all slave-holders as monsters and Northerners as their abettors in crime. He may have hoped that the books he lent Lesley, and the minister's experience of being hounded like "a hunted slave," would persuade his comrade of the need to attack evil with ferocity, and to join the cause. But when Phillips invited him to speak to Boston's Antislavery Society, Lesley declined. "I should have to say some practical truths which they would not like to hear perhaps, and which I certainly would not like to utter. I can't endure their neglect of exact truth, any more than their lack of the spirit of tenderness and love, in what they write and speak. At the same time, I see the cause, and appreciate it,—they roar by instinct like lions, and wise people must interpret."[42]

Peter Lesley was not ready, in 1849 or for most of 1850, to become an open abolitionist. What held him back was more than fastidiousness about exact truth or personal preference for a spirit of tenderness and love. Members of his own family, particularly his father and his brother, Allen Lesley, were hostile to abolitionism. To go on the circuit against slavery would pit him publicly against the two of them. Peter had already dismayed his father with his failed ordination. He confined his antislavery sentiments to private family letters, though restraint frayed on both sides. In the summer of 1849 he condemned President Zachary Taylor, the slave-holding hero of the Mexican War, as a murderer, and wounded the feelings of his father, who had voted for Taylor.[43] He engaged in heated debate with his brother about the Free Soil Party, which Allen Lesley saw as humbug and Peter Lesley saw as a symptom of the inexorable shift of the North to antislavery. To Peter, Free Soil announced, like surface ice, a chilling of sentiment down to the bottom of the pool. In ten years the whole North would act with the abolitionists. In trying to hold on to bondage, the South was like a maniac in a straitjacket. Destiny would have its course. If Peter Lesley's forecast was right, there was nothing that his proslavery brother could do, or that the iconoclastic minister needed to do, to change the future.

"The world was made for freedom and free men, for an endless movement and mingling of the races. . . . I shall live to see a black man governor of Georgia."[44]

There was a final reason the embattled minister held back. He knew that when he became passionate about a cause or an idea, he pulled out the stops, as he had when he finally and irrevocably declared war on the clerical hierarchy. He gloried in the steadiness with which he then "stood firm to my opinions in the face of all earthly interests" and "yielded to no man for an instant." But he recognized that attacks brought out the worst as well as the best in him. "My determined will, which supports me under necessity, is my own worst enemy."[45] One all-out conflict was enough.

FOR PETER LESLEY, AS FOR many Northerners who opposed slavery but avoided abolitionist involvement, the Fugitive Slave Law of 1850 forced choices, and ultimately converted millions of Northerners to the cause of antislavery and to political parties opposed to slavery. Peter Lesley's first response to the law was dismay. In early October, writing from Boston to his father, he reported on the "real horror to many here, indeed I trust to all good people everywhere, I mean of course this new and dreadful law for returning the slaves." Nonetheless he seemed uncertain whether there was anything he should or could do personally. "The only mitigation of the horror that all feel comes from the hope that, as Satan always overreaches his own ends, the very enormity of the thing will produce a speedy repeal." Peter Lesley and his wife, Susan, earnestly hoped that the law "will be evaded in every possible way."[46]

James Lesley's inquiry about Mary Walker put Peter and Susan Lesley to the test. *Would they take in a fugitive slave?*

"EVERYBODY IN BOSTON IS ARMED in one way or another, if not with dirks and pistols, at least with scripture and indignation." So

Peter Lesley wrote to a fellow minister in early November 1850. "A hundred extra fugitives have already entered the City as a place of refuge." He reported that he had joined the fray—with an indignant sermon—and indeed had given an advance copy to be published immediately in William Garrison's *Liberator,* the most outspoken antislavery newspaper in the nation.[47] What he did not reveal to his correspondent, to parishioners, or to Garrison was that he and his wife had joined the ranks of the lawbreakers.

Mary Walker was in the Lesley household, or known to be en route, when the minister rose to address his flock on October 30, 1850.[48] He began his sermon with a passage from Deuteronomy 23: *"Thou shalt not deliver unto his master the servant that is escaped from his master unto thee. He shall dwell with thee, wherever he shall choose; thou shalt not oppress him."* The minister acknowledged at once that there were those who thought he should not be speaking on this subject from the pulpit—that the pulpit and politics should stay separate. "In this, as in so many other things, people think wrong." When "the trembling slave is hunted through the land and dragged back to the bondage of a malicious revenge—where else than at the home of the altar shall he lay hold?"

Stopping short of revealing the Lesleys' decision to give refuge to Mary Walker, the minister posed the choice that all Northerners of conscience now faced. "Would Christ return fugitive slaves?"

> Imagine the Savior saying, in reply—I cannot help you, friend; it is a hard case; I pity you from my heart; but I dare not conceal you, or help you conceal yourself, for I shall be fined thousands of dollars, and probably be put in jail, if I do. We can only wait and try to repeal the law next winter. "Next winter! Lord! The hunter is at my heels—there is no judge to appeal to, no jury to listen to my case. . . . Lord, protect me, Lord . . ." Imagine the Savior still replying—I cannot, friend, it is against the law!

> Think of the risk I would run; remember that I am an American citizen. Be considerate, now, and bear your fate like a man.

"Give this law of Congress to the winds," Peter Lesley urged his Milton congregation. "Harbor, and protect the oppressed wherever you behold him."[49]

Mary Walker had found her sanctuary.

3 "In the Midst of Friends"

"My feelings have been greatly moved by Peter's having a Fugitive Slave woman sent to his care, & one of the most interesting people I ever saw." So Susan Lesley confided to her closest friend, almost two weeks after Mary Walker's arrival in Milton, Massachusetts. The Fugitive Slave Law had moved Peter Lesley from sympathy to antislavery action. For his twenty-six-year-old wife, Susan Lyman Lesley, Mary Walker herself brought "the whole subject of slavery home to me."

Clearly the minister's wife was startled that Mary Walker was a "Fugitive, for no one would guess it from her color, and her hair is quite smooth." Mary Walker spoke "the most beautiful English I ever heard, & seems like a lady. She sews beautifully, and wants to go out as a seamstress by the day or the week." Susan Lesley found the refugee to be "a truly religious person, [who] speaks of her old master and of slavery without resentment but with horror. When she thinks of her mother & her little children, whom she never expects to see on earth, for she left them in slavery, she says 'I will be patient, that I may meet them all in heaven, where we shall all be free.'" To Susan Lesley, Mary Walker's restraint only confirmed the horror of slavery—that such a fair and forbearing woman had been enslaved, that her family remained in captivity. Hearing about "the real experiences of a slave," Susan Lesley could no longer "be reconciled to the idea that slavery should exist in what we call a land of Liberty."[1]

Mary Walker eventually would reveal far more about her master, her children, and herself than she chose to disclose in the first week in Milton. For her safety, she could rely on Susan Lesley. Experience would decide if she could trust this Northern white woman with her secrets. Susan Lesley, for her part, clearly found Mary Walker a person to admire. What she had no way to foresee was that the fugitive and fugitive's family would ultimately provide the higher cause that she had long sought for her life. More than either woman could realize in November 1850, the arrival of the refugee would transform both their destinies.

SUSAN LYMAN'S QUEST FOR A cause had begun half a lifetime before, with the death of her sister in January 1837. Anne Jean Lyman, named for her mother and known as "Annie," was idealized by her family. For her mother, who was twenty-two when she married the forty-four-year-old judge and widower Joseph Lyman in 1811, her namesake daughter became the intellectual and spiritual companion that an aging husband could no longer be by the 1830s.[2] Physical fragility made Annie Lyman all the more precious.[3] Foreboding that "my holy child" was too good for this world was confirmed when rheumatic fever doomed the twenty-one-year-old daughter to an excruciating illness in the winter of 1836. Barely able to breathe, unable to sleep more than two hours in twenty-four, Annie Lyman sought to inspire thirteen-year-old Susan, who cared for her afflicted sister day and night for nine weeks. On her last day, the sister enjoined Susan Lyman to dedicate herself to a life of usefulness and benevolence to others. It was a pledge that "united me to her forever."[4]

Finding a higher destiny proved elusive for Susan. Like her sister, she was not well. Chronic headaches and endemic stomach ailments periodically forced her to bed. Her model of good works was shaped by her mother's example in the village of Northampton, Massachusetts, where they lived and where Susan had grown up. Cultivate conscience, act decently toward others, and the community would follow suit.[5] Small and conservative, Northampton was not a place where organized reform took root. When Susan Lyman first encountered a passionate social reformer in the early 1840s, she found herself wary. On the occasion of meeting Maria Weston Chapman, the outspoken abolitionist from Boston, Susan seemed to anticipate a woman who would overwhelm or dismiss her. Instead, she was "surprised to see a lady of such quiet, unobtrusive manners." "When she spoke of slavery, her manner was very fervent, and her voice deep, as if her whole soul had dwelt upon the matter." Susan found "the great Abolition woman" "so gentle and free from all violence, that though I could not feel as if she had the whole truth of the thing, yet there was a something that could not fail to excite admiration."[6] Still, Susan stood by her parents' views on slavery, hoping that "good slaveholders" and decent treatment would mitigate a system which there seemed to be no peaceable way to end.[7]

Extended trips to New York City in the mid-1840s widened Susan Lyman's horizons about the benevolent work needed in the world, but brought her no closer to finding a calling.[8] Her interest in good works was evident to her New York hosts, who arranged for her to teach eight orphaned youngsters in the basement of a church she attended on Sunday. The twenty-three-year-old Good Samaritan from Northampton had little idea how to reach such children, with "the wickedness of age and crime stamped on their young features . . . bearing witness to the sins of their parents."[9] Brought as a guest to a meeting of the New York Prison Association, Susan learned of the staggering vastness of misery and crime in the city. Undeterred, she inquired about work with fallen women whose misfortunes had produced the abandoned children. There was a refuge for those women, she was told, but not a role for anyone like her. The hardened women there despised mere "words of kindness." "All agree that no young lady ought to go to the Home. The records of crime & seduction are too sad & woeful, & the hearts of such cannot be touched easily, except by age & experience."[10]

Still seeking, she turned to two persons who had become her dearest friends in the city. Susan Lyman had first met Lydia Maria Child in 1838, when Maria Child and her husband, David, had spent a year in Northampton. One of the most versatile, prolific, and spirited reformers of the age, Child was hailed as *"the first woman in the republic"* by William Lloyd Garrison, editor of the *Liberator* and the era's most radical abolitionist.[11] Maria Child moved to New York City in 1841, to become the editor of the *National Anti-Slavery Standard.* Child hoped that her labors in New York might allow her to bridge rifts in the antislavery movement and to repair an unhappy marriage. Thwarted, she left the paper in the spring of 1843, and turned to writing about places and people of the "great Babylon."[12] Her literary career rejuvenated, she found joy as well in a fervid but platonic friendship with a wonderfully enthusiastic sunbeam of a man, John Hopper. Thirteen years younger than Maria Child, John was the son of Isaac Hopper, the famed Quaker battler on behalf of fugitive slaves in early nineteenth-century Philadelphia, who had moved to New York in 1829.[13]

The two New York friends took Susan Lyman under their wing. To Maria Child, Susan became a surrogate daughter—innocent, inquisitive, and grateful for the music and conversations they shared.[14] To John Hopper, Susan became a confidante, someone to whom he could reveal his blossoming but forbidden love for Rosa deWolfe, the daughter of a man in Bristol, Rhode Island, whose family had made its fortune in the African slave-trade.[15] John Hopper recognized that his benevolent young friend from Northampton did not want to be written off, as she had been by others, as too innocent to see the worst of New York or too infirm to do good works. So without telling anyone, he escorted her to the lairs of vice in the city. Together they "ploughed through the filth of Five Points, & through the Tombs, and into the worst of all places, the haunts of abandoned women." Susan had hoped for "a new lesson in the book of Life." In reality, the scenes struck "horror . . . upon the spirit." John Hopper "knew it would not altogether do" to leave Susan overwhelmed. So he took her from their long tramp to "some artist's studio . . . to show me something beautiful, to divert my thoughts, and these things he did in a most natural & pleasant way."[16]

Had Susan Lyman come to New York at an earlier time, she might have found her friends in the Hopper household still deeply involved in the struggle against slavery, and made their cause her life's work. But Maria Child's attempts to bridge schisms in the antislavery movement—between those who roundly denounced slavery, slave-holders, fence-sitting Northerners, and the Union itself; and those who hoped that more temperate tactics would further the cause—had left her scalded by critics. It was a sobered and distanced abolitionist that Susan encountered in the mid-1840s, who despite an occasional letter on behalf of a fugitive slave, had taken leave of the movement.[17] John Hopper, too, had found other causes. Only his father, Isaac Hopper, riveted Susan Lyman's attention to slavery, sharing with her many "strange and romantic experiences in the course of his eventful life that I shall never forget. His efforts in the antislavery cause, while he lived in Philadelphia, were wonderful."[18]

Home again in Northampton, personal traumas diminished Susan's hopes for either happiness or a higher destiny. In 1847, a family friend pursued and won her heart, only to retreat without explanation.[19] That fall, she took charge of her enfeebled father, seventy-six-year-old Judge Joseph Lyman. His death in December 1847 left her to care for her widowed mother, whom she had promised never to leave, "even for a few months, so long as you want me."[20] The cumulative impact of failed romance, her father's death, and her mother's care left Susan dispirited. She went through the motions of housekeeping and neighborliness, but inside felt vacant and mechanical.[21] Her aspirations atrophied. She imagined herself as "a little old maid" or, alternatively, wed to a kindly new suitor who had the wish and means to provide for her. She confessed herself ready "to give up the ideal of a perfect love"—indeed, ready to give up loftier visions altogether.[22]

ON THE LAST DAY OF July 1848, Susan Lyman's sights lifted. Peter Lesley arrived at the Lymans' Northampton home as the guest of Susan's older brother, Joseph. She had learned of him earlier through relatives in Boston.[23] She knew that he held the pulpit at the Milton church of her aunt and uncle, who had recruited the twenty-nine-year-old minister to take charge of their congregation. The Milton faithful soon discovered that their young clergyman was a visionary. Susan Lyman's brother Joseph and their Milton aunt and uncle knew that Peter Lesley's vision and tenacity had made him *persona non grata* to the clerical hierarchy of Massachusetts.

If Susan Lyman was aware of the circumstances that jeopardized the future of her visitor, they were immaterial. Here was a man willing to stand up for his convictions, come what may. Here was a man with a passion for truth and a willingness to act on his beliefs. She instantly sensed in Peter Lesley something she was searching for in all those she met. On the morning of August first, after a day spent in the company of the guest her brother had brought to Northampton, Susan Lyman knew she had found a man with soul. Then and there, she later confessed to Peter Lesley, she "was ready to throw my arms around you."[24]

"Why didn't you?" Peter Lesley later chided Susan Lyman. The young minister had been just as instantaneous in sensing that this was the match he'd been looking for. The family was divided over the engagement of an impetuous minister with a dubious future to a young woman of no wealth and poor health. Susan's mother, who at twenty-two had boldly married a forty-four-year-old widower with five young children, backed her daughter wholeheartedly. Her closest aunt, Cath-

erine Robbins, was deeply ambivalent, not knowing "whether to laugh or cry, to sing or croak." Susan's two brothers, sure that the headstrong minister was putting their fragile sister at risk, charged him with "threatening my death or destruction, for his own comfort."[25] Throughout the tempest, Susan Lyman "kept a tranquil spirit." "I feel in my heart I would rather suffer with him, than be happy with anyone else."[26]

Susan Lyman anticipated a happier destiny than one of shared suffering. She foresaw the beginning of "a new and better life," in which her husband-to-be would help her realize her work in the world.[27] Susan acknowledged to her fiancé that her capacity for empathy had immobilized her. "I have all my life been permitted to love & to sympathize with the good and the wicked, the humble & the exalted, & the afflicted of every description." To *act,* she needed Peter Lesley's guidance. "Oh aid me, dearest friend, in this work of life, to unite my inward aspirations to my outward life. With thoughts high enough to overpower me, yet my life has been poor, & broken into parts. I have been weak in action. Be to me a stern second conscience, as well as the dearest of friends."[28]

Susan Lyman summed up the transformation in her life in a November 1848 letter to a cherished friend, Margaret Harding White, whom she had first met at boarding school in Boston, and who would remain a correspondent for sixty years. To her friend "Meggie" she wrote that a "stronger, richer man than" Peter Lesley might better provide for "my earthly destiny." But "oh such a one could not meet the wants of my heart & soul as he does, & bring out in my character all the powers that have so long lain asleep. Meggie! I feel as if I could do & be anything now."[29] Susan Lyman and Peter Lesley wed on February 13, 1849.

A year and a half after their marriage, when her husband's Philadelphia cousin asked the Lesleys to give Mary Walker sanctuary in Massachusetts, the refugee's arrival opened the way for Susan Lyman Lesley to find her work in the world.

"HARBOR, AND PROTECT THE OPPRESSED," Peter Lesley exhorted his Milton congregation in his stirring sermon at the end of October 1850. The Lesleys did just that for Mary Walker. After their marriage, the young couple lived hand-to-mouth as boarders with relatives and as renters on their own. Susan Lesley suffered a heartrending miscarriage in April 1850; in early July, hemorrhaging brought her to the brink of death. Only God's dispensation and a nurse's care saved his wife, Peter Lesley believed, and he gratefully "received her by faith and miracle from the grave." Though the ordeal left his wife drained and "made an old man of me," both Lesleys were improving and ready to start afresh as autumn began when news came of Mary Walker's need for refuge.[30] The trio took lodging in a little house in Milton in late November, but the expectation seemed to be that for Mary Walker, their home would be a way station, while the Lesleys sought a household that could safeguard and employ her permanently.

Mary Walker came to Massachusetts with a strong letter of reference from James Lesley. She did not seek charity. Neat in her person, a high-minded woman, she was "in every way worthy of encouragement. All she asks is work, and this she is willing to perform cheerfully." An expert needlewoman who did beautiful handiwork, she could support herself. "She can make shirts as well as anyone." "Of her moral character, you may give any recommendation. Here she gained herself a high reputation for propriety of deportment." Her legal status was a more delicate matter. By Pennsylvania law at least, she was technically *not* a fugitive from slavery. Since she was "*brought here,* subsequent to the passage of the state law of '47, she was a free woman in my opinion." Nonetheless, that legal shield was rendered uncertain by the new federal law of 1850. Because "still there was a danger of her being carried off," she'd fled farther north. "Any thing, that you can do, in procuring her a situation," James Lesley concluded the letter to his cousin, "will be thankfully regarded by me."[31]

Finding another family to take in Mary Walker proved difficult. Friends were most certainly willing to help. One neighbor gave her a nice fitting-out, providing a wardrobe to see her through the New England winter. Others gave her work. But efforts to secure a good place for her fell through. The Lesleys' ministerial set of acquaintances may not have had the wherewithal to hire a new live-in worker. More fundamentally, there was surely fear about hosting her. If she *could* be claimed as a fugitive, her protectors risked being charged with a crime. The difficulties caught Susan Lesley by surprise, as she confessed to her best friend. Naively, they'd both assumed that it was "a foretaste of heaven to be able to do anything for anybody," the "sweetest pleasure the world has to give." Neither had any idea there would "be so many obstacles to our doing what we want for others."[32]

Susan Lesley's best hope for placing Mary Walker lay with Louisa Loring, the wife of New England's leading abolitionist attorney, Ellis Gray Loring. Susan Lesley had a passing acquaintance with them both, and knew the Lorings to be philanthropic persons with the resources to employ and defend Mary Walker. She wrote to them in early December and didn't hear back until the end of the month, when Louisa Loring declined. "I have constantly hoped indeed expected to be able to employ her myself or find some one else," but the Lorings already had offered a place to "an unfortunate person" some weeks before, and that woman had just accepted. Louisa Loring enclosed a small gift for the Lesleys' "protégé," adding that "I need not tell you how much I feel" for "your *Mary.*"[33]

Mary Walker would stay with the Lesleys. In early January they were joined by Susan Lesley's widowed mother, Anne Jean Robbins Lyman, and for intermittent stays by her unmarried sister, Catherine Robbins. Into that multigenerational household came another fugitive slave named Nancy, who took over the responsibilities of cook and housekeeper. Far from feeling burdened, Peter Lesley expressed deep contentment. "Our home and the air about us and our habits of life are all that we could wish," he wrote to his father at the end of January 1851. "We shall never be happier or in a better position for enjoying life than we are now." Yet if life in the Lesley household in Milton was bucolic, the moral skies of New England were anything but clear. Slave-holders had dispatched agents to hunt down fugitives in Boston, and had found sympathizers ready to help them. Lesley was "more shocked than grieved to find that in *New England,* the very sanctum and last refuge of liberty, the poor fugitive is as unsafe as elsewhere."[34]

For her part, Mary Walker sought safety in legal affidavits. She and allies in Philadelphia yet hoped that the 1847 Pennsylvania law, which declared free any slaves voluntarily brought into the state by their owners, would guard her from being claimed as a fugitive. She wrote back to friends, asking them to give depositions on her behalf, and from December 20 to January 16, four of them separately did so before a Philadelphia justice of the peace. Each deposition specified how long the witness had known Mary Walker and testified that during three separate summers, in the years 1846–1848, she had dwelt in the city from six to ten weeks at a time. Each witness affirmed that Mary Walker was voluntarily brought to Philadelphia by her master: "said Mary did not escape from a state where slavery is recognized." Mary Walker asked James Lesley also to have an affidavit made out and sent to her. Anything "calculated to relieve her mind, will of course be well worth attending to," he responded, and promised to "see to it without fail." But by late January 1851, he feared it would be of no effect, for already a Pennsylvania district court judge had ruled that the 1850 Fugitive Slave Law overrode the Pennsylvania state law.[35]

The depositions in hand, Mary Walker asked Peter Lesley to seek a legal opinion about whether they would protect her in Massachusetts. He turned again on Mary Walker's behalf to Ellis Gray Loring, the leading antislavery lawyer in New England, sent him the documents, and asked his view. Loring responded that because Mary Walker had left bondage in Pennsylvania, she technically "is not a fugitive from any state in which she owed service, & she is free by the law of Massachusetts." But he added quickly that "even in this case, she is not wholly out of danger." The U.S. Supreme Court might reverse the decision of "our own State Court, & may decide that a slave is not freed by being brought by her master into a free state."[36] The more imminent danger, Loring thought, was that Mary Walker's owner could go to a Southern court and "procure a certificate that she was a slave & escaped from his service." The Fugitive Slave Law of 1850 "makes this certificate *conclusive,* as to every point, except that of personal identity. If this course should be followed, the affidavits you produce . . . would not be admitted, as evidence for any purpose." Considering "this clause of the new law," Loring concluded, "I could not feel very safe, as to my friend, who *had ever been* a slave."[37]

SAFETY LAY WITH THE LESLEYS and their secure location just outside of staunchly antislavery Boston. Mary Walker threw herself into becoming a valued part of the Lesley household and the neighborhood around it. Work became easier to find as nearby women learned of her skill as a seamstress. They called on her to make dresses for themselves, shirts for their husbands, and garments for their children. Mary Walker typically boarded at the residence of those who hired her, where she first measured sizes and patterns and then sewed the clothes, often spending a week or more at the tasks. In other families, she was asked to help out the lady of the house or to care for young children. Mary Walker found it best not to talk about her past, lest loose lips betray her whereabouts to slave-hunters now brazenly foraging around Boston. Her reserve only deepened others' attachments to her. Mary Walker became a full-fledged human being in Milton—a literate, well-read, handsome mixed-race woman, who did beautiful work as a seamstress and could look after a household as well. With the publication of *Uncle Tom's Cabin,* which started with serialized chapters in newspapers in the fall of 1851 and culminated with the entire book in early 1852, Mary Walker came to stand for even more to the women of Milton. In their midst was a living embodiment of bondage and one who, like the character Eliza in Harriet Beecher Stowe's novel, was a "white slave" at that. Neighbors invited her to tea, and when the subject of another prominent book came up in conversation, they found that Mary Walker had just read it. It was Susan Warner's novel *The Wide, Wide World,* an immensely popular saga in which—through Christian self-mastery and a saintly woman friend—an orphaned young heroine overcomes suffering and self-pity to achieve spiritual perfection. Mary Walker had ample comments to share. "From that time her tongue ran glibly. She said when she came home that she had a beautiful time. The only trouble was that they made too much of her."[38] It seemed astonishing that such a woman should be enslaved, and shattering to think that her children were still captives.

Outwork often took Mary Walker away from the Lesley household, but then its other members were far from stationary. Peter Lesley, though devoted to the faithful of his Milton congregation, was increasingly uncertain about his future in the ministry. He accepted additional commissions for geological survey and mapmaking work that took him to the hills of Pennsylvania for weeks at a time. His mother-in-law, Anne Jean Lyman, who had moved into the Milton cottage in January 1851, proved equally nomadic. Though the sixty-one-year-old widow had the company of her daughter Susan, her sister Catherine Robbins, Mary Walker, and even a young Northampton protégé who had just finished Harvard and come to teach in the village school, she nonetheless remained in an unsettled state. With little notice, she took off for trips back to Northampton or impromptu visits to other family members.[39]

Would the care of Anne Jean Lyman fall to Mary Walker? In many ways, the two women were perfectly mismatched. Anne Jean Robbins Lyman was buoyant and always up and doing. During her married life in Northampton, she always rose early to dust the house before waking her two servant-women, darned or mended all manner of garb with what her children dubbed her "goblin tapestry," read aloud or urged others to read to her from morning to night, and kept up with village gossip from her rocker at the door, hailing all in sight to share their news or listen to a passage she had just come upon. She relished conversation, monitored the affairs of the day, and saw to it that her domestics got as much learning as she thought they could absorb and that worthy young men from Northampton went to Harvard, whether their parents wished it or not. Anne Jean Lyman had little liking for solitude, and no patience for moodiness. Mary Walker was reserved, prone to serious headaches, and given to pensive sadness—partly a matter of temperament, certainly a consequence of the circumstances of her life. Nor was Anne Jean Lyman an abolitionist. On the contrary, to her one-time Northampton neighbor, antislavery writer Lydia Maria Child, Mrs. Lyman seemed aristocratic, opposed to any social movement that would disturb the nation's peace, and disposed to view slavery as one of those lamentable things one could simply do nothing about.[40] It was no blessing to her to be harboring a fugitive slave.

Nonetheless, Mary Walker and Anne Jean Lyman found ways to touch chords in each other. Both women had arrived in the Milton household in a state of transition and uncertainty. Mary Walker had left behind her family in North Carolina and her friends in Philadelphia. Anne Jean Lyman, her husband dead and her children grown and gone, had left a Northampton that had centered her world for twenty-five years. For the New Englander, there was a deeper source of restlessness. Her mind and memory were beginning to grow erratic; she fainted one moment, woke lucid the next. Anne Jean Lyman would need safeguarding.[41] Mary Walker, who had nursed others for much of her adult life, was expert as a caregiver. What was not clear, to Mary

Walker or anyone, was which Anne Jean Lyman would hold sway—the motherly Good Samaritan eager to encourage, or the faltering widow in need of care.

"MY THOUGHTS ARE IN CONFLICT about my course." So wrote Peter Lesley the first week in April 1852, and with those words signaled that Mary Walker's life was about to change again. During the previous year, the young minister seemed to have worked out a modus vivendi with two jobs. When he was home, he served his congregation from the pulpit in Milton, albeit at the Town Hall rather than a regular church, and as a lay minister rather than an ordained one. To supplement his income, he turned ever more to geological-survey work, and agreed to complete a survey in Pennsylvania for his old mentor, Henry Rogers. But in the spring of 1852, he had come to feel that his patron was exploiting him—planning to pay him less than others, preparing to deny him credit for his work. Should he just swallow pride, he asked his wife, and regard the betrayal by his mentor as "wholesome discipline, profit from it spiritually, though not temporally?" Should he flee—going to California to start afresh? Should he match theft with theft—partnering with another mapmaking refugee from Henry Rogers and selling their survey maps to private companies? The thought of release from his pulpit and his patron exhilarated him. "If you could see my inner man, you would hardly recognize it under the energizing influences of an open season and a wide field of enterprise. The moment I am emancipated from the petty thralldom of the study chair and shake off the small responsibility of the weekly sermon, I am a man again."[42] Whichever course Peter Lesley took, his emancipation would disrupt the home that Mary Walker had just settled into.

Peter Lesley's association with Mary Walker may have prompted him to use the language of thralldom to describe his relationship to his church and his mentor. He likened neither explicitly to *slavery*—the minister surely knew *that* would be blasphemous. Yet had Mary Walker seen Peter Lesley's letters, she would have recognized the feelings that swept over her protector. His mentor sought "to make himself absolute Master of everybody & everything, recipient of all the advantages & all the fame." He had robbed others and intended to rob him of his due "renown & its results." Part of him wanted publicly to denounce the conduct of his mentor, though he acknowledged that "the 'paths of revenge lie so close to that of self redress, that it is hard to avoid them.'" Susan Lesley counseled a different course. "Here & now is the very time to call up your Christian principles" and to leave "without crimination or recrimination." Do "not have on your conscience any word or act, that shall be a sword in your memory at some future day."[43]

Peter Lesley followed his wife's advice. Unlike Mary Walker, who stole away from her master, he told his nemesis face to face that he was leaving. Even then, Peter Lesley was beset by feelings that would have been familiar to Mary Walker as she had readied to flee. "I was sick with protracted emotions." Confronted, the angry employer charged Lesley with "faithlessness." In turn, Lesley "hardly dared speak above my breath for fear of committing some violence." Even though quitting left him unemployed, he resolved to "live on bread and water" rather than "enslaving myself." His act was a form of deliverance. "[When I] took my hat and walked out, I felt . . . as if I had waked from a long and frightful nightmare to find myself in a summer morning among the trees of an orchard, & the birds."[44] Mary Walker had known the feeling.

Susan Lesley assured her husband that none of his impulses alarmed her, but privately she knew that his decision augured great changes for everyone—for herself, for her mother, and for Mary Walker. He was leaving the ministry and taking up geology "on his own hook and pursuing it for the business of his life." It would mean months of separation while he did work in the field, and risks to his health and eyesight. It was inevitable that they would leave New England. The prospect of a move, along with the deteriorating mental health of Anne Jean Lyman, prompted deep anxiety. As Susan Lesley faced uprooting, she realized the urgency of finding a "permanent home" for all those she must leave behind.[45]

MARY WALKER WAS NOT IN the Lesley household during the weeks that Peter and Susan Lesley were making their life-changing decisions. She was working at the home of a neighboring Milton minister, John Morrison, and his wife, Emily. Ironically, at the very moment that the Lesleys realized they must leave the region, Mary Walker's experience at the Morrisons' profoundly deepened her attachment to her New England hosts.

In the Morrisons' home that spring, Mary Walker saw firsthand the degree to which the Lesleys' friends would extend themselves on behalf of a servant in their employ. Mary Walker reported the experience to Susan Lesley, who shared the account with her husband in a long, detailed letter of late April 1852. The Morrisons had a young Irish servant woman, nineteen-year-old Mary Moore, who had become a treasured friend of Mary Walker during their time together in Milton. The young Irish girl had fallen ill in the Morrison household, and the minister and his wife had spared no effort to comfort and care for her. They gave her their warmest room. The minister's wife "waited on her as if she were a sister or a child." "Many a night," Mary Walker told Susan Lesley, "the poor girl seized Mrs. Morrison's hand, kissed it—& cried over it, saying, 'These dear hands were white & soft, a lady's hands, when I came here to live, but they are now coarse & rough, with doing *my* work, and waiting on me.'" When the physician attending her suggested that Mary Moore go to a hospital in Boston, Mary Walker prepared her to make the trip in a large carriage with two nurses. Her parting words "to Mary Walker . . . were full of faith in God, & love for the family." The Morrisons visited her on successive days and were reassured that she was improving, only to be told by the doctor on their next visit, "That girl of yours . . . died," with no familiar face or voice around. Mary Walker consoled the Morrisons. "Christ took her into glory, all the same as if she had left this world in the midst of friends."[46]

"Love for the family," "in the midst of friends"—surely Mary Walker had felt those impulses in bondage, only to realize that such feelings welded her more deeply to persons, however caring, for whom she was property. The example of the Morrisons and Mary Moore brought home how different human relations might be in the North. "Mary Walker looks as if she walked in another world, these last few days," Susan Lesley reported to her husband. She "says she loved Mary Moore like a sister, & her death seems to have opened the other world to her."[47]

Mary Walker had no idea when she returned to the Lesleys in early May that Peter Lesley had quickly found a new full-time job in Philadelphia, and that both husband and wife were exchanging scenarios that might cushion the change for the other women in the Milton household—mother Anne Jean Lyman, her sister Catherine Robbins, and Mary Walker. A new employer had offered Lesley $1,200 for a year of survey work in western Pennsylvania. Euphoric, he wrote that "Everything since I left home has brightened around me." His search for work ended so swiftly that he seemed to imagine quick cures for everyone. He proposed immediately to buy a home in Philadelphia, presumably with money advanced by his father and new employer. His wife's mother and aunt could then come for long visits, even move there if they wanted—though he admitted that a move would unsettle them. As to Mary Walker, if "she will come with us," "I have no fear . . . about her liberty, but I do not know what she can do to work. She must either live with us as a friend or remain in Milton." Within two weeks, he seems to have realized that he surely *should* have fears about Mary Walker's safety in Philadelphia. "She dare not come here." He proposed another panacea: they would buy Mary Walker a sewing machine. In Philadelphia, skilled seamstresses had machines. It "does work neatly," and "saves the eyes." For an investment of $100, Mary Walker could stay in New England and make a living on her own.[48]

Susan Lesley's plans for Mary Walker and her mother were less focused on logistics and more attuned to the emotional upheavals that she expected both women to experience once they learned she was leaving. She planned to stay in Milton through the summer of 1852 to make arrangements for everyone, and hoped to work things out before acquaintances learned of her husband's decision. But word got out, and almost immediately offers came in from others for Mary Walker to work and live with them, looking after children, doing household jobs.

Had it been merely a matter of employment, the former bondswoman might have viewed the surfeit of invitations as a welcome problem, and negotiated accordingly. But all her life she had accommodated others, first as an enslaved woman in the South, and then as a refugee in the North. The ability to negotiate required a readiness to decline if a match seemed wrong, and faith that there would be other offers to come. Women who had many employers knew how to do this. By upbringing and experience, Mary Walker did not. She was a refugee, about to lose her protector. She was a woman who just had begun to sense what it might be like to have employers she could regard as friends, even as family, and now found herself required to start again.

Mary Walker confessed to Susan Lesley that she felt caught, especially by one offer. She had done occasional work for a cousin of Susan Lesley—Sarah Forbes—who also lived in Milton. Sarah was the wife of James Murray Forbes, a merchant and railroad magnate whose business success had made him one of the wealthiest men in the country. When Sarah Forbes, mother of several young children and pregnant with another, learned that the Lesleys were leaving Milton, she instantly proposed that Mary Walker move in with the Forbes and care for their children. Mary Walker acknowledged that the Forbeses had "always been extremely kind to her"—it seemed "the basest ingratitude" to refuse them. But it was her "settled conviction, that she cannot live in a large family & where there are children." "Mrs. L., it is not the life I am fit for. I don't want to be with children. It is always reminding me of my own, & what shall I do?" Mary Walker agreed to attend Sarah Forbes through her pregnancy, and then looked to Susan Lesley and her aunt to explain why "I cannot stay." On her behalf, they explained to the cousin that "All this & more she has wanted to say to you a dozen times, but has not had the resolution to do so in the face of all your kindness, & knowing how ill you often are."[49]

As Susan Lesley viewed it, Mary Walker was overwhelmed. "I shall have . . . to make some good arrangement for poor Mary, who has shown herself to need it very much of late. Everybody pulls her about, and makes her do just as they like, for she has no power to say no." From Mary Walker's vantage point, however, it was resolution enough to have Susan Lesley and her aunt convey the refusal on her behalf, a refusal she understandably found difficult to express face to face. Without power, she nonetheless found her own way—a refugee's way, through intermediaries and indirection—to "say no."

Susan Lesley understood that Mary Walker needed more than a job. She needed a home. "I can never leave her in Milton without some more permanent resting place than she has now."[50] One plan might have kept Mary Walker in the household with Anne Jean Lyman, who more than ever needed a person to care for her. But her mother's situation had become so unstable that Susan Lesley had no certainty that any plan for her would take hold, and thought it unwise to make Mary Walker any part of it. In the midst of writing to her close friend Meggie White, Susan Lesley suddenly "saw mother on the floor. I got her up and her senses returned in a second." One minute she was walking; the next she "felt a spasm in her heart, mist in her eyes, and fell." Then as abruptly, she woke again and seemed "as bright and funny as ever." Six such attacks had occurred over the previous winter; in May 1852, four occurred in a single day. Perhaps small strokes, perhaps narcolepsy, perhaps symptoms of what the twentieth century would term Alzheimer's disease, the attacks took their toll. Anne Jean Lyman developed "very vague and untrue impressions of people, things, and especially of conversation." Susan Lesley now understood that there were physical reasons behind the dramatic change in her mother's behavior. "I am full of compassion and patience for facts which have disturbed and troubled me: a great falling off in that truth of character which I used to consider one of her distinguishing traits." The conclusions were inescapable. Her mother needed to remain where she had friends, preferably in Milton. And without doubt, she needed "a proper companion." Susan Lesley had in mind a woman from Northampton, Martha Swan, who had served in the Lyman household for many years, and who could supply the memories and capacity for guidance that her mother was losing.[51]

Susan Lesley thought it best to plan separately for Mary Walker. Who among her circle of acquaintances could best secure Mary Walker from all the dangers that the refugee faced? Who could comprehend Mary Walker's need for friendship, as well as work? On May 21, 1852, she wrote to Louisa Loring.

"I CANNOT TELL YOU HOW happy she made me," Susan Lesley wrote to her husband on May 25. Louisa Loring had arrived in her carriage, and for almost an hour they took "a beautiful drive." The Lorings agreed to look after Mary Walker. The antislavery lawyer and his wife promised to protect her after the Lesleys departed. She would have light work and high wages. She could visit people in Milton when she wished—on Sundays if that suited her, for longer if she desired. If serious danger threatened, they would send her where she need fear nothing. To guard them all from easy discovery, Mary Walker would change her name to that of her dear departed friend Mary Moore. During the carriage ride, Susan Lesley explained that Mary Walker had become more than a seamstress, more than a domestic helper, more than a refugee in their household and in the home of their dearest neighbors. Louisa Loring understood. She promised that she and her husband would "be the best of friends to her." They agreed that Mary Walker would join the Lorings at the end of the summer and spend the fall with them for a long visit. If after that she wished "to live with them always," she could.[52]

Relieved, Mary Walker readily concurred with the plan. She had heard the Lesleys and others speak of the dedicated antislavery couple. The plan allowed her to remain with her benefactors in the Milton household until Susan Lesley left for Philadelphia. It gave her the opportunity to regain her poise and to deflect diplomatically the entreaties of others who wanted to hire her. Freed "from the coils she was caught in," Mary Walker, according to Susan Lesley, told "folks that she considered it her duty & her privilege to stay with me, until I leave these parts, & then she does not wish to make any engagement. It will be a great comfort to have her at home."[53]

Mary Walker experienced more than relief. She felt a deepened connection to Susan Lesley, who had charted a passage to safety. For Mary Walker, it was as if all the experiences that linked the two women now flooded to the fore. They were both mothers who had lost their children, Mary Walker by exodus, Susan Lesley by miscarriage. They were both women who knew sorrow, and tried to transcend it with faith. Yet for Mary Walker, there had always been boundaries. Life in bondage had taught her to be exceedingly guarded about how much of her feelings to disclose. She also knew that hers was not a conventional story of bondage. It was clear from her color that Mary Walker's forebears included whites. Who were these white relatives and parents, and what were the circumstances of their sexual relations with enslaved women and those of the women with them? Had friends or members of the Cameron household sired any of Mary Walker's children? What had been the resistance or compliance of Mary Walker's mother, her grandmother, and Mary Walker herself—and what responsibility, if any, had white family members taken toward those they knew to be kin or children of close family friends? An angry observer had written an anonymous letter to the Camerons charging that the household was full of proud half-breeds, neither properly enslaved nor fully freed.[54] If some part of this was Mary Walker's story, it was little wonder that she chose silence, letting others imagine for themselves how she came to be a person with fair skin tending toward white and eyes tending toward blue. The Lesleys obliged by asking no questions.

The boundaries broke one evening in early June 1852. Susan Lesley lay on the sofa in her Milton home, obliged by illness to keep herself indoors and at rest. Anne Jean Lyman was away, and Peter Lesley was at his new job in Philadelphia. Darkness had fallen. Unnoticed, Mary Walker came quietly into the room. According to Susan, she "knelt down, took my hand, and pressed it to her heart. She kissed it. She stroked my hair with her other hand." Then she rose hurriedly and said, in "her low trembling voice, 'This is Mr. Lesley's place. How often I have seen him here.'" "Since then," Susan Lesley wrote to her husband, "she has told me the whole strange tragedy of her life, that it has taken two years of confidence & kindness to win from her. I would not have asked her to tell me for worlds. Poor soul, yet she has a happy spirit."[55]

A hand on the heart, the stroking of hair, the revelation of secrets—Mary Walker had crossed over into trust. She trusted the Lesleys to welcome her affection and to understand her life story without pulling back from either. "I was very much moved," Susan Lesley wrote her husband. The Lesleys never put on paper the details of "the whole strange tragedy" of Mary Walker's life. On a later occasion, Peter Lesley saw fit to divulge some of the story to his brother Joseph, partly to help Joseph Lesley understand why his older brother and sister-in-law had become fervidly antislavery, partly to put the younger brother's troubles in perspective. Peter Lesley hastened to assure his wife that he had violated no trust. There were parts of the "story which I did not tell, nor can to any ears. They are sacred and I would feel dishonored and worthy of a perpetual punishment . . . if I breathed them."[56] In years to come, clues about the mystery of Mary Walker's "strange tragedy" appeared on rare occasions, focused on the identity of her father and the paternity of her children. But in thousands of letters written and preserved from a correspondence that lasted almost sixty years, the Lesleys never wrote explicitly about the nature of that tragedy.

Her most intimate secret unburdened, "Mary Walker often sits with me now," Susan Lesley reported to her husband, "and tells me sad stories of slavery, interspersed with many characters." The New England Unitarian, who had read *Uncle Tom's Cabin* earlier that year, found herself profoundly moved by the startling intensity of Mary Walker's firsthand accounts, "full of the poetic fervor of religious faith that belongs so peculiarly to the African race."[57] The former slave could finally share tales of the world she had left and express feelings she'd long held in check.

IRONICALLY, BY SEPTEMBER 1852 IT was Susan Lesley who had to hold her feelings in check. Months earlier, she thought she had settled on a suitable living arrangement not only for Mary Walker but for Anne Jean Lyman as well. In June 1852, it appeared that Anne Jean Lyman had decided to rent the house in Milton that they all had occupied for the previous eighteen months. Her devoted sister Catherine Robbins and two recent Harvard graduates, both her protégés from Northampton, agreed to join her. Aware of her own mental lapses, Anne Jean Lyman had grown "more and more anxious to be in a home of her own for the rest of her life." Even better news was that a former Northampton housekeeper, fully aware of Anne Jean Lyman's difficulties, had agreed to look after her. But when it came time to sign the lease for the Milton house, Anne Jean Lyman backed off. She "doesn't know what she wants," reported Catherine Robbins. Tired and flustered, Anne Jean Lyman fled to Northampton and, as weeks passed, remained undecided. She "will do as she wishes without regard for others," lamented her sister Catherine. The uncertainty led the Northampton caretaker to back out. Suddenly Mary Walker emerged as the best person to look after Anne Jean Lyman, and to share the burden of her care with Catherine Robbins. But how could Susan Lesley ask her? If Mary Walker found light work, friends, and an easy life with Ellis Gray and Louisa Loring, Susan Lesley could never advise her to forgo such security to help a mother with such vague plans. Susan Lesley would not try to sway her friend.[58]

Catherine Robbins felt far less constraint. In the months she and Mary Walker had dwelt together in Milton, the two had grown close. She knew that, grateful as Mary Walker was for the chance to try life with the Lorings, she was dejected at leaving the Milton household. "She says she seems destined to be separated from everybody she becomes attached to." In Milton, according to Catherine, Mary Walker felt "she has friends, and learned to feel at home." When Mary Walker left in September to join the Lorings at their lodging house in Beverly and the ocean shore, Catherine Robbins confessed that it was "a great loss to me." In letters to Catherine Robbins, Mary Walker expressed loss as well. Life with the Lorings was proving *too* easy. She had too much time to sit over her work and reflect; the ocean and woods were her only friends; there was little variety and nowhere to go; she missed Milton. Catherine Robbins didn't hesitate to reciprocate Mary Walker's feelings. "I have constantly written her how much I wanted her. I am sure I have wanted her every day since she went, and shall write again to say so."[59]

When Mary Walker returned from the shore in early November, she had made up her mind. She was well-contented to be with the Lorings, but not ready to stay with them. Their lives were too peripatetic. Louisa Loring did not like to keep house; she preferred to dwell in lodging houses. Mary Walker wanted to remain in Milton. For a time,

Mary Walker and Anne Jean Lyman had the household to themselves. Relieved from having to look after her sister all the time, Catherine Robbins returned for a visit to the home of cousins in Cambridge, Massachusetts, where she had dwelt for the previous decade. Nancy, the former slave who had been the Milton cook and housekeeper for almost two years, left to marry a fellow fugitive employed as a carriage driver in Boston. Susan Lesley had moved to Philadelphia. In letters to her daughter, Anne Jean Lyman poured out feelings of abandonment and loneliness.[60] But that was not the side of herself she revealed to Mary Walker. On the contrary, Mother Lyman took Mary Walker under her wing. She picked books and newspapers for them to share. She revived her Northampton custom of reading aloud.

For Mary Walker, the winter of 1852–1853 became an extraordinary time. "My Dear Mrs. Lesley," she began a letter on the first Saturday of January 1853. "The dearest of friends having a leasure today I thought I could not pass my time more to my satisfaction than to write you. The time I spent with Mrs. Loring at the Sea Shore was very pleasant to me though I was glad to get home after eleven weeks absence you may be sure." She was employed constantly making new dresses for five women in the neighborhood. Though "I miss you & dear Mr. Lesley very much, [we] all have your Mother." "I have enjoyed being with your dear mother who has been a mother to me & dear Miss Robbins." Both Anne Jean Lyman and Catherine Robbins read to her and to each other in the evenings, and their exertions inspired her. "I am trying to improve my self in writing & arithmetic." On Christmas Day, Anne Jean Lyman had taken Mary Walker to the annual Antislavery Bazaar held in Boston, where they both visited with Louisa Loring, its founder. A month later, the North Carolina native seemed fully at ease in her adopted New England household, where Anne Jean Lyman had embraced her as a surrogate daughter, knitting stockings and making a nightshirt and two nightcaps for her. A snowstorm outside, a warm fire and "the dearest of friends" inside, Mary Walker occupied herself with books, writing, and talking over past times with the women who'd become like mother and sister to her. "The winter has been a very happy one to me."[61]

Yet Mary Walker's tranquillity was in jeopardy. Paralyzed by her earlier indecision, Anne Jean Lyman had failed to renew the lease for the house in Milton. Even though she now wanted to stay, the dwelling had been rented to others. They all had to move and had no idea where. When Mary Walker fully realized the circumstances in late February 1853, she felt overwhelmed once more. Where would Anne Jean Lyman and Catherine Robbins go? What would happen to her? Again, the refugee faced the loss of home and friends. She felt a strong desire to "belong to somebody." Anne Jean Lyman felt no less deserted: it would be "the end of everything if she [Mary] leaves this house." At the last moment, Anne Jean Lyman's Boston son found a house for her in Cambridge, located just a block from Anne Jean Lyman's sisters and nieces. Once the house was rented, Anne Jean Lyman had a place to stay. Immensely relieved, Mary Walker agreed to join the household.[62] For both women, all seemed well.

Then Mary Walker received news from the South.

4 "Never Reject the Claims of the Fugitive"

Duncan Cameron had died. The startling news came to the household of Mary Walker on February 24, 1853. A friend of Mary Walker's from Philadelphia, perhaps the waiter who had seen her every day in the summer of 1848, had heard the report. Mary Walker was in shock. Was it true? Could they get confirmation? She asked Peter Lesley to contact James Fells, the free black carpenter with whom Mary Walker had kept in touch, and to write to a physician who had attended the Camerons when they came north. Word came back. "The old judge is dead." Mary Walker sank into depression. Wrote Catherine Robbins: "She has seemed more excited and unhappy than I have ever known her."[1]

In the nearly five years since she had left the Camerons in Philadelphia, Mary Walker had found friends, protection, and patrons for her work as a seamstress, caregiver, and companion. She had been welcomed into a household almost as adopted kin and had begun to focus on her own self-improvement as a free woman. She had never ceased to think about her children and her mother, about her separation from them without a parting word or any correspondence since. Her periodic illnesses, her headaches and her melancholy, were rooted in the sorrow of that separation. Yet she knew there was nothing she could do. The need for secrecy concerning her whereabouts forbade contact.[2] She could only hope that in the Raleigh household of Duncan Cameron, his daughters, and her mother, Silla, there was nothing she needed to do. Duncan Cameron's death forced her to confront the fate of her family. What would happen to them? Who would inherit them? Could she—*must she*—try to reclaim them from bondage? Events would reveal that Mary Walker became a woman obsessed.

What was to be done? Almost certainly, Mary Walker hoped that possession of her family would fall to Duncan Cameron's daughters. Margaret and Mildred Cameron had known Silla all of their lives. They had seen Silla help Rebecca Cameron and Rebecca Cameron help Silla, in sickness and in health. The Cameron girls had seen Mary Walker attend their dying sisters. Margaret and Mildred Cameron and their former servant knew each other's secrets and longings as only the members of the same household could. If anyone understood why Mary Walker had left them and their angry father in Philadelphia in 1848, surely the sisters did. Might they be ready to part with those children, for a fair price? Could Mary Walker hope, with the help of Northern friends, to buy her children out of slavery?

Mary Walker focused single-mindedly on the recovery of her children. She was prepared to do all that she could—to use her own savings and enlist the aid of others—to purchase them from the Cameron sisters. She knew that for her own safety, she would have to go through an intermediary. Without hesitation, Mary Walker decided she would ask Ellis Gray Loring and his wife Louisa for help.[3] Mary Walker didn't know whether Ellis Gray Loring would write the Cameron sisters directly or seek the help of secret antislavery sympathizers in the South. She simply assumed that with Loring's experience, he would know the best approach and would make every effort to help free her children. She had no illusions about the chances of success. She knew there was "ever so little hope," but, according to Susan Lesley, "she cannot rest without making a trial." Susan Lesley likewise doubted that any plan would work, and grieved that "*we* can't do anything for her." Nonetheless, she agreed that Mary Walker should consult "Mr. Loring," who "can't advise her wrong."

Susan Lesley had one word of warning. When Mary Walker did meet with Ellis Gray Loring, she should be certain to tell him "what a person the present master is. . . . One has to be ever so careful in dealings with such a character."[4]

WHY HAD MARY WALKER CONVEYED to the Lesleys such profound fears about "the present master"—the late judge's son, Paul Cameron? Why the need to be "ever so careful in dealings with such a character"? Without a doubt, Paul Cameron did not see himself as an inhumane man. As a young planter just starting out, he had pledged to his father that "no love of money shall ever induce me to be cruel," or to expose their workers to harmful weather. "It is besides miserable economy!" He viewed himself as a considerate son and brother, a decent and just master of slaves, a worthy successor to a grandfather, father, and uncle characterized by others as "men of feeling" when it came to their human property. Following in the footsteps of his uncle Thomas Bennehan, Paul Cameron had become the field doctor for the people of the plantation. With saddlebags carrying emetics and other remedies of the day, he made the rounds of the slave-quarters, looking in on "members of our black family," and if he found them merely sick but not in a perilous state, he treated them with laxatives intended to cleanse their systems and restore them to health. When he judged someone to be "dangerously ill," he immediately sent for a professional physician from nearby Hillsboro or Raleigh. As Paul Cameron saw it, he never stinted on his workers' food, garb, blankets, or shoes. Early on, his mother had exhorted him to be attentive when "the people ought to be shod." Obligingly, he kept the plantation's shoemakers busy every spring having them make new shoes for "our faithful old slaves, and their descendants."[5]

Nevertheless, Mary Walker and members of her family had seen the emergence of a thornier side of Paul Cameron. In 1829, Mary Walker was eleven and living with her mother at the main plantation dwelling of Fairntosh. While twenty-one-year-old Paul Cameron was away at Trinity College in Hartford, Connecticut, Duncan Cameron had become exasperated with plantation life and all the elements beyond his control: the periodic epidemics that swept away waves of workers and their children; the capricious weather and crop diseases which blighted whole seasons of work. In the winter of 1829, seizing the chance to become interim president of the State Bank of North Carolina, Duncan Cameron had left his family at Fairntosh and moved temporarily to Raleigh. He delegated oversight of the plantation to overseers and to selected slaves—including Mary Walker's uncle Luke. Duncan Cameron hoped that his son Paul would want nothing to do with plantation management—it was too fickle and too monotonous—and hoped he would choose the law instead. Paul Cameron had other ideas.[6] On his arrival home from college, the son took a tour of the plantation with Mary Walker's uncle Luke. With amusement and a touch of amazement, the planter's son reported Luke's pride about all he and Duncan Cameron were doing—building tobacco barns, stables, and now tanning yards. Why didn't his father just replace the name Fairntosh with "Hodgepodgiana," Paul Cameron joked to his sister. "Yes I expect to see his man Luke declare it a regular incorporated city and himself mayor and sole sovereign."[7] Despite the lighthearted tone, the young master was signaling that he had no intention of letting Luke or anyone else "declare himself mayor and sole sovereign."

In early 1835, Mary Walker and others at Fairntosh witnessed a formative episode in Paul Cameron's career as a plantation master. Now seventeen and the mother of a three-year-old son named Frank, Mary Walker still lived at Fairntosh along with her mother, Silla. Duncan

Cameron was twenty miles away in Raleigh, preparing to move himself, his wife, Rebecca, and his daughters to the city, where he had accepted the permanent presidency of the State Bank. At twenty-seven, Paul Cameron was helping to manage Fairntosh, and eager to give up a brief and unhappy attempt at the law. On the morning of April 25, one of Cameron's workers, a man named Jim, appeared at Fairntosh. Jim had been beaten by his overseer at one of the plantation quarters a few miles away. He had come to appeal to the young master. Both master and slave knew that physical beatings were rare on the Cameron place, that the overseer was new, and that Jim was no ordinary servant; he had been the gift of Paul's grandfather and was one of the plantation's oldest workers—though also "a bad and ungovernable slave." Paul Cameron sent Jim back to his overseer with the instruction to be obedient; the young master would come by the next day. But overseer William Nichols confronted Jim: You've been to see your master. Jim admitted it. What did you say to him? "That is my own business, Mr. Nichols," and with that Jim turned his back and began to walk away. Enraged at Jim's audacity, the overseer picked up a nearby fencepost and clubbed Jim over the head. Somehow Jim staggered back to Fairntosh. Fearing that we may have "a murder on our plantation," the shaken son wrote to his father in Raleigh. "I feel a *deep* solicitude that Jim should live."[8]

Mary Walker had been among the many Fairntosh residents waiting to see whether the Cameron plantation, now in the hands of the untested young master, would tolerate such brutality. Paul Cameron himself clearly wanted guidance from his father. His father apparently came home to deal directly with the episode and his unsettled son. The new overseer was not removed; there was no mention of a reprimand; Jim recovered and was reassigned to a different quarter.[9] The lesson was basic. In a dispute between an overseer and a slave, the planter must back authority. Mary Walker and others could only assume that the outcome was the young master's choice, and his alone.

Reports followed of Paul Cameron's further hardening. On a visit two months later to a field that was in a "desperate condition," the young master had found that the slave-driver "has not worked or made others work." Suggesting an end to squeamishness about physical punishment, the son had assured his father that "a new born spirit of industry must and *shall* be infused into the people upon this establishment!" Ten years later, faced with other workers who had "not acquitted themselves of their duty," Cameron was more explicit: "I have made them *feel* as well as acknowledge their neglect." Among slaves, Paul Cameron's readiness to take to the whip soon translated into a reputation for eagerness. Rumor spread to black laborers beyond Fairntosh that young Cameron beat his slaves "for no offense, but merely, as he said, *to let them know he was their master.*"[10]

In the 1840s, as Mary Walker and others saw it, Paul Cameron's ambitions had put the fortune of the white family and the destiny of its black families at risk. In 1844, Paul Cameron had persuaded his father to allow the son to buy a cotton plantation in the Black Belt of Alabama and to carry over a hundred men, women, and children from their home place in North Carolina to be its workers. In compelling the migration of one in five of the Cameron workers, Paul Cameron had initiated the first mass breakup of families in three generations of the plantation's history.[11]

In February 1853, Mary Walker and the Lesleys could only imagine the worst when they thought of what Paul Cameron might do, now that his father was dead. What part of his inheritance would he keep, what part mortgage, what part sell or send away, to slake his ambition? Little wonder that Susan Lesley felt wary of how Paul Cameron might respond if he learned of Mary Walker's secret effort to buy her children. "One has to be ever so careful in dealings with such a character."

WHEN SUSAN LESLEY ARRIVED in Cambridge in early June 1853, to spend the summer in the household of her mother, Mary Walker greeted her with great joy. To the delight of all, Susan Lesley was pregnant, expecting a child in November. Mary Walker was to attend to her friend's needs through the summer and then accompany her back to Philadelphia for the birth in the fall. There was another source of elation. Susan Lesley had brought with her a treasured friend of Mary Walker, Sarah Elbert. A free woman of color, Sarah Elbert had come to know Mary Walker in Philadelphia after she had left the Camerons in 1848. A housekeeper who served in the home of James Lesley, Sarah Elbert had sought her employer's help in late 1850, when the new Fugitive Slave Law had compelled Mary Walker to flee the city. When the two women reunited in Cambridge on the sixth of June 1853, they were swept away, as was Susan Lesley herself by what she witnessed. They "cried and sobbed," Susan Lesley wrote home to her husband. A grateful Mary Walker "can't let me alone. Her joy is like a frolicsome child." She "manages Mother like a wife" and the fixing-up of their newly rented Cambridge dwelling "goes on famously, in spite of the ancients fussing. Oh dear! How she makes us laugh."[12]

Even as Susan Lesley rejoiced in the happiness of her summer caregivers, she remained mindful of the shadow that slavery cast over them all. The year before, when she had read *Uncle Tom's Cabin,* she had admired its "beautiful spirit, so just to slaveholder as well as slave, so fervently religious in its tone, & so capable of showing every shade of the subject." As recently as January 1853, she had praised her Philadelphia minister for his "calm, and earnest, and loving appeals" on behalf of the slave. The uncertain fate of Mary Walker's children had brought home the full "horror and nightmare of slavery." She could "now understand the intense indignation of the abolitionists, all their bitterness. Christ himself would utter the same, were he now upon earth."[13] She passed on to Peter Lesley an account given to her of the last hours of one of New England's wealthiest men, the aged Robert Gould Shaw. Considered a man "remarkable for common sense all his life time," Shaw had amassed a fortune of a million and a half dollars. An "hour before he died," Shaw had summoned his children to his bed-

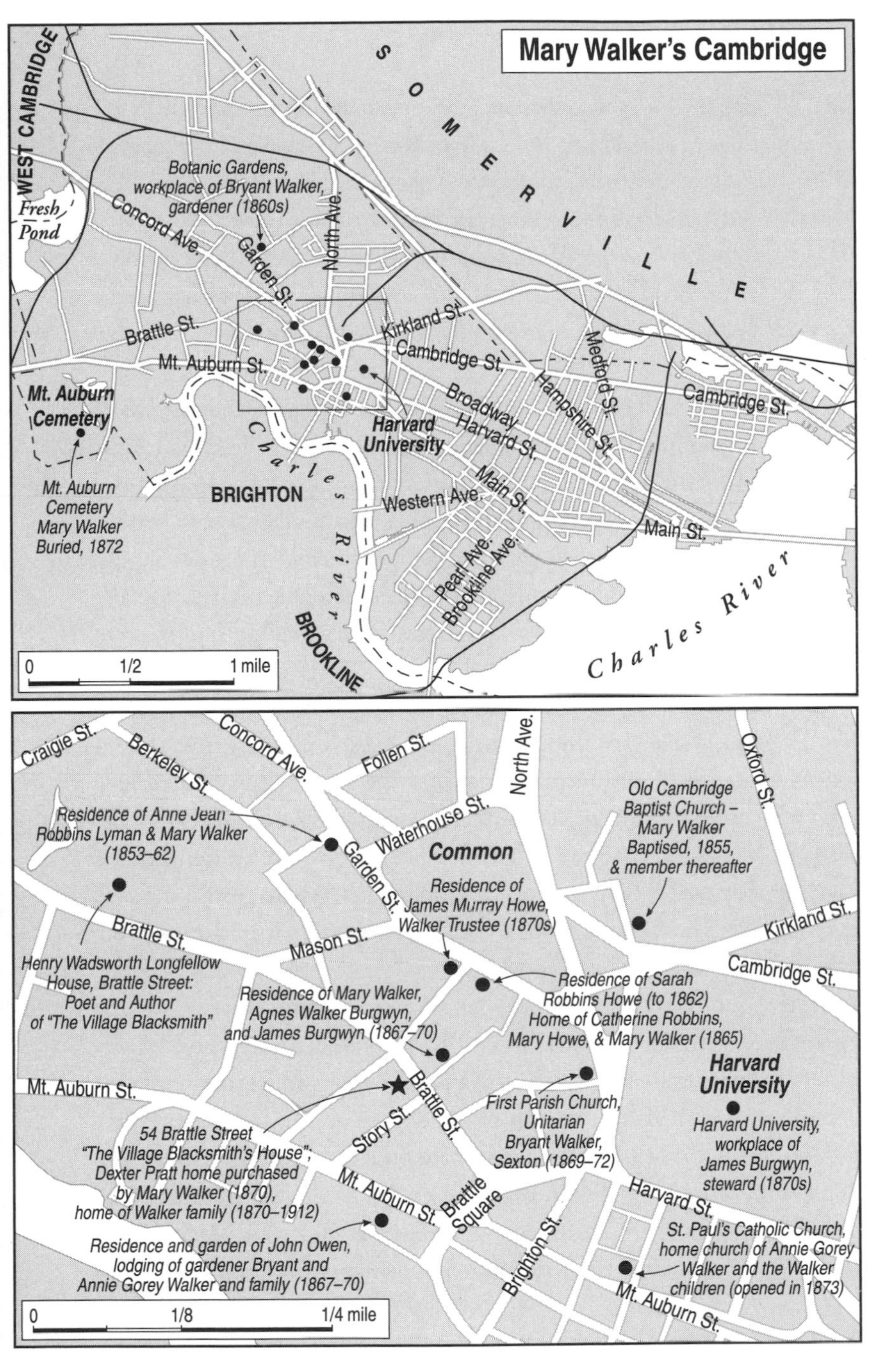
Mary Walker's Cambridge
WEST CAMBRIDGE
SOMERVILLE
Fresh Pond
Botanic Gardens, workplace of Bryant Walker, gardener (1860s)
Concord Ave.
Garden St.
North Ave.
Kirkland St.
Cambridge St.
Brattle St.
Mt. Auburn St.
Mt. Auburn Cemetery
Mt. Auburn Cemetery Mary Walker Buried, 1872
Harvard University
Broadway
Harvard St.
Hampshire St.
Medford St.
Cambridge St.
Main St.
Western Ave.
BRIGHTON
Charles River
Pearl Ave.
Brookline Ave.
Main St.
BROOKLINE
Charles River
0
1/2
1 mile
Craigie St.
Berkeley St.
Concord Ave.
Follen St.
North Ave.
Oxford St.
Waterhouse St.
Common
Residence of Anne Jean Robbins Lyman & Mary Walker (1853–62)
Garden St.
Old Cambridge Baptist Church – Mary Walker Baptised, 1855, & member thereafter
Residence of James Murray Howe, Walker Trustee (1870s)
Brattle St.
Mason St.
Kirkland St.
Cambridge St.
Henry Wadsworth Longfellow House, Brattle Street: Poet and Author of "The Village Blacksmith"
Residence of Mary Walker, Agnes Walker Burgwyn, and James Burgwyn (1867–70)
Residence of Sarah Robbins Howe (to 1862) Home of Catherine Robbins, Mary Howe, & Mary Walker (1865)
Harvard University
Mt. Auburn St.
Brattle St.
First Parish Church, Unitarian Bryant Walker, Sexton (1869–72)
Harvard University, workplace of James Burgwyn, steward (1870s)
54 Brattle Street "The Village Blacksmith's House"; Dexter Pratt home purchased by Mary Walker (1870), home of Walker family (1870–1912)
Story St.
Mt. Auburn St.
Brattle Square
Harvard St.
Brighton St.
Residence and garden of John Owen, lodging of gardener Bryant and Annie Gorey Walker and family (1867–70)
St. Paul's Catholic Church, home church of Annie Gorey Walker and the Walker children (opened in 1873)
Mt. Auburn St.
0
1/8
1/4 mile

side. "He then told them that he had just had a vision in which the other world was revealed to him. That there he had seen the multitude of fugitive slaves who had not only suffered much in this world but were still suffering from the remembrance of their woes & the sorrows they had left behind. He then solemnly charged them that whatever they neglected in life, never to reject the claims of the fugitive. Those were his last words and the crowning proof of his insanity to all but his children."[14]

It was with Shaw's exhortation fresh in her mind that Susan Lesley learned the outcome of Mary Walker's audience with Ellis Gray Loring and Louisa Loring concerning her enslaved family. Mary Walker had held the story back until her Philadelphia friend had gotten settled. Then she had poured out all that had happened since the moment she had heard of Duncan Cameron's death. Overcome with "suffering and excitement," unable to "rest day or night," Mary Walker had become possessed to "save her children at all hazard." "Her own easy position became as nothing to her—indeed increased her misery for those she loved." Mary Walker had indeed gone to see Ellis Gray Loring and his wife, the stanch abolitionist couple who the year before had offered her safety and lifetime employment in their household. She shared her distress, told them that she believed her children were in danger, and asked if they could help her find an intermediary who would offer to purchase her family with money she had saved and would raise from others.

The Lorings' answer startled Mary Walker. Though "very kind and liberal" toward Mary Walker herself, they refused. Like a good many other abolitionists—but by no means all—they declared themselves "entirely principled against putting money into the hands of slave holders." Along with most Garrisonians, the Lorings viewed ransom as a compromise with the sin of slavery; African Americans and political abolitionists took a different view. The Lorings told Mary Walker that they "had steeled their hearts against every individual case." Ellis

Gray Loring asked Mary Walker to "consider me always a friend and a brother"—but "offered no word of consolation." Louisa Loring begged Mary Walker to "give up her mother and children as if they were dead." Mary Walker kept her composure, but was "secretly indignant." She wondered: If it were the Lorings' daughter who was in slavery, would "they give her up and form other ties?" She knew that they were excellent people, committed to the "general cause of freedom." Still, Susan Lesley was sure that no power could ever induce Mary Walker to carry "her own individual sorrows to their door again."[15]

Undeterred by the Lorings' rebuff, Mary Walker turned to more sympathetic—but less experienced—allies. When she shared her plight with John Morrison, the Lesleys' friend and fellow minister from Milton, he immediately volunteered to contact an acquaintance in Baltimore, a lawyer who he was sure could obtain a copy of Duncan Cameron's will. The document would reveal whether the Cameron sisters or their brother Paul had inherited Mary Walker's children. The lawyer got the will for Mary Walker. It bequeathed her family and "all their increase forever" to the Cameron sisters. "All their increase forever"—even as the news soothed, the words scalded. "Full of sympathy for Mary," minister Morrison now "offered to make every exertion" on behalf of her family. Recognizing that Mary Walker initially could hope only to gather enough money to purchase one child, Morrison declared that "he himself would write openly to the ladies" with "a moving appeal to sell her daughter."[16]

When Susan Lesley heard about John Morrison's offer in early June 1853, she was aghast. If Morrison wrote under his own name, he would reveal where he lived and expose Mary Walker's whereabouts. He would also make himself the target of investigation, should the Camerons decide to pursue their escaped slave. The very moment she heard of Morrison's offer, Susan Lesley "put a stop to these proceedings." When she consulted with her brother Joseph Lyman, who lived nearby in Jamaica Plain, he agreed completely with his sister. "How could he?" the brother scolded. "A child ought to have more judgment." Why expose Mary Walker and her friends to the harassment that might follow the discovery of where they lived? Besides, given the influence of "the young man," any letter written to the sisters "might quite as well be cast to the winds." If there was to be a negotiation, the only way to do it was through "some person quite unconnected with the family."[17]

Firm about finding an untraceable intermediary, Joseph Lyman hedged about who that might be. The brother offered to "do any safe thing himself and to keep a look out"—hardly a plan of action. He then returned to the possibility of the Lorings, perhaps thinking that their objection was to giving any of their *own* money as ransom to a slave-holder. "Mr. Loring would be the best person, because he surely knew abolitionists in the South, of whom the northern ones keep lists, and through whom they transact business, because their sympathies are not suspected." If Loring could identify a middleman, others could raise the money. Peter Lesley agreed with his brother-in-law. "If Mr. Loring can negotiate the purchase of the little girl through any proper person (and there must be such) I am willing to put together all we have invested into his hands for the purpose. I have no scruples about paying slaveholders for the individual's freedom, altho' I would condemn any general indemnification. Single cases can do no great harm, if any." The Lesleys had $500–600 laid up. "Mary is welcome to it all for my part if it will purchase her daughter." Peter Lesley added that the money must be a gift. Mary Walker, in the effort to rescue her daughter, must not "become a slave and die prematurely to pay for her."[18]

Mary Walker knew better than to turn again to the Lorings. When "I told Mary all, that evening," Susan Lesley reported to her husband in late June, "she was dreadfully troubled. I never saw such an expression on her face." Susan Lesley tried to explain the folly of the Morrison offer to write a letter and expose her location. Mary Walker would have none of it. She had to do something and the Reverend Morrison offered action. "Why should she not run every risk rather than not save her children and her children's children (for so runs the will) from the curse of slavery? Mr. Morrison, with his warmth and sympathy, was more to her than all the advisers of better judgment in the world." Mary Walker revealed the foreboding that underlay her urgency. She feared for her daughter. Agnes had just turned sixteen. She was now approaching the age at which white owners would consider her ready to mate, voluntarily or involuntarily. Mary Walker reminded Susan Lesley that "she herself was married before she was 15." Both of the Lesleys knew the facts of this union—who the man was, whether he was a slave-owner or enslaved, what force or pressures, exchanges or consent, had been involved in the relationship. Her daughter was nearing the age where she would be at the same crossroads and face the same pressures. If a "marriage" took place, and especially if children came, her daughter would be fettered to a life in the South, as Mary Walker herself had been until the events of 1848. "She feels that another year may rivet the child's chains, and add to the impossibility of getting her."[19] There was no time to lose.

Understanding Mary Walker's urgency, Susan Lesley nonetheless implored her to look out for herself as well as her children. She took Mary Walker's hand and begged her "to leave the whole subject and its case and management" to her husband, Peter, to trust him to come up with a plan that safeguarded the mother at the same time that it sought the release of her daughter. Mary Walker was silent. The two women went to bed, but neither slept. At midnight, when Susan Lesley became ill, Mary Walker came into her room to look after her. "Her whole manner was changed to one of patient, sad resignation. She told me she had passed three hours on her knees" and reached a conclusion. She would be patient—"she would leave it all to me."[20]

5 The Rescue Plot

Over the next twenty-four months, Peter and Susan Lesley launched three attempts to free Mary Walker's children from slavery. Two efforts involved the search for intermediaries willing to propose an offer to purchase her daughter, Agnes, from the Cameron sisters. The third plan—more daring and more desperate—involved hiring an agent to go to Raleigh, to make contact with Mary Walker's mother, and to shepherd an escape from the South. The Lesleys stood ready to spend their entire savings for the purchase of the daughter, and hoped that her freedom would be granted if the price was right. "The money forthcoming there ought to be no great difficulty in the way." Peter Lesley admitted that he had no aptitude for surreptitious dealings. One thing he did understand, however: stealth was absolutely necessary to conceal the whereabouts of Mary Walker. None of their efforts should expose her to risk.[1]

Peter Lesley knew he had to find a knowledgeable go-between. "You know how ill-adapted I am for assuming a part and carrying out a diplomatic idea." His choice for an intermediary was Thomas Verner Moore, a former classmate from the time when both men had been students at the Princeton Theological Seminary in the early 1840s. He thought "my friend T. V. Moore would be a capital agent." Peter Lesley remembered Thomas Moore as a man who "used to love me," who had extraordinary talents, and who was "full of *worldly wisdom.*"[2] Born in Pennsylvania and a graduate of Dickinson College in 1834, Moore had become a minister in Richmond, Virginia, in 1847. He responded at once to Peter Lesley's letter of late June 1853. He would be willing to help—to arrange for an offer—but only if there was no deception involved. He didn't need to know the name of the mother or father, or whether the person was a fugitive, or to reveal Lesley's name. But honor would oblige him to inform the owners that he wished to buy the young girl on a parent's behalf. "I must not be made an instrument of misleading or hoodwinking the owner into an act which, did he know all that I know, he would refuse to do."[3] Taken aback, Peter Lesley nonetheless wrote immediately to assure Moore he wished him to do nothing "clandestine or improper." Moore answered that "I did not suppose you would ask me to do a thing you deemed dishonorable. But if you had become indoctrinated with 'the New England abolitionism' fully, you would regard some things as perfectly fair and honorable, which I would not." They agreed to meet at the end of July.[4]

Susan Lesley reported to her husband that Mary Walker was soothed "wonderfully" by "the thought of your sympathy & earnest desire to help her." But when Susan Lesley shared news of Moore's conditions with her brother, Joseph Lyman, and with her Boston antislavery cousin, Susan Hillard, both relatives were dismayed. Her brother scoffed at the idea of being candid with slave-owners about the motive for the purchase. "What is the good of openness with people whose bad passions would at once be aroused?" Susan Hillard was even more dismissive. "He is too conscientious," she said of Moore. Forthrightness "will never do with these people. I haven't any conscience" when it comes to a slave-holder's honor. The cousin thought the only way to save the Walker children was to *take* them. The most famous antislavery brother and sister in the country, preacher Henry Ward Beecher and author Harriet Beecher Stowe, had told Susan Hillard to her face that "they both know plenty of people who will go South and bring north anybody, for their expenses." It was "no use trying to *buy.* Such people won't sell."[5]

Susan Lesley understood the skepticism of her relatives, but was aware that a rescue plan carried its own dangers. Who knew "how many consequences this might involve for poor M"? Susan approved of her husband's decision to entrust the case to his Virginia friend, and of his many safeguards. Peter Lesley would not reveal Mary Walker's name or residence. "The darker the agent is kept (providing he has light enough) the better." He asked Susan to cease mention of Mary Walker's name in her letters to him—or, if she continued to use it, to write as if the fugitive were in Philadelphia rather than Cambridge. Moore apparently had proposed using a second intermediary—a clergyman in Raleigh—as the person who would make direct contact with the Cameron estate about a purchase. Moore would keep secret the Raleigh minister's name from Peter Lesley, and would not divulge Lesley's name to the minister. Lesley and Moore would not talk terms. Moore "shall have entire liberty to agree to any terms of sale without consulting me." Talks would be cut off at once if the Raleigh minister sought information about Mary Walker. Peter Lesley felt optimistic. "I know that if Tom undertakes it and succeeds he will do it well." But if his friend failed, Lesley added, "I shall apply to Henry Ward Beecher to learn other methods more expeditious."[6]

The two friends met at Johnstown, Pennsylvania, on the last day of July. Tom Moore looked gaunt and thin-cheeked but otherwise well, Peter Lesley told his wife. Moore was the "same man I left ten years ago at Princeton"—warm and openhearted. "He is as wise as I thought he was." Lesley decided to confirm that the offer for Agnes Walker was on behalf of her mother—a fact that Thomas Moore could reveal in the negotiations, but without knowing or divulging her whereabouts. "He knows nothing further nor did he wish to." Knowledge of other details might make Moore complicit in abetting a fugitive slave. "We said little but perfectly understood each other." Moore agreed to write at once to his clergyman colleague in Raleigh, whom he trusted to see the parties and open negotiations. He would inform his Philadelphia friend of the results.[7]

Having agreed to act as a liaison, Moore added that he had "little hope of success." A girl that age was worth a thousand dollars, he told a startled Peter Lesley. Not yet a grown woman, she can be "taught and formed." Moore did not explain what he meant by "taught and formed"—presumably he meant taught valuable skills as a house slave and formed to be a faithful servant.[8] Surely the Virginia minister did *not* refer to the cultivation of concubinage in the plantation household, though that also was a way in which certain young women were "taught and formed." While the ownership of enslaved women permitted masters to impose their will on their servants' bodies, some men sought complicity rather than submission from their servants. The fifty-year-old slave-owner who controlled the fate of Harriet Jacobs, a fifteen-year-old enslaved in Edenton, North Carolina, in the late 1820s, sought to persuade her to become his voluntary mistress. He found her attractive, conveyed his desire for sexual congress with her, and promised her comforts and privileges and all the ease in the world—her own cottage and their bed within it. She found his allures repulsive, his enticements duplicitous, and the betrayal of his wife reprehensible.[9] For whatever purpose her owners might mold Agnes Walker, Moore thought the young girl's presumed malleability would make her more valuable than an adult woman. If they sold her, it would be at a high price. Moore intimated that the interest of outsiders in Mary Walker's daughter might only steel the owners' determination to keep her. Nonetheless, he would help his old friend in the quest, though, according to Peter, he "thinks I am doing neither M nor the girl any good." "We were affectionately parted," Peter Lesley wrote his wife.[10]

Susan Lesley responded that she was fully satisfied "at all you have done" for Mary Walker; she was ready to be patient and to await the results. But just two weeks after her husband's July 31 rendezvous with Tom Moore, a startling letter came to Mary Walker from Philadelphia—and raised further doubts about whether the Camerons would be amenable to an overture to buy Agnes. The Cameron sisters had returned to Philadelphia in mid-August 1853 and brought with them an enslaved manservant from their home in the South. Unbeknownst to them, the servant made inquiries about Mary Walker and got the name of James Fells as a person who might know how to communicate information to her. He sought out Fells—who of course revealed nothing to him of her whereabouts—and reported a stunning fact. For the first time, Mary Walker learned that her oldest son, Frank Walker, had escaped the year before. According to the servant's account, Frank Walker had been harassed and mistreated "on the plantation" and had made his escape in August 1852. Had his mother's departure unsettled her son? Had extra scrutiny and perhaps retribution prompted his "mistreatment"? Whatever the cause, the escape had been a success: Frank Walker was somewhere out of the South. Somewhere, *but where?* Surely glad for her twenty-one-year-old son, Mary Walker was nonetheless dismayed for herself. "How will she ever find him?" Susan Lesley wondered. But she focused on a different consequence of Frank Walker's escape. "Will all this affect the sale of the girl?"[11]

The servant from home had shared more news, no less shocking in its own way. At the age of forty-two, five months after her father's death in early 1853, Margaret Bain Cameron had married. Her husband was George Mordecai, a Raleigh banker and business associate of her father who had succeeded Duncan Cameron as the president of the State Bank of North Carolina. Margaret Cameron Mordecai, her husband, and her invalid sister, Mildred, had taken an extensive tour of the North in the summer of 1853. Before they arrived in Philadelphia, they had traveled to New York and Boston, where they had even visited Mount Auburn Cemetery—a mile from where Mary Walker resided. The marriage meant that there was now a second patriarch in the picture—the husband of Margaret Bain Cameron Mordecai—in addition to the sisters' brother, Paul. Had Mary Walker's mother and remaining two children come under the control of the new husband? No wonder Susan Lesley reported, just two weeks after Peter Lesley's meeting with Tom Moore, that Mary Walker was agitated all over again.[12]

MERCIFULLY, MARY WALKER HAD no idea how right she was to be anxious. Her oldest son had indeed escaped slavery in the spring of 1852. No one knew how he got away or where to track him. Preoccupied by illnesses throughout 1852—Duncan Cameron had begun to fail, and Mildred Cameron remained plagued by unnerving spasms—the Camerons of Raleigh had made no effort to find Frank Walker.

Then, in the first week of March 1853, word came to Raleigh that revealed the young man's whereabouts. A letter sent by Frank Walker set in motion a determined effort to recapture Mary Walker's son and prove to the rest of the Cameron slaves that flight from their plantation was futile. Neither Mary Walker in Massachusetts nor Paul Cameron in North Carolina had any idea that in exactly the same week of March 1853, each was mobilizing friends and resources to recover one of Mary Walker's children.

Frank Walker had somehow made it to Trenton, New Jersey, had found work there, and was making a dollar a day. He knew that his mother had been in Philadelphia when she left slavery five years before; he wanted to find her. He assumed she had stayed in the city and that her mother—his grandmother Silla—knew where she was. Hence the risky letter home—to get directions from his grandmother. Now twenty-one, Frank Walker addressed the letter to a white Raleigh friend, whom he asked to speak to his grandmother. The friend was a man named Archy Drake. Drake lived just a few households away from where Frank Walker had grown up at the Cameron mansion in Raleigh; close by Drake's house lived two free black carpenters, a sawyer, and a cabinetmaker. Archy Drake ran a Raleigh grog shop and was known to ask no questions of men of color when they presented cash or bartered goods for whiskey. Minimally literate, Frank Walker may have composed the letter himself or may have had a slightly more literate acquaintance write it on his behalf. The letter's spelling was phonetic. It was addressed to "Roley," North Carolina.[13]

Either Frank Walker's trust in Archy Drake was misplaced or the phonetic spelling was a giveaway to an alert official in the Raleigh Post Office. Within days of its arrival, the letter found its way into the hands of Margaret Cameron, who then communicated it to her brother, Paul. His response was instantaneous. "Glad to hear of 'Frank' once more, tho' he is a long way off—& it maybe will cost some money & trouble to bring him *Home* once more. But as a slave holder [and] as the representative of the Estate and of my sisters I think it my duty to have the effort made." Paul Cameron intended to have Frank Walker pursued, immediately. "I will take steps at *once* to send a man who if he can be had is equal to the work. I will go to see him tomorrow."[14]

Duncan Cameron's death had made Paul Cameron the new patriarch of the plantation, and for the forty-four-year-old master, much was at stake in Frank Walker's recapture. "*His flight* has had a very bad effect here and to bring him back would render others better contented and improve the spirit of subordination." And if Frank Walker were caught? While Paul Cameron could not impose his will on his two sisters—Frank and other members of the enslaved Walker family belonged to Margaret and Mildred—his tone was peremptory. "Of course *if* he should be recovered you & Mildred must let him be sold." Clearly Paul Cameron was fed up with the whole Walker clan and with the fact that his father and sisters had taken no action against them when Mary Walker had left five years before. If Frank Walker "remains North & you keep that family near you, you will lose others if not all of it. If mine I should get them out of the way of the Post office by sending them to the Country"—or "what is better out of the way of giving me any trouble by selling them." Indulgence had failed. "They have proven themselves to be most ungrateful pets."[15]

Cameron lost no time. "What is attempted to be done, should be done and done quickly & nothing said of it in any quarter." He arranged for "the services of my neighbor" Joseph Woods, whom he thought had the bearing required for the mission. Woods had engaged in the slave-trade to the South in years past, and had successfully carried "off a large family of slaves" to sell for a neighbor. Presumably the experienced slave-trader would not be intimidated by Northerners who stood in his way, or by Frank Walker, once he found him—"and he will be found if Mr. Woods has but half a chance." Because the law of 1850 required a witness to confirm the identity of the alleged fugitive slave, Cameron also dispatched his overseer "to identify Frank if he be found." Cameron hired the two slave-catchers at four o'clock on the afternoon of March 10, and the next day they headed north on the train from Raleigh. Secrecy was imperative. "Nothing should be said about the steps to recover Frank," Cameron wrote his sisters. "The last thing I said to both [men] was to 'keep their tongue between their teeth.'"[16]

When Margaret Cameron received her brother's letter, she was still beset by grief at her father's death six weeks before and alarmed at the worsening condition of her thirty-three-year-old sister, Mildred. "Oh how sad it all is to me." Their father's death was "our overwhelming calamity our deep bitter sorrow." Her sister "Milly has spasms by the dozen" and had "so long been deprived of her voice that I begin to fear it may become a permanent thing." Margaret Cameron felt "at times as if my heart must break." Nonetheless, she kept her head when it came to her brother's decrees about the Walker family. "Of course if [Frank] is taken Mildred and myself will consent to his being sold," she wrote her brother—"but not the others. Do tell what is the source from whence you derived your information that Mary had intercourse with her mother? I do not think she has. If she had such, I think Frank would have gone immediately to see her—and it seems from his letter that he had not found her out." Paul Cameron responded that he had no information but also no doubt. "I have learnt from no one that Mary had any intercourse with her Mother but I have never doubted it—and I am now satisfied of it from the fact that Frank writes to [Archy] Drake to ask 'Cillar' to send him 'the Street and N° at which' his mother resided in Phila'd'a. This I think pretty strong proof of the fact—with me it is conclusive."[17]

All awaited word from the North. Paul Cameron had given his agent, Joseph Woods, an affidavit certifying that Frank Walker was a fugitive from his North Carolina plantation. "Frank who sometimes calls himself 'Francy' Walker is about 20 years of age." Born "a slave on The Plantation of my late father Duncan Cameron," he "fled from his masters ownership & employment some time early in the spring of 1852—and from a late letter received from him is supposed to be at Trenton New Jersey engaged in some sort of labor at a dollar a day." Cameron took the precaution of having his agent and witness stop briefly in Washington en route to Trenton, to meet with two North Carolina representatives, Congressman George Badger and Senator Willie P. Mangum. They reviewed the affidavit and Badger gave the agent a letter of introduction to former New Jersey Senator and Trenton lawyer George Stockton. Badger wrote his congressional colleague that Wood was visiting New Jersey upon a "business of difficulty & delicacy in which he may need advice and countenance [in his] behalf & in behalf of a very worthy & highly respectable family which he represents."[18]

A "business of difficulty & delicacy" may have been a euphemism for more direct language that, in 1853, might have embarrassed a Northern congressman who might not wish to be explicitly involved in the capture of a fugitive slave. But the language also may have reflected the expectation that the return of this particular person might involve special difficulty and delicacy. "Francy Walker," the affidavit declared, "is so nearly white that with ninety five men in a hundred he will pass for a white man." He "has black & straight hair—inclined to curl—especially toward the end of the hair on the neck—His eyes blue by some would be called gray . . . he was somewhat *freckeled.*" There were other parts of the description that conformed more to what one might expect of an enslaved youth. He "had the tip end of one of the fingers of the right hand bitten off by a horse"; he "seldom ever looked any one in the face when spoken to"; this "boy or man 'Francy Walker' is very fond of Whiskey & is to be found about such places." Did Cameron or his congressmen expect resistance to the re-enslavement of a young man "so nearly white that with ninety five men in a hundred he will pass for a white man"?[19]

As it turned out, Cameron's agent was blocked even before he could begin the hunt for Frank Walker, and returned to North Carolina empty-handed less than a week after he left. On his arrival in Trenton, Joseph Woods had decided to lay "his papers before an eminent lawyer and the Judge before whom the case would be brought if [an arrest] should be made." The agent was "told that his papers had not been properly authenticated by the clerk & that in New Jersey they do not recognize our scroll seals (made with a pen)." Cameron told his agent "I wish that he had remained & sent his papers back to be perfected & returned," but Woods "said he acted under the direction of his lawyer"—George Stockton—who had apparently discouraged him from pursuing the case. Reporting the failure to his sister, Cameron thought there was more to the objection than a legal technicality. When in the Senate, Stockton "was never regarded . . . as friendly to the South! I am not inclined to give it up."[20]

Cameron decided on a different approach. He'd see if he could get Frank Walker to reveal his whereabouts in Trenton. For this plan, Cameron sought to enlist the cooperation of Frank Walker's Raleigh friend and correspondent, Archy Drake. Cameron asked a young cousin to approach "Mr. Drake" and "to say to him for me that *if* he will open &

conduct a correspondence with Francis Walker *that shall be the means of finding him and recovering him* I will pay Mr. Drake $25 or 50 dollars." Cameron wished Drake to write to Frank Walker, "find out if he can at what he is employed and with whom—& that as soon as he can see his grandmother that he will give him the Street & N° at which his mother resides—and above all . . . to say nothing about the matter to any one." Drake need not know "that my agent has been sent or returned." His cousin "must not let Mr. Drake think that any one doubts his *good faith* in the matter," but he wanted the cousin to give him a candid assessment: Would Drake "come into the *service in good faith*" for fifty dollars? The cousin met with Drake, who "immediately agreed" to the scheme. He wrote a letter to Frank Walker which stated that Drake had seen Frank's "grandmother, that she had lost his mother's direction but thought she could find it in a few days that all the children would send love but she was afraid to let them know that she had heard from him . . . asking him to write soon etc." On March 23, the cousin personally mailed the letter from the Raleigh post office. The cousin thought that Drake was acting faithfully. "I have no doubt it will be answered in a few days unless the boy gets from some other source information of the intended pursuit after him."[21]

Frank Walker never responded. Did Archy Drake say something in the letter, deliberately or unintentionally, that led his drinking comrade to suspect that Drake "was playing the traitor"? Obliged by caste to seem eager to assist Cameron and to feign fidelity, Drake may have contrived to send a coded warning. A saloonkeeper that no Cameron would ever traffic with directly, Drake had more in common with his grog-shop patrons than with Raleigh patricians; he may also have had a son by a woman of color. On the other hand, Drake in 1853 may have been ready to break from his grog-shop past. Down on his luck in 1850, a decade later he would be listed as a merchant worth three thousand dollars. Could someone else have informed Frank Walker that he was in harm's way? Cameron's agent, despite instructions from his employer to keep his tongue between his teeth, had "made no secret of his business." He "talked very openly about the matter" at the bank in downtown Raleigh and again while waiting to catch the train north.[22] Even if no one from Raleigh "played the traitor" to Cameron—so as to betray Frank Walker—who knew but that someone in the judge's circle in Trenton may have put the word out that the slave-catchers from North Carolina might be back. Frank Walker was never caught.

AS IT TURNED OUT, the Camerons never made mention of an offer to buy Agnes Walker in 1853, nor did the Lesleys again correspond about Tom Moore or his mission. If Moore *did* write to his clergyman friend in Raleigh, and the cleric *did* gauge the readiness of the Camerons to consider a proposal, he would certainly have found that the premonitions of both Susan Lesley and Mary Walker were right. Frank Walker's escape had most certainly made Paul Cameron more determined than ever to deter the family's other slaves from thinking they could leave bondage. And Margaret Cameron's marriage, five months after her father died, had undeniably complicated the chances of securing Agnes Walker's release.

Margaret Cameron's marriage had tightened the vise on the family of Mary Walker, though not in the way she might have expected. Paul Cameron regarded the bequest of slaves and land from his father as an inheritance that should be kept in the family—and under his control. That stance became clear even before Duncan Cameron's death, when Paul's sister Margaret began to receive the attentions of George Mordecai. Mordecai had long worked with Duncan Cameron at the State Bank of North Carolina and had succeeded him in 1848, when shattered nerves compelled the senior Cameron to resign the presidency. Mordecai frequently visited the Cameron mansion in Raleigh and worshiped at the same Episcopal church that the Camerons attended. Although Mordecai's forebears were Jewish, he had became a prominent lawyer and banker, and along the way had converted to the Episcopal religion. Talent won him entry to the highest professional circles and gained him the presidency of the State Bank. So long as he worked and dined with Duncan Cameron as a colleague, he was cordially received.[23]

When George Mordecai began to court Margaret Cameron as a suitor, relations soured. Whether the objection came first and foremost from Duncan Cameron isn't clear. What is clear is that Paul Cameron scorned George Mordecai, not only as a Jew whose religious conversion was motivated by self-interest, but as a fortune-hunter. The son used his father's debility as the grounds on which to forbid any further visits by George Mordecai to his father's Raleigh household—and to ban all discussion of marriage. George Mordecai was stunned by the rebuff; Margaret Cameron was devastated. Yielding to the brother's demands, the lovers resorted to secret messages and meetings as the way to sustain their bond while Duncan Cameron lived.[24] A month after her father's death, Margaret Cameron announced that she had accepted the marriage proposal of George Mordecai. She sought her brother's blessings for the nuptials. He refused. Marriage would make Mordecai the legal possessor of all that Margaret Cameron had inherited from her father—hundreds of slaves, the Raleigh mansion, thousands of dollars in stocks and bonds. Mordecai was not without wealth, but clearly Margaret Cameron was one of the great heiresses in the state. Insulted by Paul Cameron's intimations—unquestionably shared by others about the convert and his motives—the couple decided to put such suspicions to rest through a prenuptial agreement that kept all of the bride's inheritance under her control, instead of surrendering the estate to her husband. Paul Cameron's father-in-law, Thomas Ruffin—who was a justice on the North Carolina Supreme Court—pronounced the document all anyone could want and urged the Cameron family to withdraw its objections. Paul Cameron declined to attend his sister's wedding.[25]

The summer of 1853, then, would have found Paul Cameron resolute against any proposal on behalf of Agnes Walker. Even if his sisters had been receptive to an offer, such a decision would have brought further friction between Margaret Cameron Mordecai and her brother. If a letter from Thomas Moore did reach the unnamed Raleigh clergyman, it would have taken little inquiry by him to conclude that any overture about the fugitive's daughter would fall on barren ground—and indeed might provoke a resumption of Paul Cameron's pursuit of the Walkers who had gotten away.

IT IS POSSIBLE THAT BY summer's end, Peter Lesley may have received word from Tom Moore that he could accomplish nothing in Raleigh. When the two men had met in July, they had agreed to keep the exchange of details about Mary Walker and her daughter to a minimum. If there was a communiqué about an impasse, it was probably cryptic. When Peter Lesley went to Cambridge to visit his wife in September 1853, where she was in the seventh month of her pregnancy and being cared for by Mary Walker, he chose to avoid discouragement. Rather, he asked Mary Walker whether there might be other ways to communicate with the Cameron sisters. Perhaps alarmed at first at what she could only take as the sign of a setback, she soon recovered. "After you left," Susan Lesley wrote her husband in late September, "Mary's wits came to her in a remarkable manner & she has given me many new facts which will be of great assistance to you in your enterprise. I will not write them"—but she would convey them when she returned home in October.[26]

Mary Walker stayed with Susan Lesley in Cambridge and then traveled with her back to Philadelphia, where she would remain until the Lesleys' baby was born. Care for the mother-to-be had been the priority of the summer for Mary Walker, and, as always, her gifts as a nurse had won admiration and gratitude. "What a treasure Mary Walker is!" wrote Susan Lesley's visiting friend, Meggie White. "She is the most tender & judicious nurse Susie could have." When at one point in the summer, illness prompted the alarmed husband to ask if he should rush to Cambridge to be with his wife, a confident Mary Walker had replied, "Oh, she is not going to be any worse, if we keep her quiet today"—and had been right.[27] The same talents made Mary Walker welcome at the bedside of those whose condition did get worse, as happened with the ailing father of the Lesleys' New York friend Rosa Hopper. Hopper was "so inexperienced in nursing that it was an unspeakable comfort" to appeal to Mary Walker. "She made the last drink my dear Father could take, & with his weak faltering voice, he asked me, who she was & said she was so kind. Dear Mary! She wrote me a beautiful, sympathizing letter a short time since."[28] In Philadelphia, both Peter and Susan Lesley witnessed Mary Walker's nursing at its best. She was "busy as a bee, taking care of Susan," Peter Lesley reported to aunt and mother in Cambridge. As the time of labor neared, Peter Lesley himself got merrily drawn into being the servant of "Your Empress. I am her perpetual slave doing little else than running to all quarters of the heavens to execute her innumerable commands. Yours till Death, Peter Walker." On November 4, 1853, the parents welcomed the birth of a blue-eyed daughter. They named her Mary.[29]

No correspondence from 1853 reveals the "new facts" that Mary Walker thought would help the enterprise of buying her daughter. With Mary Walker and the Lesleys in the same household for the month of October, communications during that time were face to face. Clues did not come until an exchange of letters nine months later, in late July 1854. In an uncharacteristic outcry to her husband, Susan Lesley wrote on July 24, "I wish it were possible to send JF to Raleigh to see that woman!" Replied her husband on July 27: "We never thought Mrs. Stephens would be traveling with the ladies this season. If so, there is no chance a letter will reach her this summer."[30]

"JF"? "Mrs. Stephens"? "A letter"?

Mary Walker may have proposed a different route to reach the Cameron sisters—and specifically Mildred Cameron, the invalid young woman whom she had cared for during the 1840s. Apparently there was someone almost as close to the youngest sister as she herself once had been, and Mary Walker had suggested conveying an appeal through that person. Perhaps this was the woman named "Stephens" in the Lesley correspondence—sometimes "Mrs. Stephens," other times "Miss Stephens," on one occasion "Lucy." Was there a "Lucy Stephens" who would have known Mary Walker, "JF," and Mildred Cameron? In 1828, when the State Bank of North Carolina almost failed, the treasurer guilty of embezzling bank funds was named M. C. Stephens.[31] Was "Mrs. Stephens" or "Miss Stephens" the wife or daughter of the disgraced treasurer, who became the friend and sometime traveling companion of the two women in the 1850s? Perhaps. But there was no woman by the name of Lucy Stephens who was listed as a resident of Raleigh in the United States Census for 1850 or 1860. There *was* a Lucy Stephens, age fifty in 1870, listed in the United States Census for 1870 and again in 1880. She lived in the hamlet of Milton, North Carolina, not far from Raleigh. The surprise? Her race was given as black. She could have been the mother of twenty-three-year-old Stephen Stephens, also of Milton, also black, who in 1870 had a one-year-old daughter named Lucy. Stephen Stephens was interviewed in the 1930s by a reporter doing a story on the Civil War in Raleigh; the reporter identified him as a former "slave in the Mordecai-Cameron family."[32]

Could Lucy Stephens have been the "Mrs. Stephens" named in the Lesley letters—an enslaved woman who attended Mildred Cameron after the departure of Mary Walker? Did Lucy Stephens accompany "the sisters" in their travels to Philadelphia and there make the acquaintance of Mary Walker's close friend and frequent correspondent, the free black carpenter James Fells—"JF"? Had Mary Walker proposed that James Fells write to Lucy Stephens to see if she could circumvent the men, to plead for the purchase of Agnes Walker? Was this the continued silence from the South that prompted Susan Lesley to explode, "I wish it were possible to send JF to Raleigh to see that woman! I don't believe she will ever answer the letter."[33]

ONE GOOD THING MAY HAVE COME from the intermediaries' overtures to Raleigh on behalf of Mary Walker. In March 1854, she received a letter—most likely sent to James Fells in Philadelphia and then forwarded to her—about her children. "She has great pleasure in hearing a good account of her daughter." Someone unnamed, prompted by knowledge of Mary Walker's anxiety about the well-being of her family, had written a letter of reassurance. Eager to share with the Lesleys the good news and perhaps the fruit of their efforts, Mary Walker sent the letter to Philadelphia for them to see firsthand, and asked them to return it after they'd read it. Mary Walker found the writer's testimony convincing. Her spirits lifted. "She seems to feel confident that all will be well with her in the end."[34]

The Lesleys found patience harder to come by, as personal and public events intensified the strain of waiting for a response from Raleigh. Peter Lesley's work on a geological survey called him to Virginia in March 1854, and for the first time he traveled to the South. He was sobered by what he found. His Southern hosts were perfectly cordial—"in all respects good men"—until conversation turned to the subject of slavery. They "at once laid aside the right and wrong of the matter." They "simply regarded it as a question of property and as such, likely to exist through all eternity." The whole episode, Susan Lesley wrote her confidante Meggie White, reinforced the sad weight of slavery on those of "us who live on its borders and are personally interested in many of the sufferers." Through "last autumn and the early winter, our hearts were so oppressed with the sufferings of those for whom we could not lift a finger, that it seemed sometimes as if they would burst." For many weeks "I could not clasp my little Mary in my arms without tears for the poor women who cannot own the children that God has given them."[35]

Enormous setbacks to the antislavery cause created growing despair for the Lesleys and thousands of others. In January 1854, Congress passed and the president signed the Kansas-Nebraska Bill, which voided the Missouri Compromise of 1820 and the Compromise of 1850, and allowed slavery to enter territory from which it had been barred since 1787. Many in Massachusetts resolved to send Yankee immigrants and arms to Kansas to confront Southerners in an effort to keep Kansas free of slaves. Then, in late May 1854, the battle over bondage abruptly came to Boston, a city which saw itself as the bastion of liberty during the American Revolution and, since the 1830s, as the capital of the antislavery movement in America. A fugitive slave from Virginia—Anthony Burns—was arrested and jailed by a federal marshal on behalf of the slave's owner. The Boston Vigilance Committee, acting quickly, stormed the city jail but failed in its attempt to rescue Burns—and killed a deputy in the attempt. A Boston judge ruled that Burns must be returned to slavery. The president ordered troops to Boston to make sure that Burns boarded the ship waiting in Boston Harbor to take the captive back to Virginia.

The events in Boston shook Mary Walker. She had been there for earlier arrests of accused fugitives. Either the cases had been dismissed or a rescue attempt had succeeded. This time, the judge and the police authorities had gone against the slave and forced Boston to submit. Would other slave-holders be emboldened to come to the heart of New England to recapture their property? "These things worry Mary very much though she has more faith than the rest of us." Faith notwithstanding, events prompted her to act with caution. Scheduled to go to Milton for two days, she decided to remain in Cambridge until the excitement subsided.[36]

For Susan Lesley, the question was "where will it all end?" Outrage at the Kansas-Nebraska Bill and the Burns case seemed to be making new converts to the antislavery cause. But when she got to Boston at the end of June 1854, she found people going about their daily lives as if nothing momentous had happened. The two setbacks focused Susan Lesley's attention on the failure of their efforts to get results from Raleigh. "This eternal patience is too much for a poor soul." Later she apologized to her husband for the outburst. "Do not mind if I expressed impatience about poor Mary's affairs. I know it will take heavenly prudence and patience to effect anything for her. She never speaks a word about it."[37]

Peter Lesley sought to soothe when he responded to his wife's letter at the end of July 1854. He explained why they might not have heard anything from the woman they hoped would be their second emissary to Raleigh. Then his tone changed. "I shall make all the necessary arrangements this week to meet any contingency. Assure Mary that neither haste nor anxiety will help us. But on the contrary [either] will be dangerous as well as distressing. The risks of failure" were great; the cost of "favorable contingencies is terribly great. But what can I say?"[38] In fact, her husband had said a good deal: "I shall make all the necessary arrangements." Elliptically, Peter Lesley signaled that he had heard his wife's *cri de coeur.* Like those who had stormed Boston's jail to free a fugitive slave, like those taking up arms to repel bondage in Kansas, Peter Lesley was ready to take bolder action. Two days later he did so.

EVEN AS THE LESLEYS UNDERTOOK attempts to buy Mary Walker's daughter, they knew there was another way. Susan Lesley's cousin had told her early on that there were "plenty of people who will go South and bring north anybody, for their expenses. No use trying to *buy.* Such people won't sell." Peter Lesley had assured his wife that he would pursue that option if the purchase plan "doesn't succeed." "I shall apply to Henry Ward Beecher," the famous antislavery minister and brother of Harriet Beecher Stowe, "to learn other methods more expeditious."[39]

Now willing to chance the bolder course, Peter Lesley detailed his plan for a new approach on July 29, 1854. He didn't turn to Henry Ward Beecher or Harriet Beecher Stowe. Instead, he inquired of antislavery friends in Philadelphia and they identified "an agent, a white man, who for say $300 will go and try to do what we wish." "I am to learn more" the next week, "probably have an interview with him then. He has succeeded at such an affair before. I need not say more at present."[40]

Peter Lesley hoped that his news "would relieve you (and Mary) of the distress of thinking nothing is doing." At the same time, he urged them to avoid "speculations about the result. Do for your own precious sake think as little about it as you can. And advise Mary seriously to try for the present to take a purely business interest in it, as a sort of anodyne diet. It will be so much better in the end. God has great good for all of us in store and we must possess our souls patiently and cheerfully."[41] Part of the great good that he envisioned was that the agent would attempt to recover not just her daughter, Agnes, but her son who remained enslaved, ten-year-old Bryant Walker. To take only one child north would clearly expose the other to almost certain reprisals.

A year before, Peter Lesley had acknowledged "how ill-adapted I am for assuming a part and carrying out a diplomatic idea." In August 1854 he received a crash course in stealth. Coded abbreviations and circuitous language marked the daily reports to his wife which detailed the unfolding plan. The Philadelphia Vigilance Committee had made the first contact with the agent on his behalf. "The man was seen yesterday," Peter Lesley reported on August 4. "He said if all was right and his information complete, he could be induced to attend to our business. I shall see him today and make final arrangements and send him on to Boston to obtain the information." Clearly an experienced member of the Philadelphia Vigilance Committee had gone over the covert operation with Peter Lesley. That advisor was the white abolitionist James McKim. McKim knew his counterpart in Boston—black abolitionist leader Lewis Hayden—and scripted an elaborate protocol for working with him. The agent "will go to LH" (meaning Hayden) with a letter "to enable him to see Mary safely. I think it very necessary that Mary should herself give him all the details." Peter Lesley was to meet the proposed agent face to face the next day. "I must judge for myself and arrange myself the plan. No one else I find can be substituted. The only real precautions to be taken are to avoid *every kind of writing about it,* and for only *two* persons to be together at each interview. Talk to *nobody* but LH about it."[42]

On August 5, Peter Lesley met the person recommended for the mission. Although fair in complexion, the man "so far identifies himself entirely with her people, and will doubtless prove as good an agent as we could desire." He was "a common carpenter doing piecework" in Philadelphia, who had spent time in Savannah some years before. He had "once before happily accomplished something similar and feels pretty confident of success in this instance." The meeting went well. "He has a peculiar countenance, inspiring respect and confidence—although I saw him at dusk." Lesley emphasized that "the people here speak with entire confidence of this man and I suppose he is quite trustworthy, but I cannot prove it. They have known him well for 4 or 5 years."[43]

Lesley and the agent met again two days later and arranged for him to travel to Boston at the end of the week to get information firsthand from Mary Walker about her family and friends in Raleigh. It was imperative that the agent get details about persons who might help—and equally vital that he learn nothing about Mary Walker's location in Massachusetts. Under no circumstances were they to meet in Cambridge or was he to know she resided there. "M. will need to take all needful precautions. In fact, be more likely to be over than undercautious." The key to making the most careful arrangements in Boston was the middleman, a go-between who could arrange the meeting at a neutral site and prevent disclosure of Mary Walker's location. Hence the choice of Lewis Hayden, one of Boston's leading antislavery men and the head of the Boston Vigilance Committee.[44]

LEWIS HAYDEN WAS HIMSELF a man who had fled bondage in 1842. With the determined aid of two white Northerners—both subsequently captured and imprisoned—Hayden, his wife, and his infant son had escaped from slavery in Kentucky. In Detroit, Michigan, he had organized a school and had become an agent for the escape of others. He had moved to Boston in 1846, opened a secondhand clothing shop, and had become an indomitable and resourceful leader of the Boston Vigilance Committee. After passage of the Fugitive Slave Law in September 1850, Hayden and the committee pledged to block any attempt in Boston to reclaim a fugitive slave. A test came when Frederic "Shadrach" Minkins was arrested in February 1851. Within hours, the Boston Vigilance Committee went into action. While some members diverted attention, Hayden and others burst into the courtroom, and in the ensuing confusion they covered Shadrach with a cape, hustled him out of the building into a waiting carriage, and sped him away to refuge in Canada. Hayden's leadership required him to be an astute judge of character. He had to know friend from foe, how to bolster the timid and calm the volcanic. He was a particular friend of Ellis Gray Loring, the abolitionist lawyer who knew Mary Walker well.[45]

Peter Lesley tried to follow his own injunction for secrecy in the letters to his wife. "LH" was the Boston go-between, "M" was Mary Walker, and "P" was the agent. But Lesley proved inconsistent at espionage. In some letters, he wrote out—and then scratched through—Lewis Hayden's full name. In other letters, he wrote out P's last name: Price. In all likelihood, the carpenter he had engaged was James M. Price, age forty-four, unmarried, whom the Census of 1850 listed as having been born in Pennsylvania. In 1850, James Price was a carpenter who dwelt in a roominghouse in Philadelphia's North Ward, living with two other carpenters, a printer, a laborer, a salesman, and the hotelkeeper's family. James Price's absence from the city directories of Philadelphia in the 1840s and 1850s seems to confirm that he was a tradesman who did odd jobs—"a common carpenter doing piece-work," in Peter Lesley's words—rather than one of the established carpenters who listed themselves in the annual directory.[46]

On August 7, 1854, Lesley and Price finalized their plan. "I shall send P. to LH and let him arrange an interview with M if M consents—not otherwise." Mary Walker had the option of giving "LH all the necessary directions," but it was "certain that a personal communication would be the desirable thing." Let "LH take P in a carriage and drive to the rendezvous . . . without letting P. know previously that he is to see M. This may be needless—but it is a sure precaution." Lesley had "told P. the whole story except the names of the parties. He has none of these yet" and would have them only in Boston. "M must be full and frank in her explanation as possible, but *not* see Mr. P. *twice,* nor give him a clue as to her residence. Nor must you appear in the case, at least by name, if it can be helped." Peter Lesley noted to his wife: "You may think it strange that I should advise these precautions." But "reflect that they are entirely for M's sake. Nor do I wish to lay straw in the way of his obtaining entire command of the case in all the details of persons & places. But I cannot divest myself of a nameless fear of failure," even though "the people here speak with entire confidence of this man." Lesley had written to Lewis Hayden to notify him that Price would go to Hayden's when he arrived. "Cannot Mary go into town that morning and meet him at Lewis Hayden's?"[47]

Lesley laid out the assignment for Mary Walker at the meeting with Price. She must be prepared with "all the most specific information she has." She also needed to give Price some personal possession "by which he can assure them"—her family in the South—"of his being the proper person." "Cannot Mary go in and see him there and take some article of dress, use or ornament by which token her mother & children may be assured of him. They are very suspicious and instances occur where fear overcomes every instinct." James McKim, Lesley's advisor from the Philadelphia Vigilance Committee, had "failed himself once on that account," although he showed a wife her husband's razor. Let her "remember every circumstance but write no letter to anybody." Aware that Mary Walker ached because she had left the Camerons without a word to her family, Lesley reiterated: "She must not write any letter by him to anybody." As Lesley sent Price off to Boston, his assurance grew. Price "has Mr. McK's confidence and mine. He has extraordinary qualifications for success. He will at least reconnoitre."[48]

On the eve of Price's departure from Philadelphia to Boston, Lesley cautioned patience. "The whole business will proceed so slowly and tediously that months may be required to bring all parties to a settlement." *"Bring all parties to a settlement"?* Was Lesley holding out the possibility that Price might locate the mysterious Miss Stephens in Raleigh and nudge her to open a negotiation with the sisters about Agnes Walker? Lesley did plan for Price, on his return from Boston, to meet with "JF" so that he would "have sufficient introduction" to Miss Stephens, and to "be entrusted with the payment to Miss S. of a legacy of $50 from her relative in New England." But those arrangements appeared to be more a cover story than Price's real mission. The phrase "bring all parties to a settlement" seemed a euphemism for what the agent really had to do—which was to gain the ear of Mary Walker's mother, to get her to listen to his case for an escape attempt, and to persuade her that a "common carpenter" from Philadelphia and Savannah was the man to bring it off. "It is possible that two journeys may be needful, one to arrange and the other to ~~complete~~ transact the business." Peter Lesley reiterated that their agent James Price "may be able to accomplish nothing" on his first visit, "but only to prepare the way for a subsequent visit a fortnight or so following."[49]

MARY WALKER HAD BEEN AT the Massachusetts shore, accompanying Susan Lesley and the Lesleys' nine-month-old daughter, Mary, when Peter Lesley dramatically changed course from a strategy to ransom Agnes Walker to a plan to rescue both of Mary Walker's children. It's not clear whether Susan Lesley received the rapid-fire series of letters while at the shore, or first learned of the rescue plan on the trio's return. At once, Susan Lesley went to see Lewis Hayden in town and "read him your letters. He will be all ready for Mr. P. and will arrange the meeting between him and Mary satisfactorily when he comes." Mary Walker was ready to do her part, even though she was ill. She'd benefited little from the excursion to the sea and had returned "nearly bent double with rheumatism."[50] On the morning of August 13, Susan Lesley devised an excuse to get her friend out of the house in Cambridge, where she was working to look after guests despite her ill-health. The two women got to the omnibus and then, alone, Mary Walker boarded the horse-drawn cars to Boston for the rendezvous with Lewis Hayden and the Philadelphia agent. "She can scarcely walk, but is strong in spirit, and carries little tokens of great age & value, which will give confidence if anything can." Susan Lesley, expectant and hopeful, wrote to her husband of her thankfulness. "For myself, dear Peter, my heart is full of love and gratitude that cannot be uttered."[51]

Mary Walker and Price met face to face, Susan Lesley reported, "as was right." She gave him details about her family and acquaintances in Raleigh. To identify Price as her emissary, she entrusted him with a treasured pair of earrings. The rest of what happened at the interview is not clear, but at some point Lewis Hayden decided that he wanted Susan Lesley to meet Price as well. "L.H. sent me a note requesting me to go. M. had come back and her interview was over." Hayden may have judged that anxiety kept Mary Walker from recalling important information and sought Susan Lesley to fill out the picture. "I went but I do not think it was of any use," she reported to her husband. "I tried to say nothing I ought not. I liked the man & thought that LH gave him some useful suggestions. . . . I advised him to return to Phil. that afternoon, as there was no use in staying longer." "Mary and I reached home at sunset, all worn out, but hoping that all essentials had been remembered, and ready to leave all now to a good providence whatever occurs."[52]

The clandestine meeting that drained the two Cambridge women had energized the agent they met with. Price arrived back in Philadelphia eager to get started south. Peter Lesley went "down to P's house this evening to give him $100 and let him be off tomorrow for he is very impatient of needless delay here. He takes his tools and seems in good spirits." Price had mentioned one subject in his Boston meeting that Susan Lesley waited a week to write about: danger. "P. said to me, if he got into trouble, he supposed Mr. L. would help him out. I said, 'oh yes,' but afterwards wondered in what way you would be called on to do so." Peter Lesley responded in detail. "The risks of our adventure are *probably* not great. It all depends on our agent. But should he be discovered, he will not implicate us unless he also be *detained.* In that case *bail* will be called for and must be raised even to the amount of $5000–$10000. For that he will look to us and as the bail of course must be forfeited for his subsequent safety, we must pay it, unless we also fly, which could hardly be done." He reminded her of a case they both knew in which the agent had been discovered and detained: "you know how hard it was to raise $5000." There was "a very remote risk of my being implicated as a principal—but so infinitely unlikely considering precautions taken and difficulty of evidence" that it was "not worth mentioning. The *bail* is the only risk of any account. His risk is from personal violence but that is also extremely small."[53]

Peter Lesley added that he thought the risks of success were as great as the dangers of discovery. Mary Walker and her friends had worked out careful safeguards to avoid disclosing her location. What would happen if her children were freed? "Mary's risk will be from the *children's letters* and I dread that more than all the rest." Of course, Peter Lesley had no idea how right he was: Frank Walker's letter home in 1853 had instantly put slave-hunters on his trail. "It will be a hundred times more difficult to keep three concealed than one as they must have connections with R[aleigh] which they will not like to break and will have access to their Mother's post office without their Mother's knowledge." All "the casualties of past years are traceable to the recklessness with which the post office has been used after a few weeks or months of freedom." Peter Lesley stifled such concerns, however. "I have shut my eyes determinedly against all this and kept in view merely the rights of the matter and the children"—and Mary Walker's "protracted agony. We must continue to do so and let things take their course and emergencies be met as they arise."[54]

6 "A Spirit Like a Dove"

Despite the efforts undertaken to reclaim her family, Mary Walker battled despair in the summer of 1854. As always, she confided her feelings to Susan Lesley, who arrived in Cambridge in July to be with her mother. For Mary Walker, it had been a "year of untold sorrows."[1]

Those sorrows had deep sources. As the nation observed almost fourscore years of independence in 1854, Mary Walker had to wonder whether independence would ever come for her children or for herself. It had been more than a year since she had first learned of the death of Duncan Cameron and initiated efforts—through the Lesleys and their network of friends—to buy her children. The intercessions of the Lesleys had deepened her debt to them, which she was determined to repay by being a dependable companion to Susan's mother, Anne Jean Lyman. That role was getting no easier. The brilliant and irrepressible Northampton widow, who had made Mary Walker her protégé and surrogate daughter in early 1853, had experienced worsening memory lapses in 1854. Frustration led to outbursts of temper and tongue at her two caregivers, companion Mary Walker and housekeeper Mary Cashman. On those occasions, reported Anne Jean Lyman's sister Catherine Robbins to her niece, Mary Walker understood "her importance to your mother" and made "sacrifices to get along." The task was nonetheless difficult, Susan Lesley would later reflect, because Mary Walker was "very proud and sensitive for a woman at service." If Mary Walker could just ignore the unintended barbs of her mother's occasional remarks, the two of them might reliably get along. As it was, her mother's slights prompted Mary Walker to brood and her mother to withdraw, until the turmoil passed. Less than a week after Susan Lesley's return to her mother's household during the first week in July, the daughter decided that a pleasure trip for Mary Walker might distract her from anxiety about her children and the burden of caregiving. Susan Lesley wanted "to give her all the happiness I can" and thought a journey away would help.[2]

Before an excursion could be arranged, however, a succession of setbacks roiled the summer for both Mary Walker and the Lesleys. On the second Sunday in July, Mary Walker reported that members of the Old Cambridge Baptist Church, which she attended regularly, had declared that they wanted all persons of color to sit in a separate section of the sanctuary. Susan Lesley overheard Mary Walker and two or three other women talking in the kitchen of her mother's house—they were hurt and inclined to leave rather than comply. They didn't mind sitting in the back—voluntarily—but bridled at the requirement that they do so. The whole episode made Susan Lesley sick to her stomach; she wrote to the minister the next day.[3] Then, near the end of the month, a dispute between Anne Jean Lyman and her Northampton protégé and boarder—Chauncey Wright—led the recent Harvard graduate to announce that he planned to leave the household. Anne Jean Lyman had encouraged Wright, when he was a precocious Northampton youth, to apply to Harvard, had personally urged Harvard's president to admit him, and had taken him in as a boarder after his graduation and her move to Cambridge. Chauncey Wright had been an incandescent presence to all. Even when his talk soared beyond comprehension, it entertained and enlivened, and kept Anne Jean Lyman in touch with the world of ideas and current events. Susan Lesley thought that her mother's refusal to "make a small concession" had prompted Chauncey Wright's decision to move, though he may have been looking for an occasion to room with a friend his own age. Whatever the cause, the "two Marys were in despair" and her mother faced what her daughter saw as self-inflicted solitude.[4]

Even after the August meeting with the agent from Philadelphia, Mary Walker's spirits remained low. She told Susan Lesley that she was hopeful the man and his mission would do some good. But ongoing symptoms of depression—weeping, refusal to eat—made Susan Lesley wonder if even the recovery of her children would make Mary Walker happy. Her "fits of morbid melancholy" seemed to be chronic. Susan Lesley conjectured that the melancholy came in part from conflict between Mary Walker's proud temperament and her role as a servant. "Truly humble before God," Mary Walker had to pray to "rectify her natural temper of mind." Susan Lesley seemed reluctant to allow that the symptoms might come from repressed resentment at Anne Jean Lyman's cavalier treatment of her caregiver. What might have been seen as grievance—grievance at the need again to oblige a capricious mistress—was perceived as unseemly pride. Susan Lesley worried that pride might induce Mary Walker "to interfere with good direction of those dearest to her, though I trust not."[5]

"The good direction of those dearest to her"—the rescue mission initiated by Peter Lesley—may well have added to Mary Walker's worry about her family's vulnerability. The plan of her choosing—a letter, an appeal, a proposal of ransom—had so far yielded nothing. The rescue mission, which she had not sought, surely raised at least as much uncertainty as hope. If the rescuer planned only to smuggle out her daughter, what would happen to her mother and remaining son? If he meant to flee with her daughter, son, and perhaps mother, what were the chances that three or four of them could make it from Raleigh to Philadelphia, four hundred miles by land and longer by sea? Heart and head told her that doing something was better than nothing, that there was no enduring sanctuary for her children in bondage. Her daughter was approaching the age when Mary Walker, and her mother, and her mother's mother, had conceived their first children by white men. Her son lived in a household where the male servants took to drink at an early age. Even if the children's grandmother was able to see them safely through the perils of youth, they all lived with the reality that slave-owners ultimately died. When they did so, their human property was bequeathed, separated, and sometimes sold—reason enough to attempt a rescue. Yet she must have wondered: Might her efforts unsettle what thin allegiances protected her mother and children from sale or reprisal? There was much reason, in September 1854, for Mary Walker to confide to Susan Lesley that her "heart longs for rest."[6]

THERE WAS ANOTHER ROOT OF Mary Walker's unrest in the fall of 1854—a man in Mary Walker's Northern life. His name is not known. Neither is his color, or his age, or whether he was a free man or a fugitive slave. What is known is that he lived in Albany, New York. Where and how he and Mary Walker met is conjecture. It could have been in Philadelphia in the late 1840s or in Boston in the early 1850s. Glimpses of their relationship come through in Susan Lesley's letters to her husband and to her confidante Margaret (Meggie) White, a classmate from their schooldays together. Mary Walker and her friend from Albany cared for each other and yet could not be together. He not only lived in Albany. He had a family. But if distance and family fealty kept them apart, they nonetheless wrote, and on rare occasions met.

Whoever the friend was, the relationship which might have brought some fullness to Mary Walker's life instead became another mirage of hope and waiting. Sometime in the summer of 1854, the acquaintance from Albany beseeched Mary Walker to allow him to visit. "He had almost died of longing to see her," Susan Lesley confided to her husband, "and she finally consented to tell him to come to Cambridge." It was arranged that he would come in early August when the Cambridge house was empty—when Anne Jean Lyman was away with friends and when her sister, Catherine Robbins, was also away. There would be "no one there and no one to question." He never came. Not until two weeks after the aborted rendezvous did Mary Walker learn that he had pleurisy.[7] For those two weeks she could only wait, wonder what had happened, and become distressed further by reports of a frightening cholera outbreak in Albany. When he resumed their correspondence, he apparently expressed a range of feelings that Mary Walker found impossible to share even with Susan Lesley. Longing, desire, admiration, frustration, success, sadness, his need for her—no letters survive. Whatever he wrote, Susan Lesley observed, the letters unfailingly set Mary Walker back emotionally. "Her letters from Albany always make her gloomy." She made it clear at such times that she had no wish to talk about the man, the tidings of his letters, or her feelings in response. She "encloses herself in such a proud reserve which is not strange. Her position will not admit of sympathy, but it is trying not to be able to fathom her moods sometimes." All Susan Lesley could do was wait until her friend's dejection passed.[8]

A crisis point came in the fall of 1854. Mary Walker agreed again to meet with her friend—this time in Albany. In early October, Mary Walker, Susan Lesley, and Susan's daughter, Mary, traveled together from Cambridge to Keene, New Hampshire, on a visit to the Lesleys' friend Meggie White. This was the trip that Susan Lesley had envisioned in early July, a trip to bring "all the happiness I can" to Mary Walker and to lighten her "year of sorrows." But Mary Walker could not shake her depression or her silence. She knew that the journey to Albany was to come after Keene, and that for her, the meeting with the man was not to revitalize the relationship but to dampen it. What temporarily loosened the grip of gloom was the carriage ride from Keene to Albany. Susan Lesley recalled that it was a day "I shall never forget. We rode through glorious scenery on the Rutland road, with heavenly sky and woods in gorgeous colors. Mary's eyes were full of tears, but her smile was beautiful." Nature's beauty, the resplendent yellows and reds and oranges of the leaves, broke through the wall that Mary Walker had built around herself. For the moment she suspended her preoccupation with past and future. "'How good in God to make the earth so lovely,' she said, and all the cold reserve of many weeks vanished."[9]

In Albany the next day, Mary Walker met her friend and told him what she had to say with dignity, compassion, and firmness. Susan Lesley was present. "I saw her tried almost beyond woman's endurance," Susan Lesley recalled, "but she stood up noble and firm beyond all compare, as I have always seen her do in great trials. Meggie! She is a woman of a thousand. I never expect to look upon her like again."[10] In keeping with her rule of never putting to paper the most intimate details of Mary Walker's life, Susan Lesley did not describe what passed between Mary Walker and her Albany friend. Did he say to her, "You have a right to your own life, to your own happiness"? Did he propose that she *come to Albany* to help him and others serve the cause of freedom, undermine bondage by subversion, and thereby help to loosen the chains of all still enslaved?[11] Albany had never lost a refugee to a slave-catcher. There must have been some such higher appeal, a call more compelling than the Lorings' counsel to imagine her children as dead and get on with her life. We can imagine that she knew she would need all her strength to say no, and that she wanted Susan Lesley there, even in silence, as a buttress when she stood her ground. As a buttress—and as a witness to the choice she was making.

But if Mary Walker made her choice—to live for her children, to live with Anne Jean Lyman, to forgo what happiness she might have found with her Albany friend—she couldn't stifle doubts. As she and Susan Lesley resumed their travels, Mary Walker "expressed to me many times how worn out she was with the life, how overburdened her mind was." Susan Lesley recognized that there was only so much she could do—that anyone could do—to boost her friend's spirits. "She has an undercurrent of melancholy in her nature, greatly aggravated by the circumstances of her life. We cannot alter those—rather can only feel for her and notice as little as possible when she is suffering. I would give worlds, if I possessed them, so as to make her happier. But there is no discharge from the great woes of her destiny."[12]

As it came time for their trip together to end, and for Susan Lesley and her daughter to return to Philadelphia, Mary Walker seemed to be clinging to them, as if reluctant to return to Cambridge, where she would again have to care for her erratic employer. Mary Walker's "proud reserve" returned; Susan Lesley "could not find out what she most wanted to do."[13] Mary Walker could not say, nor could Susan Lesley acknowledge, what they both knew to be the truth. Were it not for her debt to the Lesleys and her hope that they could yet become the lifeline to her children, Mary Walker would surely not go back to Anne Jean Lyman's household.

Return to Cambridge she nevertheless did by mid-October 1854, to care once more for Anne Jean Lyman, and to await word from her friends in Philadelphia of the fate of her family in the South. Little did anyone realize that all attention would soon center on the fate of Mary Walker herself.

IN THE SECOND WEEK OF December 1854, Mary Walker became critically ill. First a stone blocked her gallbladder. Then her bowels became inflamed. For three weeks, she was in such excruciating pain that only morphine and ether could sedate her. Two Cambridge physicians saw her every day; a nurse was with her for two weeks. Distraught, Anne Jean Lyman summoned help from her sister, Catherine Robbins, who remained by her side night and day. Letters from Catherine Robbins and Anne Jean Lyman carried the same message from Cambridge to the Lesleys in Philadelphia: prepare for Mary Walker to die.[14]

Susan Lesley agonized. "It is hard for me to sit here in Philadelphia while Mary is suffering, perhaps dying. . . . She expressed a strong wish to see us again—but said she knew it could not be." Electing to stay at home in midwinter with her daughter and her husband, Susan Lesley instead conveyed her feelings and thoughts in letters to Catherine Robbins. "I would say much to her," Susan Lesley wrote her aunt, "but she knows my heart. . . . Tell her we remember her in our prayers and in our hearts for all her love. Tell her we shall always feel that Mary"—the Lesleys' daughter—"has her name."[15]

During the first two weeks of the illness, the news from Cambridge got steadily worse. The doctors doubted that Mary Walker would live. She herself prepared to die. In response, Susan Lesley told her aunt to reassure Mary Walker that in the event of her death, "every charge that she has given . . . shall be strictly executed." The first promise concerned Mary Walker's letters. Mary Walker kept all of her correspondence in the Cambridge house. "I always promised Mary to keep her papers from every eye, & burn them unopened," save one "she wished me to see." If she died suddenly, Susan Lesley asked her aunt to place all the letters under lock and key until Susan could return to Cambridge and could destroy them. Susan Lesley promised as well that she would have personal interviews with all those friends who had helped Mary Walker attain her own freedom and pursue her children's liberty, and would convey gratitude to them. To assure Mary Walker that she knew whom to contact, Susan Lesley wrote out the names of every person—the list took three and a half lines of the letter. Then either she or Peter Lesley thought better of listing the friends of the fugitive—and meticulously inked through every single name.[16] Caution lay behind both the obliteration of the names and the planned destruction of the letters. Mary Walker's correspondents extended well beyond her friend in Albany, all of whom knew her identity as a fugitive slave. If by accident Mary Walker's letters or Susan Lesley's list of names ever fell into hostile hands—someone looking to identify Northerners who aided and abetted the fugitive in blatant violation of the 1850 law—many would be at risk. Prior to the Anthony Burns case, Mary Walker might have considered herself and her papers completely safe in Boston. Now who was to say that slave-holders could not breach the very citadel of abolitionism? The security of the Underground depended on secrecy.

Susan Lesley did not think that Mary Walker would die, but confided to her aunt that "deeply as I should miss her, I should hardly grieve to think she was at rest." If Mary Walker survived her debilitating illness—on top of recurrent rheumatism, severe headaches, and a prolapsed uterus—she would be profoundly weakened. Recovery would take a long time and might never be complete. Her emotional future seemed equally bleak. What good had come from almost two years of trying to restore her family? "If she lives, such a weary miserable life is before her, that I more often long to hear she is at rest." Susan Lesley thought that Mary Walker herself "looks forward in perfect peace to the end." Recalling the frequent expressions of deep fatigue—"how worn out she was with the life, how overburdened her mind was," "how discouraged she was all the time"—Susan Lesley thought that physical "recovery would be a sad disappointment to her." Death would bring an end to earthly troubles. Yet if Mary died—and Susan Lesley admitted she herself couldn't help thinking selfishly—if Mary died, what would happen to Susan Lesley's mother? Who would have the skill to take care of her and the patience to endure her? "I can never make her place good to mother."[17] What was to be wished for?

MARY WALKER SURVIVED. The gallbladder infection subsided, her pain receded, her nurse left. Her physicians declared that she was past the worst of her illness. But she would need time and care to recover. Whether she could ever return to full strength, they could not say.[18] In the midst of the crisis, no one broached the matter of what would happen if she lived. Who would care for her? Would the family that had employed her as a companion support her as a convalescent? Once it became clear that Mary Walker would live, such questions became unavoidable. It was Anne Jean Lyman who posed the issue to her daughter, in a letter written during the third week of January 1855. When she did so, all the tensions between mother and daughter—generated by four years of the mother's erratic emotional behavior—came to the fore.

On the surface, Anne Jean Lyman's letter seemed perfectly reasonable, a candid summary of a regrettable reality. "It is now six weeks since Mary was confined to her room," Anne Jean Lyman wrote her daughter. She had sat up *"some"* that week and for the first time was able to walk into the dining room. "I do not think Mary will ever be well and strong again—but I do not expect to take care of her. You must settle what shall be done with her—for you unwittingly drop'd her down upon me." Susan Lesley had received several earlier letters from her mother expressing the view that the Lesleys—eager to support a refugee and the antislavery cause—had imposed Mary Walker on Anne Jean Lyman. "I will pay my part for her support, but I could not undertake the care of her and I never thought that I ought to have the care of her, provided she was well."[19]

The problem went deeper than who should be taking care of whom. Anne Jean Lyman contended that Mary Walker had never been an ideal match for her. "I ought to find someone who could be a consistent companion and in some measure, an assistant, if required." Accustomed to an overflow of family and friends during her married life in Northampton, the widow had found Cambridge to be "a solitary place as far as an intimate interchange is concerned." People "of my age require something to animate them & the way they do it is to engraft some of the interests of youth upon their advanced life & dullness. If I were living with or near my children, I should not require in the evenings any other interests than that they would furnish. But . . . if I cannot keep but one person, I ought to have at my age a suitable companion." "I would not have you think because I have given you a fair exposition of my feelings and wishes, that I am unfriendly to Mary.

No one would be more ready than I am to help any good person and her in particular, than I am." Mary Walker was welcome to recuperate in the household through the winter. But come spring, the mother felt, she must find another companion.[20]

Susan Lesley had ignored similar sentiments in her mother's earlier letters, fearing that a response "would do more harm than good," and hoping that her mother's feelings would pass. By the end of January 1855, she realized that she would have to reply and wrote to Catherine Robbins—her mother's youngest sister and closest Cambridge relative—to prepare her for the explosion expected to follow. From Susan Lesley's vantage point, her mother overlooked how indispensable Mary Walker had become to the Cambridge household. No one else had stood ready to care for her mother when she fainted, to endure her kaleidoscopically changing versions of events, to oblige the endless need to repeat accounts of what was happening, whether in the household or the world. In the previous year, Susan Lesley had twice tried to find her mother a more amenable companion, not as a replacement for Mary Walker but as an additional member of the household. Yet neither arrangement had worked out.

In Susan Lesley's opinion, her mother was the author of her own troubles, and Mary Walker her mainstay rather than her burden. Given all that the daughter had witnessed—stories changing, insults inflicted and then forgotten, and Mary Walker enduring it all without family members around to share the burden—it was hard to take her mother's complaint seriously. Quite the opposite. To Susan Lesley's mind, her mother had no idea of Mary Walker's indispensable role in the household, or how rare it was to find such a person—someone who would put up with, as a free person in service, what only enslaved persons in the South endured, under pain of punishment. "What is to be done," the niece wrote to her aunt, "with a person who always willfully sees all her own relations with others in an entirely false light, and always changes her way of seeing and representing them so rapidly!! I must now and then tell her right. Yet I know it is wholly in vain." Susan Lesley warned her aunt that she planned to write a candid response to her mother; she anticipated an explosion of denial.[21] As expected, her mother was angry, both at the daughter's letter and at discovering that Susan Lesley had written her aunt "behind her back." Anne Jean Lyman said she was "much hurt by what" her daughter said, that she "has treated Mary as she would a sister and that she does not think she can bear to part with her—although in justice to herself, she ought to."[22]

Without a doubt, Anne Jean Lyman spoke truly when she expressed her feelings of attachment to Mary Walker and distress over her illness. The entries in her diary for the month of December 1854 chronicled those mounting anxieties. December 12: "Mary Walker is having a most threatening fit of illness which absorbs all our attention & takes up all our rooms." December 13: "Poor Mary Walker very sick. I am afraid she will not recover. I am truly sad." December 15: "Mary remains without alteration. I feel very sad." December 21: "No variety from the sadness of contemplating poor Mary's illness." December 30: "M. Walker continues to grow better, or rather she is in an improving condition—which is a great improvement to my state of mind." At the same time, the diary detailed Anne Jean Lyman's hunger for stimulation. During the last three weeks of the year, she attended church each Sunday, assessed the sermons and their messages ("searching discourses"), attended two lectures on Greece ("well delivered & very fine") and one on art ("very *original* and very *striking*"), and made calls or received visitors almost every day.[23] Clearly, she would have benefited from a companion with whom she had more in common—someone widely read, able to discourse on people and events of the day, capable of distilling the latest works of history or biography, fiction or philosophy. When it came right down to it, she *had* inherited the custody of a refugee taken in—and then left behind—by her conscience-driven daughter and son-in-law. But all this was to ignore the vital role that Mary Walker had come to play in Anne Jean Lyman's life and in the lives of her children. Mary Walker's dedication and skill meant that they could all rest easy knowing that their mother had devoted care while in the throes of an illness that slowly eroded her predictability to herself and those around her.

Her mother's stance toward Mary Walker left Susan Lesley conflicted. On the one hand, she felt "quite unwilling to have poor Mary, with her broken health and heart, live and struggle" any longer in Anne Jean Lyman's household. "I know she has staid there from gratitude to me and Mr. Lesley." Given "this last sickness of hers" and now Anne Jean Lyman's reluctance to keep her, "It seems to me . . . utterly improper to claim" an obligation "of her any longer." On the other hand—"on Mother's account"—Susan Lesley nonetheless wanted Mary Walker to stay, if she could physically and emotionally manage to do so.[24] Despite uncertainty about when or whether she would regain her strength, Mary Walker would remain in the household.

MARY WALKER'S ILLNESS, which had imperiled her life and depleted her physically, had an unexpected outcome. It set her on a road to spiritual redemption. While Susan Lesley had waited in December for the outcome of Mary Walker's struggle for life, it had seemed to her that death might be the only way for Mary Walker to be "at rest. I fear she is one of those who must drink the cup of sorrow to the dregs, before she is permitted to enter the heavenly Kingdom. Why? It is not permitted us to know." It did not surprise her when her aunt reported that Mary Walker, too, saw death as a means of release. "She had made all her arrangements . . . in case of her death and looks forward in perfect peace to the end." Survival meant that she would have to seek "perfect peace" in *this* world—and set the stage for her to do so.[25]

Finding faith was the answer. Without question, Mary Walker had always been a religious woman. When serving the Cameron family in Raleigh, she had accompanied the Cameron sisters and their mother to the city's Episcopal church. She had acted as intermediary to bring a black preacher to the aid of a dying Cameron daughter. In the Cambridge household, religion continued to be a central part of her life. She spent spare hours and Sundays in the kitchen of the house, reading to herself passages from the Bible or singing hymns. In moments of trial, she prayed and sought answers from on high—as she had in 1853 when wrestling with the news about Duncan Cameron's death and with surging fear and despair about her children.

The supreme burden for Mary Walker was that she understood her suffering as something she had brought on herself. However imperative the reasons, she had left her children in bondage. They were now at the mercy of new owners. She could neither rid herself of obsession with their fate nor, so far, do anything to change it. Had she grown up true to her mother's religious roots, her African-American religious roots, she might have felt the sustaining power of God and community to see her through all trials. But her long association with the Camerons and with their Episcopal ways—what her mother had scorned as "your white folk's religion"—had placed her between religious traditions. She could study the King James Bible in every spare moment, could pray on her knees in crisis, and could receive temporary answers and respite. But when hopes proved mirages, self-blame deepened.

The illness brought catharsis. Mary Walker had been through a month of excruciating pain. Prayer and the love of others had sustained her. Though she had been ready to die, God decided she should live. Was it simply to punish her more? The minister of the Baptist church that she attended in Cambridge offered her a more redemptive understanding of God's purpose—and hers. She had come to know the Reverend John Pryor the year before, when she had begun to visit the Old Cambridge Baptist Church. This was not the church of the Lesleys, who were now both Unitarian and distanced from traditional religion, nor was it the faith of Anne Jean Lyman, who attended Cambridge's Congregational churches. When Susan Lesley accompanied

Mary Walker to hear the Reverend Pryor preach in the summer of 1854, skepticism mixed with admiration in the account she gave to her husband, the ex-minister turned geologist. Pryor gave a sermon on "the oft repeated scheme of redemption as he called it. But his warmth of manner was good to see. Mary enjoys him so I say not a word." Susan Lesley could understand the Baptist minister's appeal: he was a "joyful Christian." John Pryor had steadfastly prayed with and for Mary Walker throughout the December ordeal.[26] Given the gift of life, she turned to him for her soul's salvation.

As she recovered her strength, Mary Walker began conversations about Baptist beliefs with her Cambridge minister. Baptist doctrine held out the promise of forgiveness, cleansing, and a fresh start for those who sought and accepted Jesus. By mid-May 1855, Mary Walker had made a momentous decision: she would be baptized in the Old Cambridge Baptist Church. Catherine Robbins worried that the physical act of baptism—immersion in cold water—would cause Mary Walker to relapse into illness. Mary Walker asserted she was willing to risk her health "in such a cause." Susan Lesley, coming from a faith with no such rite or route to salvation, knew that she "ought to be glad, but somehow feel as if she would be more separated from me." Nonetheless, she understood that Mary Walker's soul required this step, despite the risks: "whatever gives her peace." When Mary Walker informed Susan Lesley that she wanted her to be present for the baptism—and would delay the date until her arrival in Cambridge—her Philadelphia friend readily agreed. As the date of the baptism approached, Anne Jean Lyman reported a great turn in Mary Walker's temperament. "[Mother] speaks of her as a saint, and says the impression she makes on everyone is the same."[27]

The Old Cambridge Baptist Church was full on June 23, 1855, the morning of Mary Walker's baptism. Mary Walker asked Susan Lesley to be at her side for the immersion ceremony. Standing next to her friend, Susan Lesley observed the completion of the change that had been in the making since January. Watching Mary Walker, Susan Lesley saw "the most beautiful expression of faith & hope I ever saw in any human face. She looked quite unconscious of the people around her, and I do not believe once thought of the crowded church." When "she came up from the water, I supported her in her heavy clothes, down the steps to the vestry, and disrobed her. She was quiet and I never saw her so happy." Mary Walker made use of many scriptural "expressions, and very glowing imagery seemed to float through her mind. She thanked her savior for giving her a seat in his kingdom, for sending his spirit like a dove, and clothing her in a robe of righteousness."[28] Touched by a spirit like a dove, Mary Walker at last experienced the rapture felt by her mother at secret midnight prayer meetings in slavery, where they had sung:

> Jesus shall break the chain
> And bear us to the throne
> By & bye, by & bye.
> There friends shall meet again
> Who have loved, who have loved
> Their union shall be sweet
> At their dear Redeemer's feet,
> And they meet to part no more,
> Who have loved, who have loved.

Welcomed to her dear Redeemer's feet, Mary Walker was joyous and spoke "as if she had fulfilled a duty that has long haunted her."[29] Whatever her mistakes, she was forgiven. Whatever her faults, she was redeemed.

The changed disposition sustained Mary Walker in continuing her care of Anne Jean Lyman, whose behavior became more erratic and taxing in July 1855. Present in the household in Cambridge, Susan Lesley described her mother as pushing away the people she wanted and needed, alienating them with words or deeds, then despairing at her loneliness. As "reason diminishes and memory and hope vanish entirely, we must have the pain of seeing her will [become] more and more and more overbearing." What was remarkable to Susan Lesley was Mary Walker's response to Mother Lyman's emotional deterioration. "Mary's patience becomes more complete, as the situation becomes more and more painful. She realizes that Mother's friends must be friends in spite of her." Susan Lesley found herself pushed to the limit. How "unnatural and sad, to have the relation of parent and child so marred. I hope our little Mary will never have to speak such words to me, as I did to mother this morning." Throughout this trying time, Mary Walker demonstrated transcendent patience. "Mary is far more quiet and happy since her baptism, more equable, than I have ever known her."[30]

As Susan Lesley's summer in Cambridge came to a close, she could only marvel at the transformation she had witnessed. Mary Walker "picks up and folds to her heart every passing flower or sunbeam." She "never seemed to me so perfect in her goodness and sweetness as this summer. She has found the peace that passeth understanding, and enjoys as only those who can, who have known the deepest sorrows."[31]

7 A Season of Silence

Mary Walker needed all her new reserves of faith.

In September 1855, Peter Lesley wrote from Philadelphia to say that he'd just met with the rescuer they had hired to recover Mary Walker's children in North Carolina—and that the mission had ended in utter failure. "P" (James Price) had gone down to Raleigh for a second time, had stayed for weeks, but had made contact with no one and come back without a lead. "I have not a moment to spare and can only tell you how fruitless all our hopes are. Seventy dollars more are thrown away and not a word of information obtained." Price had gone down, stayed till "'his money was out,' and on inquiry for 'Lucy' learned that she was very ill—dropsy or consumption. He walked around but saw no one and so came away. He is a humbug and we must apply to Mrs. S[towe]'s man."[1]

NEITHER MARY WALKER NOR THE Lesleys had expected this outcome. While carpenter James Price was on his first reconnaissance to Raleigh in August 1854, the Lesleys had been hopeful enough to make contingency plans for the arrival of Mary Walker's daughter. Susan Lesley's friends George and Mary Stearns had agreed to give Mary Walker's daughter safe haven and work in nearby Medford.[2] Peter Lesley had stood ready to leave his geological fieldwork at a moment's notice to meet the children in Philadelphia and escort them to New England. In case Price needed money in a hurry, Lesley asked Mary Walker to send $100 to abolitionist James McKim in Philadelphia, who had already received $100 from the Lesleys to "meet any emergency." The rest of her savings she "will want . . . if she can get her children." Peter Lesley spoke for all of them in mid-August when he wrote his wife that "I try to keep cool about P and his adventure but begin to desire to hear from him"—even as he knew that contact was impossible. To protect against discovery or prosecution under federal law, Lesley and Price had agreed that "No letters were to pass between us." Criminal liability was one thing; moral right was another. "God bless and protect us in our *lawful* undertakings and a speedy success."[3]

It is entirely possible that James Price was a swindler, an impostor who deluded James McKim and Peter Lesley with the claim that he had accomplished a slave-rescue once before and was ready to do so again. In William Still's 1872 account of the Underground Railroad in Philadelphia, there are several mentions of a "P" who came under suspicion as an untrustworthy agent.[4] Yet it seems doubtful that Price set out to fleece the Lesleys and Mary Walker. Had he meant to take no risks, there would have been no need for him to ask the Lesleys—as he did in August 1854—whether they stood ready to bail him out if he got caught. On his first mission to Raleigh, he may well have received signals that there were people willing to help him, and that the logistics of flight were feasible.

It seems more likely that none of the parties to the rescue mission had a full idea of what the agent was up against. Here was a perfect stranger in a Southern capital that was hardly more than an oversized village; most of its 4,400 inhabitants were known to one another. Artisans seeking work were not unusual, because two devastating Raleigh fires in the early 1850s had prompted extensive rebuilding.[5] Nonetheless, outsiders were sure to be noticed, all the more if they asked questions about the family of a fugitive slave. Of course, Price was mainly interested in making contact with one person—Mary Walker's mother, Silla—and had received a pair of Mary's earrings to identify himself to her. Still, he needed to find someone, perhaps black friends whom Mary Walker had identified as intermediaries, to set up a rendezvous. Almost certainly, some of those people had to know what Price, Mary Walker, and the Lesleys did not: that there had been a letter from Frank Walker in 1853 and an unsuccessful attempt to recapture him, that his grandmother Silla had come under suspicion as knowing the whereabouts of her daughter, and that although exonerated by her owners, she remained under scrutiny. The grandmother herself may well have directed her friends to deflect the stranger, without a word as to why. Did Price run into a wall of silence, sustained by friends of the grandmother, to insulate her and the children from repercussions which they knew might follow contact?

If carpenter Price had made inquiries among his fellow artisans, he'd have found them no more helpful. White workingmen of Raleigh had little goodwill toward free or fugitive blacks trying to get their children out of slavery. When Raleigh ex-slave Lunsford Lane, who traveled north to raise a ransom to buy his family, returned to Raleigh in 1842 to bargain for his wife and children, he found the leading gentlemen of the place sympathetic. But the artisans of Raleigh were bitterly opposed to him and his mission. Seized by a mob, Lane feared for his life until assured that tarring and feathering was the limit of the injury the artisans planned to inflict on him. They explained that he was to them the symbol of free blacks and their white patrons lording it over the working class of whites.[6] The agent of a former slave from Raleigh would win no help from workers in the white community.

Without someone from the inside to explain the source of the shutout, Price would have had no way of knowing what was obstructing his efforts. Had Price been told bluntly that no one in Raleigh would help him—that the black community had decided to protect the Walkers from meddling outsiders—he would have exonerated himself to Peter Lesley. As it was, Peter Lesley dismissed Price as a charlatan, and concluded that they needed a truer man for the job.

No one gave up on the possibility of a rescue—not Mary Walker, not Susan Lesley, not Peter Lesley. Yet all had to deal with the strain that Price's failure placed on their hopes and their relations with one another. For Mary Walker, it meant an end to her summer of emotional euphoria and put to the test her "peace that passeth all understanding." Without elaboration, Susan Lesley simply reported Mary Walker's "disappointment" at the news. Peter Lesley responded that he too felt disappointment, "very great disappointment." Since the meeting with Price, there'd been "not a day I have not thought of her more or less." At the same time, he was clearly frustrated. He'd not written to Mary. "I did not know what to say. Nothing can be said."[7]

For her part, Susan Lesley was ready to act at once on her husband's suggestion that "we must apply to Mrs. Stowe's man." She proposed to contact her cousin Susan Hillard, a personal acquaintance of Harriet Beecher Stowe. Earlier that summer, Susan Hillard had hosted a memorable "day of days" in which Mary Walker had met the famed author and heard a black presenter read aloud from *Uncle Tom's Cabin* in the Hillard living room. It had been after Mary Walker left the gathering that Stowe had learned the Walker story and volunteered that she knew of a man who had "succeeded in getting off hundreds—and who never fails."[8] In the wake of Price's failure, Susan Lesley proposed to arrange with "cousin Susan" to "ask Mrs. Stowe about her man." She asked Peter whether they had the funds to pursue the business now or needed to wait for another season.[9] Peter Lesley's response was that of a man who had reached the end of his tether. Do whatever you want, whenever you want, he responded. "Let Mrs. Stowe's man operate as he pleases. I am willing to board this winter," to endure suffocating quarters and sickening bad air, to save "three or four hundred dollars which we can employ in the South." Perhaps boarding would give him "all the home comfort I can get to make this life endurable." But perhaps not. "To be absent from you one half of the year and to board with you the other half—I may as well hire the next rattlesnake to do me a kind turn and have done with it." Susan Hillard promised to write to Harriet Beecher Stowe.[10] But in subsequent letters, Susan Lesley made no more mention of "Mrs. Stowe's man." This was a defeat her husband had taken hard. He needed a break from the whole crusade.

Neither of the Lesleys told Mary Walker about Stowe's secret agent. There was no reason to get her hopes up again, until they knew more about whether he really existed, whether he would undertake the mission, and what he would cost. What greeted Mary Walker instead was a season of silence on the whole subject. Peter Lesley did not contact her: "Nothing can be said." When Susan Lesley returned to her home in Philadelphia, she wrote to her aunt Catherine Robbins—her "Aunt Kitty"—and noted in her letter of January 1856 that it had been some time since she'd written to Mary Walker. She "must think my long silence strange." In March she reiterated, through her aunt, that Mary Walker "is never far from my thoughts, though I give her small evidence of it."[11]

MARY WALKER TOOK MATTERS into her own hands. Independently, she too had heard there were persons willing to go south on rescue missions. She wrote her Philadelphia friend James Fells and gave him the name of a contact woman in the city who reportedly knew an agent. Fells responded that he "saw the woman. She said she did not know the man's name but would try and find out and write."[12] Apparently, a willing individual was found. Mary Walker now knew the modus operandi for a rescue venture. In mid-May, she sent to Philadelphia a box with items that would allow the person to identify himself as her representative. More important, she sent detailed information about friends who could help the agent to make contact with her mother. She asked Cambridge friend Chauncey Wright to set down exact instructions:

> Uncle Zack belongs to the Presbyterian minister Mr. La/sa [I spell it by the pronouncing dictionary], and is the sexton of the Baptist church. Willis Haywood, waiter at the largest hotel in the place, will direct to him; or any other waiter at any other hotel will direct to Mr. L's. If Aunt Lucy should be dead, inquire for Glasgow, one of the colored deacons of the Baptist church, who belongs to Mr. Saunders. Either he or Uncle Zack may be trusted.[13]

It is unclear who "Uncle Zack" was, but his owner—the phonetically spelled "Mr. La/sa"—was the Reverend Drury Lacy, minister of the Presbyterian church of Raleigh. The friends who "may be trusted" were both "colored" members and leaders of Raleigh's Baptist church, one a sexton and the other a deacon.[14] The mysterious "Aunt Lucy" remained a central figure in the rescue scheme.

While hoping for word about her two enslaved children in Raleigh, Mary Walker also sought to locate the son who had escaped—to where she knew not. In the hope that Frank Walker may have fled to Canada, she spent some of her savings to have a person there inquire about him. Having heard nothing, "she talks of sending some person to Canada to hunt for him." Susan Lesley begged her "to spend no more money in that way. Every inquiry has been made there." The Lesleys thought it more likely that Frank Walker had either emigrated to England or gone underground in the North. Susan Lesley asked if her husband could have a scientific colleague check in Britain; she herself wrote Frederick Douglass to see if he could assist in the North. "Although I have no hope of finding him," she admitted to her husband, "yet I think it will be a satisfaction to her to feel that all possible ways have been tried."[15] Frederick Douglass responded compassionately.

> It will give me pleasure to serve you and your friend in bringing Mother and Son together so far as I am able. At present, I am totally ignorant of the young man's whereabouts, but I have several acquaintances in different parts of the country from North Carolina of whom I will gladly make enquiries. And should any trace of him reach me, I will gladly inform you of all the facts. It is, however, exceedingly difficulty to find colored people from the South. They change their names and conceal their origins for obvious reasons. I have been looking for a friend of mind from slavery this 18 years—and in a measure, know how to sympathise with your poor friend in search of her son.[16]

So far as is known, nothing came of either quest.

MARY WALKER'S HEALTH SEEMED to wax and wane with the prospects for regaining her children. In Cambridge in early July 1856, Susan Lesley at first found Mary Walker "remarkably well & in good spirits." The good health of her mother's caregiver was an immense relief to the daughter, for Anne Jean Lyman's condition had deteriorated further. Susan found her mother's mind "now just like a sieve, it retains nothing a moment." She had been asked to read the same newspaper column to her mother seven times. The daughter found herself all the more grateful to Mary Walker, "now my sole dependence."[17]

But in mid-July, Mary Walker took a turn for the worse. "I see that all her consumptive symptoms have made sure though slow progress since last year," Susan Lesley reported to her husband. She coughed with every change of air, she bleeds a little, her shoulder had sharp pains. "Yet she seems unaware herself of the progress of the disease." A heat wave exacerbated her symptoms: further bleeding from the lungs, loss of strength and appetite, her "whole body showered with pain." Susan Lesley rubbed the throbbing shoulder, encouraged her quietly, and called in a physician. He reported that Mary Walker might live years with the amount of the disease she had now—with "very great care." Susan Lesley hoped the doctor was right. "Oh we are selfish mortals," she admitted, "for what could I do without her, while Mother lives"?[18]

Almost certainly, Mary Walker did suffer from tuberculosis. Any combination of circumstances could have made it worse. Stifling heat, and the ongoing burden of caring for a woman with dementia, doubtless contributed to the flareups. Yet it would be folly to ignore the role of disappointment and frustration in precipitating the "severe ill turn" in Mary Walker's health. Susan Lesley seemed to recognize that nurture was what Mary Walker needed—and that she was not going to get better in the Cambridge cottage. It's not that Anne Jean Lyman was incessantly demanding. On the contrary, when Mary Walker became ill, her employer turned caregiver herself. In Anne Jean Lyman's condition, however, that attentiveness may have become as manic and repetitive as asking to have the same newspaper column read seven times. *Are you all right? Can I do something? How about now?* Such may have been the circumstances that led Susan Lesley to decide that when she returned home to Philadelphia in early October, she would bring Mary Walker with her. In Philadelphia, Susan Lesley would "try to build her up a little in a few weeks of care."[19]

Then came a bombshell. In early September 1856, Mary Walker told Catherine Robbins, who lived in Cambridge and looked in on her older sister every day, that she was ready to quit the household. Catherine Robbins conveyed the news to Peter Lesley, who was doing geological work in New Hampshire. If she gave him Mary Walker's justification, he chose to ignore it. Instead he attempted a kind of moral geology to get to the bedrock reason for what he took as the disloyalty of the refugee woman whom they had sheltered and befriended. "Believe me dearest," he wrote to his wife, "there are very few hearts *entirely* faithful to us in this world. But then we must accept our friends with what they can bring and look always for less than we should hope for. Old friendships are not subject to such casualties. . . . Not so new friendship—especially between different orders, races, and classes of humankind." Doubtless he tried to stifle the impulse to charge *ingratitude* or to sigh, *Well what did we expect?* Rather, he wrote, "the want of homogenuousness [*sic*] is itself a ground of suspicion on both sides."[20]

A crossroads? So it seemed. It was inevitable that at some point Mary Walker would ask whether she should or could continue with Mrs. Lyman, whose condition was getting nothing but worse. Even with all the patience in the world, buoyed by her baptism and her renewed faith, she had to wonder whether it was the will of Providence that in the North as in the South, in freedom as in bondage, her fate was always to be the caregiver of invalid women. Despite knowing that few employers would give her the attention, medical care, sympathy, and support she received in the Lyman household—where she wasn't docked for time away and where fellow domestic Mary Cashman did the heavy work around the house—she must have wondered about the toll imposed on her health by the needs of her employer. Should she perhaps quit before she became worn down altogether?

Susan Lesley did not accept her husband's view of the fragility of friendship "between different orders, races, and classes of humankind." Instead, she spoke with Mary Walker to try to fathom what had precipitated her decision to leave. Out of the conversation came a belief that Mary Walker needed time away from the Lyman household. She agreed to come with the Lesleys on a trip back to Philadelphia, where Susan Lesley hoped to care for her and "to build her up." All of them seemed prepared to put off the question of whether she would stay with Anne Jean Lyman on her return. But more came out of the talk. The dwelling that Mary Walker, Mary Cashman, and Anne Jean Lyman lived in was small and without the amenities of a well-outfitted mid-nineteenth-century household. Happily, at the very time of this crisis in the fall of 1856, Joseph Lyman—Susan's brother, who lived in Jamaica Plain, on the periphery of Boston—learned that a nearby residence in Cambridge had come up for sale and made the decision to bid on it for his mother. Knowing that Joseph demanded secrecy until he had completed the purchase, Susan Lesley could not tell Mary Walker about the possibility of a dwelling with more conveniences. But she knew that the new house would be wonderful and that the garden and yard would be appealing to all. She encouraged her brother's efforts and cheered his success.[21]

There was one more matter that seemed crucial to Mary Walker, for reasons one can only guess. "I have told her," reported Susan to Joseph, "to stay home through the winter and that you and Edward will pay her $1.50 a week from the first of December."[22] A salary of $1.50 a week was no more than average for a domestic servant in Boston or Philadelphia. The fact that Susan Lesley made special note of this suggests that it may have been an increase over what Mary Walker was already receiving. The caregiver had been in the habit of looking after Anne Jean Lyman and taking on extra work—usually dressmaking done in the homes of others, sometimes sewing done in her own household. Mary Walker always had permission to do this outwork and thus to accumulate ransom money for her children. It may be that the extra income, however small, was welcomed as a way to make up for the sewing work she had lost to illness—and to keep a flow of rescue money into her savings account. A vacation, a place to be cared for, a small raise in salary, a more agreeable dwelling on her return, and time to think it all over with Philadelphia friends around her—all these

Susan Lesley hoped might sway Mary Walker to stay at her difficult post.

"TERRIBLE THINGS SURROUND US like demons in the valley of the Shadow." So wrote Peter Lesley to his wife Susan in mid-July 1856. He was writing about the larger political world in which the Lesleys and Mary Walker found themselves as events of that year unfolded. For the Lesleys, confrontations taking place on the plains of Kansas, in the halls of Congress, and closer to home in Massachusetts and Pennsylvania were coming to overshadow Mary Walker's personal struggle to free her children from bondage. A thousand miles away in Kansas, the Kansas-Nebraska Bill passed by Congress in 1854 had opened the way for supporters and opponents of slavery to fight it out over whether the territory would become a state that allowed slavery. Immigrants poured in from New England to create farms and claim Kansas for freedom, backed by Emigrant Aid Societies and supplied with "Beecher's Bibles"—long rifles sent in cases and named after the leading ministerial opponent of slavery's expansion, Henry Ward Beecher. In equal numbers, migrants came from the adjacent state of Missouri and from deeper in the South, no less determined to make Kansas a state open to slavery. They brought their sidearms and shotguns with them. Violence in Kansas ensued, and the cycle of attacks and reprisals triggered the murders of five Southerners (several of them non-slaveholders) by John Brown and his sons on May 24, 1856. Two days earlier, after Massachusetts senator Charles Sumner had delivered a blistering attack against the South and a South Carolina fellow senator, violence had come to the nation's capital. South Carolina congressman Preston Brooks had attacked Sumner on the floor of the Senate with a cane and beat him senseless at his Senate desk. "What are we living into," Peter Lesley brooded, "but an age of blood and anarchy?"[23]

For three years, Mary Walker and the Lesleys had waged a private struggle in the shadow of slavery for the freedom of her two children.

Events now led the Lesleys to focus on larger stakes and larger hopes in 1856. "Personal interests however dear [are] swallowed up in public interests when the race and its last best gains of the ages are at stake," Peter Lesley wrote to his wife. "For ourselves we are safe come what may." But "for the country—we tremble and may well be willing to fight. This Teutonic blood is one that does not readily *endure forever.* It always in time *rebels.*" The elemental conflicts raging in Kansas and in Washington raised the possibility of freedom's ultimate triumph in the country. "I hope to live to see a northern army sweep with a majestic irresistible movement over the South, and remodel at a blow the monstrous frame of society that has grinned at us across the line and lashed at us from above for so long. What will a few thousand lives lost be in comparison with a saved age, an emancipated race, a regenerated tone of sentiment in America?" He did not forget Mary Walker, and proposed to mail her a check for $25. But he intended to send money as well to support those in New York and Pennsylvania stumping for the newly formed Republican Party, which had nominated antislavery candidate John C. Fremont as its choice for president. Susan Lesley, well aware of the peril and promise of the moment, reported that her brother Joseph Lyman had become a major fundraiser for the Kansas Emigrant Aid Society—and even "poor unsettled mother sews [garments] for the Kansas sufferers."[24]

The preoccupation with Kansas and national politics intensified through the summer of 1856. Writing to his wife from Philadelphia, Peter Lesley reported good news: he had just landed a new job which promised a $1,200 stipend—an enormous relief to a household that had just been getting by. But bad news from the battlefront in Kansas dimmed elation over his personal success. "My heart breaks and sinks about the poor people in Kansas. May the curses of the righteous destroy our tyrants. I have no heart to write on personal topics. What is our interest compared with this immense crisis—this impending fate of all American hope and life." In Boston, too, Susan Lesley reported, the political eclipsed the personal. While she was sitting at tea with friends, family friend and Kansas emigrant backer George Stearns "walked into our tea" and told of a Kansas meeting that was about to take place. Chauncey Wright went to fetch "Aunt Kitty" and the neighboring Howe relatives, and "we all proceeded in a body to the Hall." The Reverend Theodore Parker, a leader of the Boston Vigilance Committee, came in and sat down next to Susan Lesley, and together they listened to the featured speaker: Ralph Waldo Emerson. He spoke "very well," but with great sadness. "He evidently feels the wrongs of Kansas to the heart's core." Throughout the fall, "Greatest excitement is kept up about political affairs." People "can't keep quiet."[25]

PEOPLE COULD NOT KEEP QUIET about politics in Philadelphia, any more than they could in Boston, but discord spoiled the hope that Mary Walker's visit there would revive her health and spirits. Certainly there was logic to the change of scene. What no one had counted on was that Mary Walker, who "had been a great invalid" before her arrival, would remain so throughout a stay that lengthened to six weeks. As it turned out, the house was never quiet. "We are quite a hotel, with visitors coming and going." One of the visitors was the younger brother of Peter Lesley, the Delaware physician Allen Lesley, who himself suffered from what was described as "incurable gout of the heart" and had become a "wretched invalid." The two brothers held diametrically opposite political views. Susan Lesley wrote that she found her brother-in-law's "ideas and ideals sadly perverted—he was always on the wrong side of every great moral question of importance." As they were all under the same roof for nearly a month, Susan and Peter Lesley came to like the physician and his wife, from whom they had kept a distance because of the differences between the brothers. But Allen Lesley made no effort to hide his political views. Not only did he favor the election of the proslavery Democratic presidential nominee, James Buchanan, but during conversations in the household

—with Mary Walker present—he had called for a "renewal of the slave trade" and said he was eager to see "the time when every free Negro shall be enslaved."[26]

Because of the supposedly desperate medical condition of their guest and kinsman, the host Lesleys held back from asserting their own views. The Lesleys and Mary Walker felt "almost hopeless here," but had to keep to themselves their growing despair during October 1856, as it became clear that the new Republican Party and its presidential candidate, John C. Fremont, would lose the election. They tried to take the long view. Even "if the worst happens, God can bring good out of seeming evil. He alone knows what is best for us." As political results blighted their hopes, neither the Lesleys nor Mary Walker could vent their feelings or console one another. They felt compelled "all through this trying election to keep under [wraps] our varying emotions, and to see one we cared for, rejoicing in Buchanan's election." Mary Walker told Susan Lesley that it was "a great lesson to her, and one she should never forget, to see Peter's patience and tenderness" with his reactionary brother. To Susan Lesley, patience seemed the only option. Added to the motive of family tranquillity, there was the "knowledge that a moment's excitement might induce Death" in the ailing brother. Yet she added: "I would have given more than I can tell, had Mary W's visit not been at the same time with his."[27]

Toward the end of the visit, Mary Walker had "the severest headache she has ever had in her life. Indeed for some hours, I feared congestion." Much of the time, Susan Lesley reported back to her aunt in Cambridge, Mary Walker "was sick and sad. I tried to build her up, mind and body, but fear I failed." The struggle for change proved no more successful in the public domain. The "sad 4th of November is over and we are doomed to four more years of waiting to renew our hope." When she saw Mary Walker off on the boat to Boston on November 12—a week after the coincidence of the migraine headache and the Republican defeat at the polls—Susan Lesley confessed that her "heart is full of sympathy for her, and a desire to serve her as long as we both live. I still felt a weight lifted from my spirit when she had gone."[28]

FROM 1857 UNTIL THE MIDDLE of 1859, the Lesleys' letters mentioned no further initiatives on their part or that of Mary Walker to pursue her children. Mary Walker returned to Cambridge to resume caregiving, as Anne Jean Lyman descended further into confusion and need. In the meantime, the personal circumstances of Peter and Susan Lesley took a drastic turn for the worse. The depression of 1857, which struck in September of that year, made Peter Lesley's employment and income uncertain. At one point, the geologist's future looked so bleak that he considered a return to the ministry. Susan Lesley hoped her husband would just take a direction and stay with it. The Lesleys had had another child—a second daughter, Margaret Lesley. Thankfully, she came without the trauma of two previous pregnancies that had ended in miscarriages. Still, the experience taxed Susan Lesley's constitution, and she needed time to recover at the very moment when her husband was himself struggling to make ends meet. Depression dogged him, as it always did when setbacks mounted.[29] Mary Walker's silence on the subject of her children suggests she knew the toll that economic and emotional crises had taken on her friends and patrons. The Lesleys themselves needed help.

Help came from Cambridge. In September 1858, Catherine Robbins journeyed to Philadelphia to assist Susan Lesley and her newborn daughter. Mary Walker remained at home to look after Anne Jean Lyman, and to assure family members in Philadelphia that all was well in Cambridge. Masterfully, she did so. In one of only three surviving letters that Mary Walker wrote, she carefully sought to give ease to all. Well aware of her phonetic spelling and grammatical errors, Mary Walker apologized for them: "dear Miss Robins I hope you wil be able to read this poor letter excuse all mistake." What it lacked in polish, the letter made up for in attentiveness.

Mary Walker wrote Catherine Robbins that she was "glad to hear you [are] safe with Mrs. Lesley. I no it is a great comfort to her to have you with her." She assured them both: "we ar all very well hear and ar getting along very nice." She recognized that candor and details would provide the most satisfaction. "Mrs. Lyman is as well as when you left ous. She is very nervous. The first too or three days after you left, she was in rather unhappy state and wish you told her in time to go with you." Mary Walker knew there was good reason that Mrs. Lyman was not told of the departure of her sister to Philadelphia—she would have insisted on going. "She has forgotten all about it and says she had to persuade you to go with out her." Friends made certain that "She has a good deal of company." Mary Walker named those who came to visit. One acquaintance "has bin in twice and made a long visit both times." Her protégé from Northampton, Harvard graduate Chauncey Wright, "was in. tha had very pleasant evening talking of thing too high for me to take in. Mrs. Lyman was very much please and wish you was home to hear them." Miss Stearns would soon arrive and make an overnight stay.

As Mary Walker knew they would, the particulars gave comfort. "Dear Miss Robbins I write you all these little things that you may feel easy to stay with dear Mrs Lesley as long as it will be convenient for her to have you with her." That might be a while, since Catherine Robbins had written that "dear little baby is so poorly. How very glad I am you are with dear Mrs Lesley. I no how much she injoys having you with please give my dear love to her and tell her she is in my thoughts." Mary Walker wanted to take both Lesley children under her wing in the summer ahead. "I long to help her with the dear little baby. She must come on early nex summer and stay with ous." The Lesleys' older daughter "Mary can have a little bed in my Room." Mary Walker assured Susan Lesley that she need not bring a servant to New England to look after her children: "she can come with out eny girl." The other domestic in the Lyman household, Mary Cashman, "and I will help her. We can get along nicely." As if she knew the question on the mind of her two readers, Mary Walker noted immediately: "My Cold is much beter and I take my biters evey morning and hope to grow strong soon." In a postscript, she added that Anne Jean Lyman had Mary Walker's undivided attention: the caregiver had relinquished the dressmaking jobs that sometimes took her out of the house. "Mr. Wright reads every night til ten and I am no longer seamstress but reads through the day." In ways subtle yet all-embracing, Mary Walker's letter conveyed that Anne Jean Lyman was in good hands.[30]

FOR ALMOST THREE YEARS, Mary Walker dealt with such vicissitudes while rarely mentioning her children in the South. She understood that the years were harsh ones for her Philadelphia friends. By July 1859, however, when Susan Lesley came for her summer visit to her mother, the Lesleys' circumstances had stabilized: Peter Lesley had received an appointment as professor of mining at the University of Pennsylvania.

Mary Walker, long "silent about her own affairs," decided to reopen the subject of her children.

1. Fairntosh

Mary Walker was born in slavery in 1818 on the Fairntosh Plantation of Duncan and Rebecca Cameron, located in the piedmont of North Carolina. Her mother, Priscilla—called "Silla" by her owners—worked in the Fairntosh main house, pictured here. Courtesy of Preservation North Carolina; photo by Tim Buchman, ca. 1972.

Raleigh

1 Daney	17 Mary
2 Luke	18 Frank
3 Grace	19 Agnes
4 Molly	20 Edward
5 Emeline	21 Bryant
6 Milley	22 Caroline
7 Susan	23 Frank
8 John	24 Virge
9 Lizzy	25 Jack
10 Elick	26 Henry
11 Delia	
12 Silva	
13 Amey	
14 John jr	
15 Becky	
16 Cillar	

2. Raleigh slave register, 1845

In 1836, Mary Walker and her mother, Silla, became domestic servants in Raleigh, where Duncan Cameron moved his family after assuming the presidency of the Bank of North Carolina. She was listed with her mother and her four young children on the 1845 Raleigh slave register. By 1848, her son Edward had died. Courtesy of the Southern Historical Collection.

3. Duncan Cameron
One of North Carolina's richest and most powerful men, Duncan Cameron was both a planter and the president of the state bank in the 1840s. Three times in the years 1846–1848, Cameron took his invalid daughter to Philadelphia for medical treatment, and brought Mary Walker as their servant. Courtesy of the Southern Historical Collection.

Commonwealth of Pennsylvania

City of Philadelphia S.S.

Nicholas Boston aged forty two years being duly sworn according to law doth depose and say that he is acquainted with a woman named Mary Walker who formerly was said to be the Slave of Judge Camden or Campbell who lives as deponent was informed in one of the Southern ~~[illegible]~~ states – Mary was a very bright coloured woman almost white with good straight hair same as a white woman – not overly full in the face tolerably good features but rather lean I should say she was about from thirty to thirty three years of age. This description applies to her in the year 1848 which was the time I saw her at Cape May where she was waiting on Judge Campbell and family – Mary and the family she waited on left Cape May about the middle of August and came in the Mountaineer Steamboat (I believe) to Philadelphia – I came up about two weeks afterwards to this city and then I understood ~~that~~ Mary had left him Mary told me before she left Judge Campbell that ~~they~~ he threatened to send her to his farm in Alabama and because of that she resolved to leave him knowing that as she was brought on here that she was free by the law –

Sworn and subscribed before me an Alderman and exofficio a Justice of the peace December 27th 1850 [illegible]

Nicholas his X mark Boston

4. Nicholas Boston's deposition

In his 1850 deposition, Nicholas Boston, a free man of color in Philadelphia who waited on vacationers summering at nearby Cape May, reported Duncan Cameron's July 1848 threat to send Mary Walker to the Deep South, and her resolve to escape. Ellis Gray Loring Papers, Schlesinger Library, Harvard University.

W Still

5. William Still

William Still arranged sanctuary for escaped slaves in the late 1840s and became the head of Philadelphia's Underground Railroad in 1853. After Mary Walker left Philadelphia for Massachusetts, he kept contact with her through the 1850s. Lithograph from William Still, *The Underground Railroad* (Philadelphia: Porter and Coates, 1872).

6. *Conquering Prejudice,* 1850
Daniel Webster, senator from Massachusetts, defended the Fugitive Slave Law of 1850 and pursued its strict enforcement after his appointment as U.S. secretary of state in 1850. *Conquering Prejudice,* an 1850 lithograph by Peter Kramer, captures Northerners' sense of betrayal by one of their own—and the danger that led Mary Walker to seek refuge farther north. Courtesy of the Worcester Art Museum.

7 and 8. J. Peter Lesley and Susan Lyman Lesley
Daguerreotypes taken of J. Peter Lesley and Susan Inches Lyman Lesley around the time they gave sanctuary to Mary Walker in late 1850. Howe Family Collection; courtesy of Margaret Howe Ewing.

9 and 10. Ellis Gray Loring and Louisa Loring
Ellis Gray Loring was the leading antislavery attorney in Massachusetts, and his wife, Louisa Loring, was a cofounder of the Women's Antislavery Bazaar of Boston. The Lorings offered legal counsel, protection, and employment to Mary Walker—but balked when it came to helping with the ransom or rescue of her children. Courtesy of the Massachusetts Historical Society.

225

my Dear Mrs Lesley

the dearest of friends leaving a
leisure to day I thought I couldnt pass my time more to
my satisfaction than to write to you — the time I spent
with Mrs Loring at the Sea Shore were very pleasant
to me though I was glad to get home after eleven
weeks absence you may be sure — I have been divi
ding my time between Mrs Morison & Miss L wo
... with a week fitting Miss M & Miss F. Fo
to England & dear Mrs Lesley I miss you & dear Mr
Lesley very much we all have your mother particula
but I have enjoyed being with your dear mother ho has
bin a mother to me & dear Miss Robbins the winter has
bin a very happy one to me tha booth read to me
queechy & other books & I am trying to improve my se
in writing & arithmetic & you cannot think how
much I enjoy Mr James Lesley pleas give my
best regards to him & I went in town on Christ
Mrs Lyman took me to the antislavery Fai
see Mrs Loring tho I did not enjoy my self a
much as I expected I had one of my old headach
I have been to see Anne & found her ...

11. Letter by Mary Walker

One of three surviving letters written by Mary Walker, this note to Susan Lesley reflects her contentment at the outset of 1853 when, after a time away, she returned to the household of Susan Lesley's mother and aunt. Courtesy of the American Philosophical Society, Philadelphia.

12. Anne Jean Lyman
Widowed after thirty-six years of marriage and residence in Northampton, Massachusetts, Anne Jean Robbins Lyman—mother of Susan Lyman Lesley—moved to Cambridge in 1853, where Mary Walker became her caregiver for the rest of the decade. Howe Family Collection; courtesy of Margaret Howe Ewing.

13. Catherine Robbins
Cambridge resident Catherine Robbins was the youngest sister of Anne Jean Robbins Lyman and the lifelong confidante of her niece Susan Lyman Lesley. After Mary Walker moved to Cambridge in 1853, Catherine Robbins became the family member closest to her. Howe Family Collection; courtesy of Margaret Howe Ewing.

14. Chauncey Wright

Chauncey Wright was a protégé of Anne Jean Lyman, who insisted that he enroll at Harvard. A student and later a Harvard instructor, he visited the Cambridge household of Anne Jean Lyman and Mary Walker throughout the 1850s and brightened their lives—as he did those of Henry James and Harvard friends—with dazzling conversation. Howe Family Collection; courtesy of Margaret Howe Ewing.

Fairntosh Tuesday night.

My dear Sister

Virgil delivered your letter this afternoon about 5 o'clock— Glad to hear of Frank, once more tho' he be a long way off—& it may be will cost some Money & trouble to bring him Home once more. But as a Slave holder as the representative of the Estate and of my sisters I think it my duty to have the effort made. His flight has had a very bad effect here and to bring him back would render others better contented and improve the spirit of Subordination.

I will take steps at once to send a Man one who if he can be had is equal to the work— I will go to see him tomorrow at Hillsboro— & be back home tomorrow night—. Of course if he should be recovered you & Mildred must let him be sold— If he remains North & you keep that family near you, you will loose others if not all of it— If mine I should get them out of the way of Post office by sending them to the Country or what is better out of the way of giving me any trouble by selling them—they have proven them selves to be most ungrateful pets—

15. Letter by Paul Cameron

In March 1853, Paul Cameron sent two men north to attempt the recapture of Mary Walker's escaped son Frank Walker. He urged his sisters to sell the remainder of her family—her mother and two children—whom he regarded as "ungrateful pets." The sisters refused. Courtesy of the Southern Historical Collection.

16. Lewis Hayden

Lewis Hayden, who with his wife escaped bondage in the 1840s, became leader of the Underground Railroad in Boston in the 1850s, and led defiance of the Fugitive Slave Law in the city. In 1854 he met with Mary Walker and the agent hired to attempt the rescue of her children. Lithograph courtesy of The Bostonian Society / Old State House Museum.

Mildred Cameron
Raleigh
N. Carolina

To Miss Mildred Cameron
of Raleigh. N.C.

Philadelphia Sep 4/59

Dear Madame

I beg leave to introduce myself for the sake of my subject, which I know will interest you, and which I hope will elicit your warmest sympathies.

I have been lately touched to the heart with a case of heartbreaking distress which you have it entirely in your power I find to cure. And I know by my own mother my sister and my wife that there can be no surer confidence placed in any thing on earth than that which a man instinct=ively places upon the delight with which women find they can alleviate or remove distress. In this case the misery has been so protracted and is so deep that, if I can only present it clearly I feel sure that you will stretch out your hand to it to

17. Letter by Peter Lesley

In September 1859, Peter Lesley wrote to the owner of Mary Walker's children, Mildred Cameron, seeking their release and an end to their mother's "silent heartbreak." No response ever came. Courtesy of the Southern Historical Collection.

18. Coffin Point Plantation

Mary Walker spent the summer of 1864 at the Coffin Point Plantation on St. Helena Island, South Carolina, where she joined Northern reformers who had gone south to teach school and instruct ex-slaves at free labor. Coffin Point, photographed here in 1882, looked much like this when Mary Walker was there. Courtesy of Cecily McMillan.

19. James Burgwyn
James Burgwyn married Mary Walker's daughter Agnes when Raleigh was liberated in April 1865, and together with Bryant Walker they moved to Cambridge that summer. By the 1870s, Burgwyn was a porter for students, a carpenter for professors, and—as depicted here in 1878—an admired "Character about Harvard." Courtesy of the Harvard University Archives.

20. Brattle Street house, ca. 1937

Built in 1808, the Brattle Street house was the home of Dexter Pratt, the village blacksmith of Cambridge, from 1827 to 1847. Mary Walker purchased 54 Brattle Street in 1870 and her family dwelt there until 1912. Courtesy of the Cambridge Center for Adult Education.

21. Brattle Street, 1873
View of Brattle Street and the "spreading chestnut tree" of Longfellow's poem "The Village Blacksmith." The chestnut tree is in front of the blacksmith's dwelling, which is not visible in this photograph. From W. J. Stillman, *Poetic Localities of Cambridge* (Boston: James R. Osgood, 1876).

22. Cemetery marker
Mary Walker's cemetery marker—an obelisk with a winged dove on top—is in Mount Auburn Cemetery, Cambridge. Fifty feet away are the graves of her friends and fellow North Carolinians, Harriet and Louisa Jacobs. Photo by Sydney Nathans.

23. Frederick Walker
Born in 1868, Frederick Walker was the grandson of Mary Walker. He grew up at the family home on Brattle Street and was a Cambridge postman for twenty-five years. He is depicted here with his great-nephew. Courtesy of Clare Dubé Kenney.

24. Eleanor Roosevelt at the Window Shop
Eleanor Roosevelt visited 54 Brattle Street in May 1950, when it had become the Window Shop, a bakery and showplace for handmade crafts and garments embroidered by women refugees from Europe. Courtesy of the Schlesinger Library, Harvard University.

25. Village Blacksmith Bakery
The house at 54 Brattle Street is now a state historic site, an eatery, and part of the Cambridge Center for Adult Education. Photo by Sydney Nathans.

8 "A Case of Heart Breaking Distress"

She "hates to worry you and me any more about it," Susan Lesley wrote her husband in July 1859. But "the truth is, it is the undercurrent of all her thoughts & she cannot give it up, while there is any life or hope. She told me today it was a silent heartbreak." Mary Walker's heartbreak was exacerbated by accounts of the success of other former slaves in reuniting their families. "She says she often hears of the purchase of slaves by people here, and of cases where even more obdurate hearts than those of her mistress have yielded to much importunity, & she cannot help but wishing an effort be made." It "breaks her heart to go in to see Mrs. Gall & other friends, & hear so many of them talking of friends restored by so many different methods & she doing nothing."[1]

WHO WAS THIS "MRS. GALL" who talked so freely "of friends restored"? Mary Walker had become close to one of the best-connected refugees in the entire North. Phillis Gault of Norfolk, Virginia, had fled slavery to Philadelphia in late 1855 and had come to Boston shortly thereafter. She had connections at every point along the Underground Railroad that conveyed fugitives from the South to freedom—friends and fellow fugitives in Massachusetts, leaders of the Philadelphia Vigilance Committee, a bold ship captain who carried "cargo" north from ports in Virginia and North Carolina, and persons back in Norfolk who could be trusted to rescue relatives. Aggressively the Virginia runaway had used them all to ferry family members to freedom.

Mary Walker met Phillis Gault in 1856, when Gault became part of the household of Susan Hillard, cousin of Susan Lesley and one of the most undaunted "friends of the fugitive" in Boston. The Hillard household at 62 Pinckney Street in Boston was a place of paradox. Susan Hillard's husband, lawyer George Stillman Hillard, had spoken out against slavery in the 1830s and had argued against segregation in Boston's public schools in the 1840s. But by 1850 he had become a public defender of the Compromise of 1850 as indispensable to restoring comity between North and South. In contrast, the Fugitive Slave Law provision of that compromise had driven Susan Hillard to become an adamant abolitionist—and to make the Hillard home a safe house for refugees who made it to Boston.[2] Phillis Gault had come to the Hillard home through the agency of Susan and Peter Lesley. A schooner with a daring captain and a secret hold had brought Gault and twenty other escaping slaves out of Norfolk to Philadelphia in November 1855; the Philadelphia Vigilance Committee, eager to get fugitives to safety farther north, had contacted the Lesleys, well known for their abolitionist sympathies and Boston connections; and the Lesleys had arranged to place Gault with their Boston cousin.[3]

Mary Walker and Phillis Gault quickly found that they had much in common. A depiction of Phillis Gault came from the head of the Philadelphia Vigilance Committee, William Still. Starting in 1852, Still kept a secret journal about all fugitives assisted by the committee. His description of Phillis Gault, first in his handwritten journal and later amplified in his published history *The Underground Railroad* (1872), suggested why she and Mary Walker took to each other. Like Mary Walker,

Phillis Gault was an "excellent dressmaker." As with Mary Walker, the "blood of two races flowed . . . through her veins. Such was her personal appearance, refinement, manners, and intelligence, that had the facts of her slave-life been unknown, she would readily have passed for one who had possessed superior advantages." In Boston, Phillis Gault had "sustained a good Christian character" and a reputation as an "industrious, upright, and intelligent woman," "respected by all those who know her."[4] Both women kept up their connection with those in Philadelphia who had given them their first foothold in freedom. Mary Walker's tie was the black carpenter James Fells, with whom she corresponded throughout the 1850s; Phillis Gault's link was William Still, who once lived across the street from Fells and who in 1852 had become the full-time secretary and first African-American leader of the Philadelphia Vigilance Committee. Both women had left family members in the South—Mary Walker her mother and children, Phillis Gault her nieces and nephews—and both wanted desperately to bring them out of bondage.

The great difference between Phillis Gault and Mary Walker was the means they had to redeem their families. Phillis Gault came from the Virginia port city of Norfolk, which with the nearby city of Portsmouth had hemorrhaged so many slaves to the North that the *American Beacon* of Norfolk had complained in 1854 that slave-escapes were almost a daily occurrence. Most of the escapees were "salt-water fugitives" who stole away aboard ships. Many escaped on the vessel captained by Alfred Fountain, who made dozens of voyages to Philadelphia and to New Bedford, Massachusetts, with his human cargo hidden in a small compartment below deck. Historian Gary Collison established that fully a quarter of the four hundred fugitives aided by the Philadelphia Vigilance Committee in the 1850s came from the Norfolk area, and that Alfred Fountain, despite close calls, was the one sea captain never found out as a smuggler of fugitive slaves. For those considering escape from Norfolk to the North, reported William Still, "Captain Fountain appeared as if an angel amongst them." If a Virginia slave could get the means—a hundred dollars in cash—and arrange the location and timing of a pickup, Fountain could get him or her to freedom.[5] Letters to William Still from fugitives Phillis Gault and a nephew of hers, Thomas Page, indicate that a key middleman in Norfolk named William Bagnal was the crucial figure in arranging seaborne escapes. Bagnal was a white, well-to-do bank cashier with a family of four.[6] He could correspond with ship captains and with persons in Philadelphia while evoking no questions or suspicions. Refugees from Norfolk could thus communicate with friends or family by writing to William Still and asking him to convey news to or from home through William Bagnal. In this way they could direct letters to the South and avoid exposing any of the parties.

When Mary Walker visited Phillis Gault, she invariably learned of the "many different methods" that Gault employed to pursue the freedom of her nephews in Norfolk. Her oldest nephew, Thomas Page, had escaped just four months after his aunt, arriving on Alfred Fountain's ship in late March 1856. A "more apt, ready-witted, active, intelligent and self-reliant fellow is not often seen," commented William Still. In early 1857, Thomas Page wrote Still from Boston that his aunt "Mrs. Gault requested" the Philadelphian to "ask Mr. Bagnal if he will see father and what he says about the children."[7] A subsequent letter from Phillis Gault herself illuminated the purpose of her request. Through the middleman, she sought the father's cooperation in freeing "the children"—her remaining two nephews—by getting a price from the owner. In the meantime, her resourceful ten-year-old nephew, Dick Page, had escaped on his own, making it to Philadelphia as a stowaway. Convinced that the youngster belonged with his aunt, the Philadelphia Vigilance Committee worked through the Lesleys to have the youth sent on to Susan Hillard.[8] This left only "little Johny" in Norfolk, and for him the owner was demanding an exorbitant price—perhaps as compensation for all of his losses. "I think to raise nine or ten hundred dollars for such a child is outraigust," Phillis Gault wrote William Still in March 1858. Aware that the Vigilance Committee as a matter of policy did "not send agents South to incite slaves to run away," Gault also knew that Still had a close friend—the black dentist Harry Lundy—who was less fastidious. "I wish you would see the Doctor for me and ask him if he could carefully find out any way that we could steal little Johny. . . . I feel as if I would rather steal him than buy him. Give my kind regards to the Dr. and his family." Phillis Gault closed her letter by adding that "Miss Walker that spent the evening with me in Cambridge sens much love to yoo and Mrs. Landy."[9]

Mary Walker knew every detail of her friend's labors to free her Norfolk relatives. No wonder it "breaks her heart to go in to see Mrs. Gall & other friends, & hear so many of them talking of friends restored by them by so many different methods & she doing nothing." It was indeed "a silent heartbreak."

WHAT WAS TO BE DONE? Mary Walker had nothing like the network of contacts that existed for Phillis Gault and her counterparts from the port cities of Virginia. Mary Walker's children were landlocked in Raleigh. Nonetheless, she had ideas which she now thought it timely to propose. Mary Walker did not ask that Peter Lesley open a correspondence with her former owner. Rather, she hoped the Lesleys would make connections for her that she could not make for herself. Most likely through Phillis Gault, who resided in Susan Hillard's household, Mary Walker had heard about the legendary New York minister Henry Ward Beecher, who was often able to help fugitive slaves. As Susan Lesley told her husband, "She suggested applying to Henry Ward Beecher as he has often been successful." Mary Walker had in mind, as a first resort, an offer to purchase her children. She thought

Beecher knew a "certain Dr. Hawkes an Episcopal minister in Philadelphia, who knows her people." Mary Walker thought Dr. Hawkes might "state [a] wish to buy them." "These were only suggestions"—Beecher "might perhaps know some emissary who would do it some other way." She did not specify the "other way." No matter what the method, Mary Walker understood that money would be needed and assured the Lesleys that she would provide the funds. She "works hard, lays by every penny," wrote Susan, "& I do not doubt has over five hundred dollars in the bank, possibly more."[10]

Susan Lesley recalled that four years earlier, in May 1855, she herself had spoken with Beecher's sister, Harriet Beecher Stowe, about Mary Walker's children. "Mrs. Stowe told me" that her brother "knew three or four men who had been employed to go & bring people from there." Susan Lesley had never mentioned Stowe's claim to Mary Walker. But she realized in 1859 that Mary Walker had "evidently heard of Mr. Beecher in connection with some of these matters." "I think it would please her much if you could see him, & ask his advice or help," Susan wrote to Peter. Knowing that her husband was soon to depart from Philadelphia for a summer trip to Cambridge, Susan Lesley asked if he could route his trip through New York and "see Mr. Beecher, & talk with him." Doubtless she remembered that four years before, when Peter's own attempt to find an emissary to rescue Mary Walker's children had ended in failure, he had felt exasperated by a sense of his own impotence. Raising the issue anew, Susan Lesley closed her entreaty with a gentle affirmation of her husband's strength. "My dear Love, I cannot write any more. I feel weak as a kitten & only wish I could lay my head on your shoulder & go to sleep."[11]

Peter Lesley agreed at once to take the train to New York and to "see Beecher that day if he be in town, and perhaps get through my business, so as to reach Boston Friday morning." He cautioned that any "detention in Philadelphia or New York will make me late."[12] The language of Peter Lesley's response—he would try to "get through my business" and avoid "detention"—seemed that of a man complying with his wife's request rather than responding to the stirrings of his own heart. When he finally reached Cambridge, he reported in person on the outcome. Almost certainly, nothing came of the effort. No letters between the Lesleys ever again mentioned either Henry Ward Beecher or Harriet Beecher Stowe as intermediaries who might help Mary Walker or her children.

HAVING ONCE MORE FOUND NO satisfactory agent to restore Mary Walker's children to their mother, Peter Lesley might well have decided that further effort was futile. Remarkably, he seemed to have come to the opposite conclusion. On September 4, 1859, six and a half years after the death of Duncan Cameron, he wrote directly to the children's owner on Mary Walker's behalf.[13]

Addressing "Miss Mildred Cameron of Raleigh N.C.," Lesley begged "leave to introduce myself for the sake of my subject, which I know will interest you, and which I hope will elicit your warmest sympathies." In fact, the letter that followed hardly introduced Peter Lesley at all, in any conventional sense. Only in the letter's very last line did he identify himself as "J. P. Lesley, Professor of Mining in the University of Pennsylvania." Nor was his "subject," strictly speaking, Mary Walker. Rather his focus was "a case of heart breaking distress"—and Mildred Cameron's ability to heal it. Not until well into the letter did he mention Mary Walker's name.

> I have been lately touched to the heart with a case of heart breaking distress which you have it entirely in your power I find to cure. And I know by my own mother my sister and my wife that there can be no surer confidence placed in any thing on earth than that which a man instinctively places upon the delight with which women find they can alleviate or remove distress. In this case the misery has been so protracted and is so

> deep that if I can only present it clearly I feel sure that you will stretch out your hand to it to heal it up at once.
>
> I have come to know one Mary Walker formerly in your family.

Peter Lesley wrote in a language of the heart that was widely shared among women and men of the North in the 1840s and 1850s—language that Lesley hoped could also touch the heart of a Southern slave-owning woman. Yet he knew that differences of region and race and views of bondage delimited whatever sentiments might have allowed him to appeal to Mildred Cameron as he would to a middle-class woman of the mid-nineteenth-century North. He had to elicit Mildred Cameron's "warmest sympathies" in a different way. His first mention of Mary Walker sought to reweave ties between the two women, ties frayed but hopefully not entirely broken by Mary Walker's departure in 1848. He did not identify her as Mildred Cameron's former slave. Rather, she was *"Mary Walker formerly in your family."* Lesley chose language that mirrored the way enlightened slave-owners preferred to think of their "people." They spoke of "our family black and white," wrote about "our white family and the black family," preferred the term "servant" to the word "slave." Lesley may have sensed that this is the way Mary Walker herself would reach out to her former owner: "formerly in your family."

Peter Lesley anticipated that mention of Mary Walker's name to Mildred Cameron might trigger mixed emotions. Even if both sisters knew why Mary Walker had left in 1848, did they nonetheless think her callous to desert her mother and children? Did they imagine that she had since led a carefree life in the North? Lesley addressed both presumptions.

> I have seen how sick at heart she is about her mother and especially her two children (if I remember their names aright) who

> are still with you, Agnes and Briant. She has been herself in miserable health for some years and sometimes ready to die; but is now in her usual health, able to go about and do her daily work, but very frail and often very suffering.

"Very frail and often very suffering": Mildred Cameron could certainly understand that condition. Such words described her own existence since she had first experienced debilitating spasms after the death of her mother in 1843. As Peter Lesley described Mary Walker's response to frailty and suffering, he sensed that Mildred Cameron would recognize a forbearance very like her own.

> She is a sincere & elevated Christian, bears everything without complaint, with a sweet smile and a pleasant word for everybody; and her winning ladylike & conscientious carriage has made her a large circle of friends.

If a basis for empathy remained between the two women, Peter Lesley was laying the groundwork for its renewal.

But faith, forbearance, and friendships had not brought happiness to Mary Walker any more than they had to Mildred Cameron.

> With all this her heart is slowly breaking. She thinks of nothing but her children, and speaks of nothing else when she speaks of herself at all, which is very seldom. Her mother-heart yearns unspeakably after them and her eyes fail with looking towards the South, over the dreary interval which separates them from her.

This was the anguish, "so protracted and so deep," that Peter Lesley hoped to convey: "if I can only present it clearly I feel sure you will stretch out your hand to heal it up at once."

> She has saved a considerable sum of money to buy them, can command more from her friends, and will sacrifice anything to see them once again and have their young lives renew the freshness of her own weary spirit. It is in this behalf that I address you,—to realize this hope of hers.

Yet why expect Mildred Cameron to pay attention to Mary Walker's hope?

> She says you were always kind and good. I can imagine that *her* children must be valuable, in fact *invaluable;* that any value named for them must be merely nominal. Therefore I must trust in your goodness of heart and in your own

And here the letter stopped for a moment. Lesley crossed out "your own" and added a crucial phrase which suggested a reason for Mildred Cameron's help that went beyond generosity.

> Therefore I must trust in your goodness of heart and in ~~your own~~ the remembrance of any sufferings you may have had, and in your own hopes of future happiness, to suggest the various arguments which I could urge for letting this mother buy her children back to her own bosom.

The former minister and meticulous scientist had chosen his words with care. Whatever afflictions Mildred Cameron "may have had"—or more likely still had—could be relieved by this act of compassion toward her suffering former servant. Mildred Cameron not only had it "entirely in your power to cure" the distress of Mary Walker. She had a chance to heal herself.

Peter Lesley added a final argument for "letting this mother buy her children back to her own bosom."

> She has suffered & still must the exquisite pain of fearing night and day some terrible calamity befalling either or both of her children and especially her daughter; whose blooming womanhood exposes her more terribly than the worst adventures happening to a young man.

There was no need for him to spell out what he meant. The Cameron sisters had grown up with Mary Walker at their side. They had taken lessons in writing and reading from the same private family tutor. They knew she had borne her first child at fifteen. What knowledge they had of the father or fathers of her four children, of the circumstances of her pregnancies, can only be conjectured. Given the language Peter Lesley used, it seems that he expected the Cameron sisters to agree that pregnancy so young was indeed a "terribly calamity."

Whatever the circumstances of their begetting, the children of Mary Walker had come to mean the world to her. Peter Lesley sought to convey to the childless Mildred Cameron what it meant for this mother to be deprived of the "fruit of her womb, the joys of her youth, the staff and stay of her declining age." His plea reflected the Lesleys' intimate knowledge of Mary Walker's years of pain.

> She feels as if she must die of anxiety and grief and longing love, unless she can get her children with her soon. Not that I think she will die. It would perhaps be better if she could. But she is so well situated, in all merely worldly particulars, that she may perhaps live ten or twenty years; but if she must live so—these years will all be years of lingering heartbreak.

The letter's conclusion was artful. Peter Lesley was well acquainted with the annual pilgrimage Mildred Cameron and her sister made to the North each summer in search of treatment for her spasms, though he discreetly referred to the purpose of her journey as travel rather than a cure.

> I have delayed writing until it was probable that the cooler weather had invited you home from travel. I need not add how anxiously I will await your kind reply, and pray for your health and happiness . . .

The finale, like the entire appeal, inextricably linked the freeing of Mary Walker's children with Mildred Cameron's own deliverance.

Peter asked Susan to let Mary Walker know that he had written to Mildred Cameron, but cautioned them both against high expectations. Even if the letter did "touch her heart," Mildred Cameron might well be wary about its unknown author and want to know more about him before replying. "Perhaps the reply will be wrathful," he conjectured to his wife. Having treated their servants as "family," some slave-owners viewed runaways as ingrates. Mary Walker's misery, seen as self-inflicted, might be of no interest to the Camerons.

While Peter Lesley encouraged Mary Walker to "not think too much about it," he himself couldn't avoid thinking about the outcome. "I should feel quite young & strong again if I could get these children for her," he confided to his wife. But at the same time the geologist wondered if the North would be the best home for the two young people, "moulded to the soil & the sky of the South." "Well, well, we must do what we can. . . . We can . . . open this correspondence at any rate, and perhaps it will result in a free interchange of letters at last between mother and daughter, if nothing better."[14]

NO INTERCHANGE OF LETTERS opened up between Mary Walker and her children, nor did a reply ever come to Peter Lesley's letter. Even if the appeal to Mildred Cameron had touched her heart, as it was carefully crafted to do, complicated family dynamics within the Cameron family stood in the way of a decision on her part to release the two remaining Walker children. In 1859, as when Mary Walker had left the Camerons in Philadelphia eleven years before, Mildred Cameron remained an invalid. She continued to be cared for by her older sister, Margaret, and after Margaret Cameron's marriage in 1853 to banker George Mordecai, by Margaret's husband as well. Dependent as Mildred Cameron was on her sister and brother-in-law and her brother Paul Cameron, any response to Lesley's portrait of Mary Walker's plight—"her mother-heart yearns unspeakably" after her children—would have to come from four slave-owners and not one. The brothers-in-law rarely spoke throughout the decade of the 1850s, and in their few exchanges by letter, they clashed. Given the bad blood between the men, any act of tenderness toward Mary Walker and her children—whom Paul Cameron regarded as "ungrateful pets"—risked exacerbating tensions in that family of slave-holders. It is possible that, to avoid further friction, Mildred Cameron and her sister Margaret Mordecai turned Peter Lesley's letter over to their brother.

SIX WEEKS AFTER PETER LESLEY wrote his letter, a cataclysmic event ended whatever chance there might have been for negotiating the freedom of Mary Walker's children. On the night of October 16, 1859, eighteen men led by John Brown entered the United States Armory at Harpers Ferry, Virginia, and took over the federal arsenal with the intent of inciting a slave-insurrection. Less than twenty-four hours later, most of Brown's men were dead and all but two of the rest were captured and held for trial. John Brown's raid and his subsequent trial and death sentence polarized feelings in both the North and the South. To Southern whites, Brown's raid was the lethal climax of thirty years of abolitionist agitation, and his sentence was a fitting penalty for murder and sedition. Most Northerners and abolitionists distanced themselves from Brown's action, yet many honored his goal and his boldness. Susan Lesley typified the ambivalence in a letter to her Boston aunt,

Catherine Robbins. "I can't tell you how distressed Peter and I have been with the dreadful Harpers Ferry affair. . . . It is rare to disapprove so entirely of a man's deed, and yet have such entire sympathy with his motives and character. Truly it is a long time since we have witnessed anything like the heroic exaltation of John Brown's purpose."[15]

At the end of November, the Lesleys unexpectedly found themselves firsthand witnesses to part of the John Brown drama, and described their encounter in a letter to Catherine Robbins. John Brown's wife, Mary, had come to Philadelphia to await her husband's execution. "Tell Mary Walker that last Sunday Wm. Still came round and told us that Mrs. Brown was staying at his house and he wished we would go and see her . . . so we went at once. I shall never forget the poor woman's face. . . . She looked stunned with grief. She spoke very little, said it was a bitter disappointment to her not to go to her husband, but she thought he was right about it. Perhaps we would like to see his letter about it. So she took it from her pocket and I read it first then Peter." Anticipating his execution by hanging on December 2, John Brown begged his wife and children "never to feel disgraced by the manner of his death, to remember the ignominious method by which the Savior . . . perished. He spoke of his own soul as being calm, nay even joyful." Very quiet and patient as she awaited the execution, Mary Brown broke down when she spoke of their two sons who fell in the fighting. "She said that although their father never urged them to go with him . . . yet they were in such entire sympathy with him, they would go. And yet she said when they bade her farewell, it was as if they went to certain death. She heard their sobs for ¼ of a mile after they left her."[16] As Mary Walker listened to this description, did she ponder the destiny of her own children, now also altered by the deed of John Brown?

Mary Walker and others in Boston who had freed themselves from slavery doubtless discussed the import of Harpers Ferry for their hopes to rescue or ransom their family members still in bondage. John Brown's remedy went far beyond individual redemptions: we must "purge this land with blood." As it turned out, at the Thanksgiving Day service of the Unitarian church in Philadelphia that the Lesleys had joined in the mid-1850s, Mary Brown accompanied the Lesleys to hear the reflections of their famed antislavery minister, William Furness, on the meaning of John Brown's deed. "Out of the grim cloud that hangs over the South, a bolt has darted, and blood has flowed, and the place where lightning has struck, is wild with fear." *Never,* Furness reflected later, "was there a greater cause for which to speak, to suffer and to die. . . . There is no trouble that can befall us, no, not the loss of property, of idolized parents or children, or life itself, that we shall not count a blessed privilege."[17]

On the day of John Brown's martyrdom, Susan Lesley went to National Hall—now Independence Hall—and sat in a seat with "four or five excellent looking colored women who seemed very much moved at the idea of John Brown's suffering for their race, as they said." To Susan Lesley's dismay, students from the South tried to disrupt the meeting. "I said to one [of the women], 'We should have had a good meeting if it had not been for those young men.' O Never mind Mamm, said one, with a pleasant smile. . . . They'se only here for the winter, them Virginny students, but we're in a free state all year round. I wrote to Mary Walker this afternoon."[18]

John Brown's lightning strike brought to an end the era of individual rescues of "idolized parents or children." The future would determine whether his deed would ultimately bring freedom all year round to Mary Walker's family—and to all her people.

9 If They Die for Their Freedom, Amen

For Mary Walker, the years ahead were to prove those of greatest hope and greatest trial. Along with thousands who had escaped slavery and millions still in bondage, she could nurture hopes that the outcome of events would bring freedom to all. Yet for her personally, all illusion of agency seemed at an end. Civil war would cut her off completely from her children. There would be no more visits by Cameron servants to the North with news of her family in Raleigh. She could no longer think that a message or messenger could possibly make it to sympathetic ears in the South. What was left to her was life in Cambridge as the caregiver for Anne Jean Lyman—and there, too, great trial lay ahead. In 1860 and 1861, as the country fissured, Anne Jean Lyman's condition deteriorated further. For Mary Walker, as for the country, events beyond anyone's control buffeted her fate and that of her family.

Mary Walker nonetheless persisted in her efforts to free her children. She followed the fortunes of the Union army as it seized coastal towns and territory in the Carolinas. After Union troops in early 1862 occupied New Bern, North Carolina—scarcely more than a hundred miles from Raleigh—she found a Massachusetts officer stationed there who could inquire after her son and daughter. Had they fled to Union lines? Had anyone escaped who knew them? Could someone get word back to them? Yet even as she continued to seek a lifeline to her family, she also steeled herself for news of their death, if die they must to end their bondage. When Catherine Robbins talked with Mary Walker after Abraham Lincoln's Emancipation Proclamation in January 1863, Mary Walker's Cambridge friend was both jubilant and fearful. Might news of the proclamation prompt a rising of Southern slaves and lead to a massacre by their owners? Indeed it might, Mary Walker agreed. Then she stunned her friend: she said she hoped her children would strike first.[1]

MILITANCY HAD NEVER characterized the Mary Walker that Catherine Robbins and the Lesleys saw in the 1850s, nor did it mark the approach she took as the new decade began, when her main preoccupation was to help an increasingly erratic Anne Jean Lyman continue to live in her home at the corner of Garden Street and Phillips Place, half a block west of the Cambridge Common. To do that required not confrontation but delicate give and take with family members about what was best for their mother.

When Susan Lesley came for her summer visit to Cambridge in August 1860, Mary Walker urged that the time had come to install running water in the house—on all of its floors. Susan Lesley broached the subject to her brother, Joseph Lyman, who categorically rejected the proposal. It would cost too much to be practical. Susan Lesley, straddling the middle, presented her brother's objection to Mary Walker, whose response was polite but firm—and brimmed with details. She had no problem continuing to carry basins of water upstairs for Susan's mother to use for her toilette in her second-story room. The problem was that Anne Jean Lyman no longer accepted that routine. Instead, she insisted on coming down to the kitchen, going out on the porch, and using the water on the first floor to wash up. That in itself could be accommodated, Mary Walker agreed, except for one thing: their mother's washing and dressing downstairs was clearly visible through the large window of the kitchen. And when the weather was warm, she went out on the porch, where she washed and dressed outside, in plain sight of any stranger who wandered by.[2] Mary Walker didn't have to ask the obvious question. Was this what they wanted for their mother?

Mary Walker knew that she could not argue with her patrons. She simply mustered facts. Joseph Lyman claimed that the expense of hooking up to the main water line was beyond their means. Mary Walker offered Susan Lesley facts to suggest that her brother was mistaken—their aunt Sarah Howe, who lived nearby, had installed a line to her house at modest cost. Joseph insisted that running water required endless care, especially in winter. Summer's solution could turn into winter's disaster: burst pipes. Mary Walker responded, again through Susan Lesley, that she was well aware of the danger, and would of course drain the pipes whenever freezing was a danger and carry water upstairs by hand. She reiterated what was going on now. Every day, Joseph Lyman's mother was exposing herself to the elements, to neighbors, and to passersby, and Mary Walker was hard-pressed to prevent it.[3] Dealing with patriarchs in the South and employers in the North had taught Mary Walker that they did not abide challenge from those in their service. Her hope was that command of details would win the case where the opinion of a servant would not. The water line was installed.

Mary Walker's intervention cushioned the consequences of Anne Jean Lyman's illness, but could not stop her decline. Her worsening condition, along with the unfolding of the political events of the 1860s, found a remarkable chronicler in her youngest sister, Catherine Robbins. Living with her unmarried niece Mary Howe, just a few doors down from Anne Jean Lyman, Catherine Robbins kept a private journal throughout the 1860s and reported daily on events in the troubled household of her sister and Mary Walker, as well as on the secession crisis and the outbreak of war. The Robbins diary bore witness to the strains of a family struggling with the dementia of its matriarch and central figure. Whenever Catherine took her sister out of the house, Anne Jean became "very bewildered & strange in her conduct . . . it is a great cross to have to go anywhere with her." Yet if they only "staid at home," it "was ever so wearisome a task as going over the same monotonous round, forever & ever. She seems more than ever restless & driven." Friends and family members who had once welcomed Anne Jean Lyman into their homes asked that she be kept away, and left it to Catherine Robbins to deter her. There was only so much the sister could do to "prevent her from annoying other people. . . . Poor soul. It is sad that she has not a friend or relative in the world except myself, who is able or willing to bear with her any portion of the time."[4]

In fact, two other women bore the burden of Anne Jean Lyman most of the time—her caregiver, Mary Walker, and her housekeeper, Mary Cashman. The "two Marys" were unstinting in their attentions, but the pressure of living in the home of a demented person took its toll. The caretakers began to quarrel, doubtless displacing onto each other the frustration that they could not direct at the person causing it. Such surely was what occurred when Catherine Robbins witnessed a furious donnybrook between the two Marys on November 5, 1860—the day before that year's momentous presidential election.

> Discords & quarrels are always terrible to me. Today the two women at Mrs. L's have had such a fearful quarrel, berated & abused each other to such an extent, as actually to terrify me, & to keep me in a nervous tremor all day. Each coming to tell me they will no longer live in the house with the other, that they will go away, & each accusing each other in the most frightful terms.

What seemed to shock most was that "MW [was] not a bit behind the other." Face to face with Nova Scotian Mary Cashman—who was taller, stouter, large-boned, and probably outweighed her by a hundred pounds—the more fragile Mary Walker gave no ground in the fight. "I know not what will come of it. They have quarreled a great deal before, but never so badly as this, I think. It does not seem possible that this should ever heal." For Catherine Robbins, the "troubles of yesterday" overshadowed "Election day, a day of the greatest importance to the welfare of the country." What would happen to her sister if either Mary departed? She spent election day "at Mrs. L's to keep the peace. There was silence today, which is some improvement."[5] Mary Walker and Mary Cashman stayed in the house. Neither had much option for another job in the uncertain winter of 1860–1861, with cold weather setting in and all wondering if there would still be a country by the time the new president and his party took power a few months later.

In language that was startling, Catherine Robbins agonized in her journal over the personal toll of caring for her sister. Did she give voice to feelings that Mary Walker silently shared? How "can one make it seem pleasant or even tolerable to spend the greater part of their life with a person whose mind is nearly gone, yet not so entirely as to be treated like an insane person. On the contrary, is to be kept in the position of the head of a family." Who "can have an idea what [a burden] it is, to be bound to help along such a family, & have such a person hanging upon one like a dead weight all the time?"[6] To Anne Jean Lyman's illness, they were all in thrall.

IN THE NATION, AS IN the Lyman household, uncertainty reigned during the winter of 1860–1861, and as Catherine Robbins followed the unraveling of the Union and "discords abroad," she became equally exasperated with national affairs. Devouring daily newspapers as the country's crisis unfolded—"I must see what is going on in these stirring times"—she read passages aloud when she visited her sister and

Mary Walker. Just a week after the November 6 election of Abraham Lincoln, she recorded that the papers "are full of the southern discontents & serious threats of secession." "Foolish creatures. I wish we were rid of them all," but "trust in no kind of concession from republicans."[7] At November's end, the papers were even more "full of the violence of southern men & disunion projects. I hope our people will have the character to be firm." Discord came to Boston itself in early December, when an antislavery meeting to memorialize the deeds and death of John Brown was broken up by a mob—"merchants & bruisers"—who "took possession & carried it on their own way." South Carolina's fateful passage of its Ordinance of Secession on December 20, 1860, prompted her conclusion that these "madmen are in serious earnest"—"they will not return, unless conquered by force of arms." Yet like many Northerners, she was not yet ready to resort to force. "I should be truly thankful to have the cotton states all go, if they could go in peace. We want none of them, & as [to] union with such a people, it is nothing but a word."[8]

For Mary Walker, the fugitive slave with family still captive in the South, "good riddance" was hardly a welcome solution to the country's crisis. No wonder that in January 1861 Catherine Robbins found Mary Walker "low-spirited & discouraged, which always troubles me. 'How long O Lord, how long?'" "How long . . ."—Was that the diarist's lament or Mary Walker's?[9] As weeks passed and more Southern states seceded, the mood in the household changed. Determination replaced the impulse to separate peaceably. In late January 1861, Catherine Robbins was appalled at the efforts by some Northern leaders to placate Southerners with soothing words and the promise of new constitutional guarantees. "I wish they would stand as one man upon the Constitution as it is, & not yield a point." When yet another meeting of abolitionists "was broken up in Boston and the Hall taken from them," she realized that even in the North, they had to "fight all the old battles over again." "Kind heaven avert" giving "the South another victory over freedom." The task of the North and the new president was to have the "strength & wisdom to control these discordant elements, & direct the course of things aright."[10]

From the vantage point of Mary Walker, as the country waited out the months between Abraham Lincoln's election in November 1860 and his inauguration in March 1861, what course was "aright"? Did she, too, hope that the new leaders would have the "strength & wisdom to control these discordant elements"? No letters of hers or entries by Catherine Robbins reveal her thoughts. What is known is that Mary Walker's other friends—white abolitionists and fugitive slaves—were less eager to control disputes than to make the most of them—indeed to bring them to a decisive climax. Two of Mary Walker's acquaintances in particular led a push in early 1861 to counter Northern conciliation with an explicit revelation of what Southern bondage was like for women.

In February 1861, the renowned antislavery author Lydia Maria Child mailed a new book to her friends Susan and Peter Lesley. "I am much mistaken if it does not prove a very useful missionary in the antislavery cause." After months of escalating slave-state demands and departures, the antislavery cause needed bolstering: "The worst thing that can happen is to have all this excitement settled down into a miserable mush of concession." Maria Child "also sent [the book] to Mary Walker." Like Mary Walker, the book's writer was from North Carolina, the mother of children born in bondage, and a fugitive from slavery. But there was a personal reason that Maria Child thought the Lesleys' friend would be interested: Mary Walker "had talked with the writer."[11]

Under the pseudonym "Linda Brent," author Harriet Jacobs had written the book—a remarkable autobiography of an enslaved woman, entitled *Incidents in the Life of a Slave Girl.* Jacobs had grown up in Edenton, North Carolina, where at an early age she had found herself the object of her owner's sexual attentions and demands. While the married master had the power to impose his desire on her, he wanted her to become his concubine willingly. Desperate for a way to thwart his demands, she responded to the affections of a young white lawyer in the community who found her attractive, took him rather than her master as her lover, and became pregnant by him. Far from giving up, the owner became enraged, demanded the name of her lover, and redoubled his insistence that she submit. Her resistance continued; she and the lawyer had another child. When it became clear that her owner planned to remove her and her children from the town where her free black grandmother and others could help protect them, and that he intended to send them to a remote plantation where he and his son could "break them," she escaped. The flight was not out of state or out of the South. Instead, she hid in the cramped attic of her grandmother's dwelling in Edenton itself, where she could watch over the welfare of her young son, Joseph, and daughter, Louisa, through a small window. After seven years of waiting and enduring, suffering and planning, she prevailed when, through a ruse, the white lawyer purchased her children from her old master and promised to free them. Then, escaping by ship, she fled north in June 1842, landing first in Philadelphia and finally reuniting with Louisa in New York City.[12]

Sometime during the 1850s, Harriet Jacobs and Mary Walker had met and talked. Harriet Jacobs had lived in Boston in the late 1840s. After moving away, she returned there frequently to visit friends and her daughter, who had come to Boston to work.[13] How much the two North Carolina mothers shared of their lives as enslaved women and then as Northern refugees from bondage is unknown. Both had borne mixed-race children. Both had left slavery before their children were free and both had devoted years of their lives to pursuing the freedom of their families. There the lives of the two refugees diverged. Harriet Jacobs described in *Incidents* how she was able to avoid the snare of forced concubinage and eventually to achieve freedom for her daughter and son. Mary Walker had yet to achieve the reunion she so ardently sought.

In 1852, Harriet Jacobs found herself encouraged to tell her story to the world. Her firsthand account could expose the treacheries—committed against white women as well as black women—at the heart of bondage. With her children safely in the North and her freedom purchased by friends, she could write without fear of reprisals from the South. Looking after her employer's household and family by day, Jacobs wrote at night, and over four years' time completed the better part of a manuscript. Her writing stalled for a while in early 1857, but the U.S. Supreme Court's Dred Scott decision refueled her energies. In that decision, the court declared that blacks were not and could never be American citizens; they had not and could never possess "rights which a white man was bound to respect." Fury drove her to finish the draft. "When I see the evil that is spreading throughout the land," Harriet Jacobs wrote her close abolitionist friend Amy Kirby Post of Rochester, New York, "sometimes I am almost ready to exclaim—where dwells that just Father—whom I love—and in whom I believe?" How could "all these high handed outrages reign supreme law throughout the land"? "I see nothing for the Black Man—to look forward to—but to forget his old Motto—and learn a new one his long patient hope—must be might—and Strength—Liberty—or Death." Anger propelled Jacobs to finish her narrative of a "soul that burned for freedom." In the summer of 1860, Lydia Maria Child agreed to write a preface and volunteered to edit the book. After the publisher went bankrupt in November 1860, Child helped find funds to underwrite its publication in early 1861.[14]

When Mary Walker received and read the book, did it reawaken her own anguish over what she and her mother and her grandmother had endured? Did it remind her again of the risks her daughter still faced? Did it kindle in her the anger that drove her fellow fugitive from North

Carolina to complete her narrative—to forget the "old Motto" of "long patient hope" and live by a new Rule of "might—and Strength —Liberty—or Death"?[15] If such were Mary Walker's responses to *Incidents in the Life of a Slave Girl*—and the empathetic response of white readers as well—then Harriet Jacobs and Lydia Maria Child would have thought their work well done. Such readers would stand firm in 1861 against the "mush of concession." Such readers would stay the course until slavery's end.

ALL TALK OF COMPROMISE ENDED on the morning of April 15, 1861, when cannons of the newly declared Confederate States of America opened fire on Fort Sumter in the harbor of Charleston, South Carolina. Both North and South mobilized to fight. Abraham Lincoln called on his countrymen to maintain the Union, while Southern leaders rallied followers to defend their independence. Antislavery advocates spoke immediately of war as the means for emancipating the enslaved. But Northern whites, though ready to put down "Southern violence & disunion projects" once and for all, divided deeply over whether persons of color were fit for freedom in a white republic. Neither Lincoln nor his party embraced black freedom as a war goal in 1861. Rather, both governments called for troops to preserve their nations, and each side saw itself as the certain winner of a short, decisive conflict. Peter Lesley was among the confident, certain "that in three months the war will be at an end. The Southern army must melt away, like snow before the sun's advance toward the equinox."[16]

War reverberated quickly down to the Garden Street cottage in Cambridge, as it did to households throughout the country. Mary Walker and Catherine Robbins had to redouble their role as the guardians of Anne Jean Lyman, who, "hearing the talk about war & not knowing what it meant," was "quite frightened & fancies her house is in danger." "She wants to stay down at our house all the time," the sister wrote in her journal, "& is very troublesome. I try to keep her at home & stay with her, but she comes back here before I can get out & it is difficult to make her go home." Little wonder that Anne Jean Lyman was disoriented; just two weeks after Fort Sumter, Cambridge was preparing for battles to come. "Ladies here & in town have been working for the army," sewing shirts for soldiers, while the men were "drilling & regiments forming." When accounts came that a pro-Southern mob in Baltimore had attacked and derailed Massachusetts troops en route to reinforce Washington, "it seemed like a nightmare." Catherine Robbins kept Mary Walker abreast of the latest news, "reading papers most of the time" while at her sister's house. Mary Walker was doubtless gratified that for Catherine Robbins, lines had hardened by the end of April 1861. The rebels "need to be effectually put down, & made to feel their own folly if possible."[17]

FROM APRIL TO JULY, citizens of both North and South sewed, armed, drilled, and readied their soldiers for combat, little realizing how elusive a decisive battle would prove to be. A conclusion edged closer for the household in Cambridge. For months, Catherine Robbins had been writing to her niece Susan Lesley about the degenerating condition of Anne Jean Lyman. During the first half of 1861, however, the Lesley household in Philadelphia was as distracted as the one in Cambridge. Seven months pregnant in January 1861, Susan Lesley was exceedingly fragile. "Perhaps I am wrong to perplex her any about these things, when she has troubles of her own," her aunt worried, "but there is no one else to tell."[18] The Lesleys' infant son was stillborn in March 1861. Faith consoled Susan Lesley that her loss had a higher purpose. "It seemed very important to me to have that little child, but no doubt the lessons of this last year of suffering were more important to me, in the harmonious plan of eternal Providence."[19]

Recovery inevitably took time, complicated by the uncertainties that war created concerning Peter Lesley's employment. Catherine Robbins heard that Philadelphia "is in terrible turmoil, & I suppose P's business put a stop to entirely." She doubted that she'd hear back from her niece "for many months to come, indeed not much ever, with her exceeding feebleness [and] the many cares she has." All along, however, Susan Lesley was paying careful attention to her aunt's painful reports, to "all of the things you mention over and over again," and mulling how "to do the right thing for Mother and all those who have been so close to her for years," especially "both of the Maries." By July 1861, a recuperated Susan Lesley was ready to act.[20]

"I received a letter," Catherine Robbins confided to her journal on July 3, "which actually startled me." Susan Lesley had written with "a definite proposal to send her mother away from home this autumn, & asking my aid to do it." The sister was shocked—and torn. "I know not what to do or say about it. It is wretched to live along as we do, & takes all the life out of existence to me. Still to take her from every familiar thing & person, & put her in confinement, it seems too hard. I do not feel as if I could decide upon it." Two days later she wrote to her niece, "saying all I could about her plan." It was "impracticable. If she were sent among strangers, & detained against her will, she would become violent & outrageous, & have to be taken care of regularly as an insane person, & be deprived of all the little comforts she now has. Still to keep her as she is . . . fixes me in perpetual bondage, & is a great evil to many persons." She didn't need to name Mary Walker and Mary Cashman. "How decide, when the evils on both sides are so strong"?[21]

On the battlefield and in the Cambridge household, harsh realities crystallized in late July 1861. The first battle of the war, fought at Manassas Junction, Virginia, on July 21, ended with a rout of the Union forces. Writing in her journal two days later, Catherine Robbins described her response. "Early in the morning we got a report that our army was defeated with terrible loss, had retreated, & many actually fled. I felt heartsick." Though a later report stated that the "loss was much exaggerated, from thousands it was diminished to hundreds, still it was very bad. Rhode Island regiment dreadfully cut up, many officers killed." By the end of the week, Catherine Robbins, like many Northerners, had conceded: "Those people are stronger than we had given them credit for, have more means, & are determined to fight. It will be a long & hard struggle."[22]

No less sobering was a letter she received the same week from Susan Lesley. Susan had conferred with Joseph about their mother. He not only agreed that Anne Jean Lyman should be sent away. "He even proposed to send his Mother to the Asylum," rather than to a private institution. Catherine Robbins agonized to her journal: "I cannot bear the thought of taking her to that place . . . shutting her out from everything she has ever known & enjoyed, & undoubtedly in the process of change taking from her the last remnant of reason that she has left. Yet what can I say? What have I to propose?" Catherine Robbins knew that neither she nor Mary Walker could continue to take care of her as they had done. Yet "I feel it to be a sort of treachery to consent to this plan, & to abandon her, when she relies so implicitly upon me." When she thought of "how she clung to Mary & me, & was never easy except one of us was with her, I know there is no one to whom she can feel so in that place."[23]

Susan Lesley understood that the removal of her mother would be "the most trying thing I ever look to pass through." "But my mind never wavers as to the necessity of a change." Joseph Lyman left the execution of a plan entirely to his sister. She was to come to Cambridge and arrange a place in an asylum for their mother; she was to deal with "Aunt Kitty," whose "nerves have all given out" (Joseph "says he *won't* talk about it" with Catherine); she was to deal with "all those who have been so close to her for years." When Susan Lesley asked her brother about having Mary Walker accompany their mother to the asylum, he summarily rejected the idea. He didn't "think they would have her"; he urged "not a word" to the "two Maries" until the deed was done. Shortly after Susan Lesley arrived in Boston in early October 1861, her brother left for two weeks away. She took her aunt to see the

McLean Asylum in Somerville (right next to Cambridge), where a "long and satisfactory talk" with the supervising doctor "did Kitty a great deal of good and removed her last lingering doubt about Mother's removal." On October 10, the two women took Anne Jean Lyman on a carriage "ride from which she is not to return." The aunt left first—"the easiest plan for her and the best way of avoiding an appearance of force"—and Susan Lesley next, "quickly," in the hope that "in a half hour, she'll not recall how she came or anything about it." To her husband, Peter, Susan Lesley penciled a simple note: "All well over."[24]

AND WHAT OF MARY WALKER and Mary Cashman? "After Mother is established I am prepared for my breezes with the Maries," Susan Lesley wrote her husband. Her brother had "not the faintest idea of concerning" himself "at all about their future. Joseph says they have been in one place as long as they would expect. Few domestics live as long in the same place, & they can hunt up others." Susan Lesley had no intention of leaving Mary Walker to fend for herself, or Mary Cashman either. "I could not reconcile it in my mind to not do all I can to comfort the girls, and give them the best advice in my power. They have been the bridges that have carried us through eight trying years, and Mary Walker has been invaluable."[25] The two women were not to depart the Garden Street cottage but to remain. Susan Lesley sought boarders to help defray the cost and upkeep of the house, but found no takers; by October 1861, Harvard students and professors had already made their arrangements.[26] The "two Maries" nonetheless stayed put. In early December, Catherine Robbins reported that "the mixed up family down at the cottage are getting along very well thus far. I was sorry to have them try the experiment, but thus far [they] have had no trouble." Taking in sewing, "Mary W. has had as much work as she could do," and doing domestic work, "Mary C. the same. They have a housekeeping by themselves, and MW says she could not possibly do her own work, make the fire, and cook her food, and do work enough to earn anything."[27] The "Maries" were fine. The winter experiment was working.

Far more than earning a living occupied Mary Walker's attention. She was keeping close watch on the war. Though she no longer had Catherine Robbins to read the papers aloud in the Garden Street cottage, she had her own sources of news from white friends in Cambridge and black friends in Boston. During the winter of 1860–1861, Mary Walker had frequently gone "to town" to visit unspecified acquaintances, sometimes much to the annoyance of Catherine Robbins, who had to tend Anne Jean Lyman in her place.[28] One of those persons doubtless was Lewis Hayden, the militant black antislavery leader in Boston, who in 1854 had helped Mary Walker to make contact with the agent hired to liberate her children, and who had visited and kept up ties with her thereafter. Throughout the 1850s, Hayden had overseen the Underground Railroad in Boston, had harbored and defended fugitives in his well-armed house on Southac Street (now Phillips Street) at the base of Beacon Hill, and had fearlessly fought to free fugitives arrested and jailed in the city. The moment war broke out, Hayden approached the newly elected governor of Massachusetts—antislavery lawyer John Andrew—and suggested that he urge the president to approve a black regiment to fight for the Union.[29] Others whom Mary Walker most certainly visited in town included her friend Phillis Gault and fellow Norfolk fugitives given sanctuary by Susan and George Hillard at 62 Pinckney Street. "So many of my acquaintances" dwelt at the Hillards, wrote one black resident, "that I almost imagine my self to bee in the old country."[30] From Secession on, Mary Walker and her black Boston friends riveted their attention on news from "the old country."

Battle outcomes grabbed the headlines, but for blacks in Boston and elsewhere, there was a no less urgent question: How would people of color be dealt with as the war unfolded? Answers came soon—and were contradictory. The highest-ranking officer from Massachusetts was Benjamin Butler, named a general when the Civil War began. Butler had gained notoriety in the spring of 1861, when there was a rumor of slave-insurrection in southern Maryland, a slave-holding state that had not seceded. Butler had ordered his troops to suppress any black rebellion ruthlessly, and found himself excoriated at home. That summer, Butler got a chance for redemption. In late May, he led Massachusetts troops to victory at Fortress Monroe, Virginia. Triumph brought hundreds of slaves into his lines and raised the question of what to do with them. If those who fled were not free, what was their status? Were they then to be returned to their owners? Butler devised a way to hold on to escaped slaves without declaring them liberated. He decreed that they were "contraband of war"—property confiscated as one would confiscate weapons or crops or livestock or warhorses, in order to prevent the use of that property by the enemy and convert it to use by the Union. The designation became official policy. From August 1861 onward, black men, women, and children who escaped to Union lines were termed and treated as "contrabands." The nation's leading antislavery newspaper, William Lloyd Garrison's Boston-based *Liberator,* celebrated General Butler's "master-stroke."[31]

Could Mary Walker find hope that Benjamin Butler's declaration, ratified by the U.S. secretary of war, might open a reconnection with her children? The answer was conditional. If war came to North Carolina, there was a chance that her children would see and seize the chance to become "contraband of war," or that others who became "contrabands" might know of them or how to reach them. Given the rebuffs to the Union army in 1861, however, it hardly seemed likely that the war would come soon to either of the Carolinas. "Our army still stands inactive on the banks of the Potomac," Catherine Robbins fretted from Cambridge. "One cannot but feel an intense desire that there should be some forward movement, some success, & show of power & energy."[32] In fact, while the main army recovered and drilled and prepared interminably for renewed battle in Virginia, opportunities opened for attacks on less protected outposts of the Confederacy. The Union navy and army targeted the Carolinas, with the goal of bringing the war home to the South and creating havoc within. On November 7, 1861, it took only a day's bombardment for the Union navy to seize the Sea Islands off of the South Carolina coast—less than fifty miles from Charleston. Fleeing planters left behind acres full of cotton, as well as ten thousand enslaved workers—all now contraband of war. Five months later, on March 13, 1862, the Union navy and Massachusetts soldiers under the command of General Ambrose Burnside attacked the port of New Bern, North Carolina, and within less than a week had won control of the coastal town.[33]

Mary Walker realized at once that there might be a chance her children would be among those to seek refuge as contrabands in the sanctuary created at New Bern. But Cambridge was about 780 miles from New Bern. How could she find out if her children were there or get word to them about herself? As it so often turned out, she sought and found a connection. Chauncey Wright, the Northampton protégé of Anne Jean Lyman who never ceased to be a faithful visitor to the Cambridge household, had a brother in the Union army. Twenty-two-year-old Frederick Wright had volunteered for service immediately after Fort Sumter. He had come to visit Chauncey in the summer of 1861 and had met Mary Walker at the Garden Street house. Off to war with the Massachusetts Tenth Regiment, he was wounded, returned home, recuperated, was promoted to lieutenant, and reenlisted in a new Massachusetts regiment, the Massachusetts Twenty-Seventh. Frederick Wright was with the Massachusetts Twenty-Seventh when it occupied New Bern in March 1862.[34] Mary Walker had a lifeline to the South.

As soon as Mary Walker learned that the Twenty-Seventh Massachusetts had taken New Bern and that Frederick Wright was stationed there, she asked Chauncey to send a letter to his younger brother on her behalf. On April 29, 1862, he did so, in a characteristically jaunty and seemingly casual way. After describing himself as a "looker-on, leading a very dull life and finding nothing of interest but the newspapers," the Cambridge brother got to the point. "There is one thing in which I hope to interest you if you have the leisure to attend to it—a little 'contraband' business."

> You remember Mrs. Mary Walker whom you saw at Mrs. Lyman's last summer. She is a native of Raleigh, and once the "property" of a Mr. Cameron, now deceased,—and one of the wealthy first men of the place. Her mother and her children (some of them) are still in the possession of the old gentleman's heirs,—a Mr. Cameron, Jr. and a Mr. Mordecai in Raleigh. If you can make it convenient to inquire of any escaped "contrabands," who hail from Raleigh or vicinity, if they know any such people, and where or who they are, and all that is known about them—whether they have escaped or are likely to escape; and if you can find it possible to communicate with them and inform them of what you know about Mrs. Walker; or if you can find it possible and convenient to befriend them in any way, you will do a good thing, and put me and all concerned under great obligations to you; and please write me all that you find out as soon as your leisure will allow.

Chauncey added that "an agent at New Bern keeps a list and an account of all 'contrabands' that come into your lines."[35]

Chauncey Wright had written the letter but Mary Walker had scripted it, and had left nothing to chance. She gave the names and location of the heirs who owned her family. She knew exactly how the processing of contrabands worked: an agent took the refugees' names, kept account of where they'd come from, and itemized their provisions and work assignments. Because only letters from Chauncey and no letters to him have survived, it's not known whether Lieutenant Wright checked the list of New Bern contrabands. Had he done so, he would have found very few refugees from Raleigh and no Walker children among them. Though Raleigh was little more than a hundred miles from New Bern, the terrain was full of armed Confederate troops and Home Guards. It would have involved risk to the point of folly to attempt to get to the Union lines. Not logistics but the strength of her own hopes led Mary Walker to wish that her children had escaped or that someone who knew them had made their way to New Bern. Yet the request to the brothers Wright revealed much. It revealed her ongoing passion for reconnection. It conveyed her readiness for her family members to risk danger for their freedom. It projected onto her children her own—and her Boston friends'—deepening will to war.

LOCATED IN THE NEIGHBORHOOD of Mary Walker's friend Lewis Hayden were two-thirds of Boston's twenty-three hundred black residents, most of its black voluntary associations, and all five of its black churches in 1860. When Mary Walker went to visit friends in town, she likely spent some of her time with acquaintances who lived in the "West End Negro colony," on the north slope of Boston's Beacon Hill.[36] From the outset of the Civil War, the city's black antislavery leaders had seen the conflict as the means to destroy slavery. Lewis Hayden's friend and neighbor William Cooper Nell, the brilliant historian of black soldiers in the American Revolution and battler for the desegregation of Boston's schools and theaters, wrote in the *Liberator* that "the page of history is emphatic in its testimony, that civil wars have always resulted in liberating the slave." Only a few months into the war, both leaders urged the "propriety, if not indeed the necessity, of the employment of colored soldiers in the Federal armies." That opportunity finally came with the Emancipation Proclamation in January 1863, twenty months after the fall of Fort Sumter. The federal government decreed that it was ready to organize and arm black regiments. Immediately, William Nell exhorted Boston's black men: "What wait we for?" Lewis Hayden became the foremost recruiter of Boston's black troops.[37]

But what of those still enslaved in the South itself? What should their role be in the war? Mary Walker must have asked that question and heard others debate it. Always incendiary, the debate had a long history. Bitter frustrations prompted a vocal minority of black leaders, in Boston and beyond, to call for insurrection by their brethren in the South. "The man who would not fight . . . to be delivered from the most wretched, abject and servile slavery" deserved his chains, wrote David Walker (no relation to Mary) in his famous *Appeal* of 1829. In 1843, Bostonians attending the National Negro Convention in Buffalo heard black minister Henry Highland Garnet of Troy, New York, denounce as "sinful in the extreme" those enslaved men who made "voluntary submission" to white owners. "You act as though your daughters were born to pamper to the lusts of your masters and overseers," he charged. "And worst of all, you tidily submit while your lords tear your wives from your embraces, and defile them before your eyes. In the name of God, we ask, are you men?" In response to the Reverend Garnet, Massachusetts delegates Charles Redmond of Salem and William Wells Brown of Boston opposed his 1843 summons to violence. "Bloody confrontation" would bring "bloody retribution" upon slaves and Southern free blacks alike.[38]

In 1858, a year after the Supreme Court's Dred Scott decision, Charles Redmond reversed course, and pressed other Massachusetts blacks to join with him. At the "Convention of the Colored Citizens of Massachusetts," held in New Bedford in August 1858 and attended by dozens of delegates from Boston, Redmond moved "that a committee of five be appointed to prepare an address suggesting to the slaves at the South to create an insurrection." Though he knew his motion was "revolutionary" and "treasonable" and doubted it would carry, he wanted to see "the half-way fellows take themselves away, and leave the field to men who would encourage their brethren at the South to rise with bowie-knife and revolver and musket." Opponents retorted that the call for insurrection was ridiculous. Slaves "had nothing to fight with at the South—no weapons, no education." Thousands would be "hung before their time," and in the end "everything would be lost." Redmond responded that he "had counted the cost. If he had one hundred relatives at the South, he would rather see them die to-day than live in bondage. He would rather stand over their graves, than feel that any pale-faced scoundrel might violate his mother or his sister in pleasure." The motion produced "by far the most spirited discussion of the Convention." Eventually it lost, but the subject and the anger fueling it did not die.[39] At the Boston commemoration of John Brown's martyrdom in December 1860, Frederick Douglass was roundly "cheered when he gave support to slave uprisings in the South."

As Mary Walker, her fellow fugitives from the old country, and Harriet Jacobs heard of these debates among black men in the North, what might they have thought? Did they accept or resent the description of enslaved women who yielded to their owners as defiled and violated? Did they welcome or dismiss as suicidal the goads to Southern bondsmen no longer to "tidily submit" to rapacious masters? Did they cheer or recoil at the proclaimed readiness of a Northern black leader (who surely had not a single Southern cousin he could name) to "stand over the graves" of a "hundred relatives at the South," rather than see them live another day in bondage?

For Mary Walker and her friends, the possibilities so heatedly debated in the 1850s became real choices with the outbreak of war. At first, there were doubts that black men in the North or South would be needed to bring slavery to an end. In early 1862, despite the inconclusiveness of the first year of battle, Peter Lesley forecast that the all-white-man's war would inevitably erode slavery. Equally likely was that war would force "the practical condemnation or limitation of concubinage and amalgamation of the races throughout the south."[40] Lesley seemed certain that with thousands of Southerners summoned from farms and plantations to fight, the white men left would back off sexual demands for their own safety. Susan Lesley worried that if the North prevailed before official Emancipation, there would have to be an "agitation . . . such as the Country never dreamed of," to secure slavery's end. "Let us not croak about the war coming too rapidly to an end," responded her husband. "God will know how to complete the work."[41]

But as the war ground on and Northern armies did not complete the work, Peter Lesley conceded that a long war may be "needful . . . to ripen the fruits." An immensely costly victory at the battle of Antietam on September 17, 1862, where 6,000 deaths and 17,000 casualties made it the bloodiest single day of fighting in American history, set the stage for Abraham Lincoln's preliminary Emancipation Proclamation five days later, on September 22. Lincoln let it be known that in all states still in rebellion on January 1, 1863, he would as a war measure declare all slaves free. September's realities stunned Peter Lesley. First came the "carnage and victories of the last few days," which left him "moved with joy and grief and horror." Then followed the "great proclamation which has suddenly come at last" and "converts the war into what we wished it to be at first, a holy crusade for human liberties." But at what price? "How many wives are inconsolable! How many children are adrift for life!" To his wife, Peter Lesley confided his guilt at remaining outside the crusade. While "others suffer, we are safe. I feel as if this ought not to be." "I feel a continual shame and desire to take part in the war, much as I shrink from bloody deeds and the violent way of doing good."[42]

The "violent way of doing good" likewise preoccupied Mary Walker's Cambridge friend Catherine Robbins as she penned reflections into her journal on December 31, 1862. "The last day of the year, a wild and stormy day, the close of a wild & stormy year," she began.

> What a year. When I have read in history long ago of wars & revolutions, battles & bloodshed, they filled me with horror. I felt that life would be of no value in the midst of such events, I felt that we were far removed from them, that they would never come to us. But now . . . our nearest friends & neighbors are engaged in it, & the saddest calamities come to our kindred. All the fearful scenes of which we have read are enacted in our own country, upon a larger scale than was ever known. Our best & bravest young men are cut down, thousands & thousands lie mutilated & suffering with wounds & disease.

Yet Mary Walker's friend of a dozen years also knew that "We stand on the brink of a stupendous event." On the next day, January 1, 1863, Abraham Lincoln would make final his proclamation declaring American slaves forever free. "To-morrow the Emancipation edict goes into effect. The slaves in all the rebel states will be actually free, although unable to avail themselves of liberty." "It is the greatest event of modern times," though "I know not what to expect . . ."[43]

ON NEW YEAR'S DAY, 1863, Mary Walker and Catherine Robbins attended different meetings to await and celebrate the president's promised Emancipation Proclamation. Catherine Robbins went to a grand concert at the Music Hall, the largest venue in Boston. Convened by poet Henry Wadsworth Longfellow and former mayor Josiah Quincy, Jr., the event was meant to show the support of the cultured class of Boston for the proclamation. Triumphal music marked the afternoon of hope and anticipation. Beethoven's Fifth Symphony and the Hallelujah Chorus from Handel's *Messiah* matched the moment far better, Catherine Robbins thought, than "much talk." The concert began with a solo call and choral response from Mendelssohn's "Hymn of Praise." In a plaintive voice, the soloist sang: "Watchman, will the night soon pass?" Again and yet again, the voice asked, "Will the night soon pass?" Finally the chorus answered, victoriously. "The night is departing! The night is departing; the day is approaching."[44] Until that point in the concert, Catherine Robbins reported to her niece Susan Lesley, "Nothing had been heard from Washington" and "there were misgivings that all might not be well. But in a pause of the music a person came in & announced that a telegram was received, the Proclamation had been issued, & was coming over the wires. There was tremendous shouting & cheering & waving of handkerchiefs." Men and women sprang to their feet and gave nine cheers for Abraham Lincoln and three for Boston abolitionist William Lloyd Garrison. Overcome, Catherine Robbins "never expected to live to see the day when our Government should take a decidedly Anti-Slavery stand, & itself strike a death-blow to the Institution. Heaven be praised that it is so."[45]

Mary Walker went to a quite different meeting that day, a rousing afternoon and evening gathering of black and radical white Bostonians at Tremont Temple, facing the Boston Common. Leaders of the city's black community were on the stage, including Mary Walker's friend Lewis Hayden and presiding officer William C. Nell. The tone of the assembly was martial rather than musical, militant as well as celebratory. The president's "decree for universal emancipation in all rebellious states" was a prelude, William Nell declared. The finale would come when, from the Atlantic to the Pacific, "there shall not be found a tyrant to wield the lash, nor a slave to wear the chain." To those who doubted that the proclamation had accomplished anything, Nell likened the document to a weapon which cut a man apart without his knowing it. The skeptic might not feel anything, but one shake and his body fell to pieces. For people of color, the Emancipation Proclamation had transformed New Year's Day. It would no longer be known, as

Mary Walker knew it was in the South, as Heart Break Day—the time when parents and children, husbands and wives, were parted by sales and separations. This January First "inaugurated a national era of fair play for the black man." Nell summoned people of color to join the fight, to "die, if need be, at Freedom's shrine."[46]

For Mary Walker, the New Year's Day meeting completed a transformation two years in the making. She returned from Tremont Temple "anxious for the Negroes to fight, & would not be sorry if they were to punish their masters in the severest ways." Catherine Robbins, Mary Walker's friend of a dozen years, was startled. "I told Mary that I feared there would be a great deal of cruel & savage treatment of the slaves, where they were caught trying to leave, & then when they were murdered & ill-used, it would of course excite others, & it would be strange if they did not commit acts of violence & outrage, when their passions were roused."[47]

Mary Walker's response was instantaneous. The year before, while the war was exclusively a war to save the Union, she had hoped that her children would use the chaos to escape and end their separation of fifteen years. Now there were new choices, and more dangerous ones. Deep currents that had moved the country had also moved Mary Walker. Yes, a bloodbath was likely, she agreed—but "it was not to be considered at all, if many of them had to suffer & die that all might be free. It was not to be thought of as an objection to emancipation." And if the bloodbath included her own children? She "wished her children to know how to die for their freedom. If she heard they were dead in the cause, or attempting to escape, she should say, Amen. It is best so."[48]

10 "The Welfare of Her Race"

Until early 1864, Mary Walker seemed destined to witness the Civil War from the sidelines. Then an extraordinary opportunity came—an invitation to join Northern reformers working to uplift former slaves in the South. In April 1864, Mary Walker sailed to the Sea Islands off the coast of South Carolina. There she found, in midcourse, a social experiment that historian Willie Lee Rose has called the wartime nation's "Rehearsal for Reconstruction."[1]

Mary Walker came south with high hopes that she might contribute to "the welfare of her race." What she witnessed, however, was an experiment coming apart—and a black militancy that neither she nor anyone else had dreamt of when Emancipation first came. Her time on the Sea Islands made it clear that liberation for plantation people everywhere would involve a protracted struggle. Though during those weeks she herself experienced the greatest liberty she had known in her entire life, the summer of 1864 made her all the more desperate to rescue her family from the South.

UNTIL 1864, THE OPTIONS for Mary Walker were familiar ones: working, waiting, hoping. After Anne Jean Lyman's removal to the McLean Asylum in late 1861, Mary Walker and her co-worker Mary

Cashman had remained in the Garden Street cottage in Cambridge through the early months of 1862, thanks to the decision of Susan Lesley. Susan felt that this was the least the family could do for the two women who had been the "bridges that carried us over" during her mother's descent into dementia. But in the spring of 1862, it was expected that they would find new homes and new employers.

Mary Walker had an invitation to go back to Milton, Massachusetts, and work in the household of Mary Elizabeth (Lissie) Ware, the eldest member of a family for whom Mary Walker had worked on and off since she'd arrived in New England in 1850.[2] Though not blood relatives, the Wares were close enough to Susan Lesley to call her "cousin Susie." Mary Walker was expected in Milton in the spring of 1862, but before she could make the move she received one last communication from the family of Anne Jean Lyman. It was an appeal that ultimately would intertwine the lives of Anne Jean Lyman's family and Mary Walker's for another generation. The older sister of Anne Jean Robbins Lyman—Sarah Robbins Howe—was in failing health in early 1862. The two sisters had been close all of their lives. Widowed in 1828, Sarah Howe moved her family to Cambridge, bought a house, and took in boarders to support her sons, James Murray Howe and Estes Howe, and her daughter, Mary. When Anne Jean Lyman moved to Cambridge in 1853, proximity to her sisters—Sarah Howe and Catherine Robbins—played a large role in her decision. The three sisters lived within blocks of one another for almost a decade. The Howes saw what an extraordinary companion Mary Walker had been for all those years, and knew from the reports of others what a compassionate caregiver she was for those who were dying. The Howe children asked Mary Walker to look after their mother in her last illness.[3] She stayed with Sarah Howe until Sarah died on June 10, 1862.

Mary Walker's delay obliged Lissie Ware in Milton to hire another housekeeper. After Sarah Howe's death, Mary Walker and Mary Cashman went to work instead for a different Ware sister—Ann Ware

Winsor—when her physician husband, Frederick Winsor, joined the Forty-Ninth Massachusetts Volunteers as its regimental surgeon. Learning of the arrangement, Susan Lesley was pleased for "the two Marys. We should all be grateful for roof, clothes, and food in inflationary times."[4]

Being in the household of Ann Ware Winsor meant more than the fact that Mary Walker would have a roof over her head in the fall of 1862. It also meant that she became privy to reports from the South by the two members of the Ware family who had joined fifty Northerners in overseeing the path to freedom of former slaves on the Sea Islands.

THE SEA ISLANDS OF South Carolina were the site of one of the most extraordinary experiments of the Civil War. Located south of Charleston and just north of Savannah, the coastal islands produced the most prized cotton in the South. Each of the sixty-five islands of different sizes was level and sandy, and full of marshes and creeks. The creeks abounded with fish, the larger islands with game, but for aspiring aristocrats, the soil was the draw. Perfect for the cultivation of long-staple cotton, the islands attracted ambitious planters to the Low Country. The planters imported thousands of enslaved workers from Africa, who brought with them their culture and folkways. In two generations, these workers had fashioned a hybrid African-American language called "Gullah" and, blending West African and Christian religious traditions, created expressive new ways of worship and song.

Most Sea Islands planters had welcomed the secession movement that took South Carolina out of the Union in December 1860, and had cheered at the firing on Fort Sumter in April 1861. Little did any of them suspect that seven months later, on November 7, 1861, a fleet of Union gunboats would sail to Port Royal Sound, bombard the two forts guarding its entrance, and take over the Sea Islands in scarcely more than a day. The "Day of the Big Gun Shoot" was the way the black people on the islands referred to the dramatic Union triumph.

Resident planters fled for their lives, leaving behind plantation houses and harvests, land and livestock, and ten thousand workers.[5]

Boston engineer Edward Philbrick was among the first to recruit Northerners to make the Sea Islands a testing ground for freedom. Given control in early 1862 of half a dozen plantations and hundreds of former slaves, he sought volunteers who were able to go at once and who could be trusted. In Harriet Ware and her brother Charles Ware, he found ready recruits—and relatives close to home. By 1862, both marriage and professional partnership connected Edward Philbrick to the Wares of Milton. Philbrick was married to Helen Winsor, a relative of Frederick Winsor, who had married Ann Ware. Of equal importance, the partner in Edward Philbrick's Boston engineering firm was architect William Ware, who a few years later would found the School of Architecture at the newly established Massachusetts Institute of Technology.[6]

Philbrick undoubtedly conveyed to his partner his excitement at the chance to go to the Sea Islands "to prove that the blacks will work for other motives than the lash." "You don't know what a satisfaction it is," he wrote in February 1862, "for me to *do something* in this great work that is going on."[7] He was thrilled that such a number of earnest recruits should agree on short notice "to devote themselves, as they certainly do, with a will, to this holy work."[8] Philbrick agreed to have his wife, Helen, join him in the Sea Islands, but only if she had no reservations about being around persons of color. "If you feel any hesitation about coming in contact with them you shouldn't come, for they are sharp enough to detect apathy or lurking repugnance, which would render any amount of theoretical sympathy about worthless."[9] William Ware encouraged his sister Harriet (Hatty) to join the mission, both as a companion for Helen Philbrick and as a teacher for the "contraband" children. By keeping the freed slaves at work in the South, the New Englanders' efforts would deter fugitives "from coming north as pauper emigrants where they are not wanted." William Ware knew from experience that Harriet was a good listener, always "ready to hear anything I've got to say, & understand & respond, friendly-like." He counted on her attentiveness to serve her well in the South—and to give the family back home a firsthand glimpse of her Sea Islands work. "Keep a minute journal & put down all the nigger talk you can remember. Quotations are the spice of journals. . . . Keep your thoughts & feelings in your little book, & send home what you find time to write."[10] Soon to join the Sea Islands mission as well was twenty-one-year-old Charles Ware, the younger brother of Harriet and William Ware. He had plodded through much of his last year at Harvard and had no particular plans for his future.[11] Two weeks after commencement, the new graduate was off to the Sea Islands.

Both Charles and Harriet compiled "journals" of their letters home, with the expectation that those letters would be read and passed around to all in the family. Working for Ware family members, Mary Walker would certainly have heard about Hatty's Sea Islands experiences, and perhaps even been invited to read her letters.[12] Harriet Ware reported that within weeks she found herself teacher, face-washer, medic, scribe, storekeeper—and listener. "They do not talk much unless we question them, when they tell freely." Recognizing that there was an infinite amount she didn't understand, ranging from dialect to religious worship, she sought to avoid judgments about the world she was encountering. Not so the "Baptist minister, who came out with us," who was "very much puzzled what to do about the religious feeling of these people and their habits and customs. I hope he will let them alone."[13] If Mary Walker read the Sea Islands letters, she surely would have detected that Hatty Ware's openness and her walks through the quarters four times a day had made her a welcome presence among the people. When "Old Peggy," the religious leader from one of the plantations, came over to see the school, all she could do was exclaim, "Oh Lord!"[14] Mutual appreciation marked Harriet Ware's Sea Islands beginning.

The same could not be said for her brother Charles, at least initially. On the six-day boat trip from New York to South Carolina in the first week of July 1862, with a Cotton Manual as his constant companion, the young Bostonian hurriedly read up about cultivation of the Sea Islands' principal crop. By the end of July, three weeks in the South had prompted mixed responses—and surely mixed responses from Mary Walker, too, if she had a look at his letters. "At present I find the nigs rather more agreeable on the whole than I expected, much preferred to the Irish." He was pleased that black as they were, he could now begin to tell them apart. Though he found their manners "offensively servile—with Sir and Maussa in every sentence"—he also found himself paying acute attention to the character and judgment of the plantations' black drivers, who were the foremen he had to rely on. Easing the transition to his new setting was the goodwill generated by his sister among the people. Everywhere he basked as "M's Hayyet's brudder," and was greeted with ovations and gifts of eggs.[15] By the end of 1862, Charles Ware's Yankee detachment had given way to paternalistic affection. Uncertain about the future of Edward Philbrick's Sea Islands project in 1863—and his own continued employment—he confessed that "sometimes I feel like taking myself slyly or secretly away, without seeing my people again. I shall hate to break from them or to tell them I must go & leave them to others." If the young Harvard planter had to go, the greatest hardship would be "leaving my colored friends here forever."[16]

"YOU KNOW I HAVE ALWAYS wished to have Mary Walker here with me," Harriet Ware wrote her older sister, Lissie, the first week of February 1864. "I think she would be invaluable—if I could afford the salary. I would make her housekeeper & then could do as I pleased about being off."[17] In early April 1864, forty-six-year-old Mary Walker arrived on the Sea Islands. Much had changed since Harriet and

Charles Ware had arrived two years before, and those changes would make Mary Walker's encounters vastly different from the first experiences of her Sea Islands employers.

"Being off" was actually the last thing that Harriet Ware wished to discuss in early February 1864. Her motherly older sister, Mary Elizabeth, almost twenty years her senior, had fretted about Harriet's health in the South almost from the first, not without reason. Illness had forced the younger sister to come home once in 1862 and to cut back and finally drop her teaching in the summer of 1863. But her health was perfectly fine in early 1864. She had abridged her duties to those of full-time housekeeper for her brother, his fellow plantation supervisor Richard Soule, and the elegant Coffin Point dwelling that they all occupied. Harriet Ware knew that the summons home was more for her lonely sister's sake than her own. Obligingly, she had given notice that she *might* be going home in mid-February 1864.

But on February 6 she wrote to say she could not leave. Testiness replaced her normal deference to her older sister. "I always meant to come when I could, but it had not been possible before, though equally impossible to make you understand the whys and wherefores." In his postscript to the letter, her younger brother was even more peremptory. "We can hardly expect you to appreciate fully the indefinite character of our status; it is as unsatisfactory to us as it is perplexing to you. It is not worth while to attempt to explain all the peculiar circumstances in which we are living; but what H. has written ought to satisfy you of the futility of any attempt to form, still [less to] carry out, any plans of future action."[18]

It was half in anticipation of such a rebuff—that Harriet Ware might not feel at liberty to leave her brother and her housekeeping duties—that Lissie Ware had suggested Mary Walker go to the Sea Islands as a temporary replacement. Harriet Ware had to agree. Mary Walker's coming would certainly make her life in the South easier and a visit to the North more feasible. That agreed, she ended the letter to her sister on a note of strained reassurance. "Believe me I do not purposely disregard your wishes."[19]

Lissie Ware's invitation to Mary Walker came in mid-March and seemed to catch her off guard. As almost always happened in the New England winter, her respiratory ailments had worsened. What would a sea voyage down the Atlantic Coast and a drastic change of climate do to her health? She may have wondered whether this Union enclave in South Carolina was really safe. As a domestic servant both in North Carolina and New England and a mixed-race woman of color in both worlds, what did she have in common with Sea Islands field hands? No wonder Mary Walker's longtime friend Catherine Robbins found her ambivalent about returning to the South.[20]

Yet she decided to go. She had watched her Boston friends, black and white, successfully recruit soldiers among fugitive slaves and free men of color in the North. She knew of the remarkable results of that summons. Governor John Andrew had authorized the formation of an all-black regiment from Massachusetts, the Massachusetts Fifty-Fourth, to take the fight to the South. Led and drilled by white officers just outside Boston, the regiment had dazzled Catherine Robbins—and perhaps Mary Walker, if she accompanied her—on a visit to the training ground in May 1863. It "was a wonderful sight indeed, a thousand Negroes, admirably equipped & drilled, & officered by some of the finest young men in the country. . . . We have called on the Negro to help us in trouble & must admit his manhood & capabilities as they have never been before."[21] Sent to South Carolina, the Massachusetts Fifty-Fourth was stationed on the Sea Islands, where in 1863 its officers had gathered with the missionaries, including Harriet and Charles Ware, and with the emancipated slaves for an extraordinary Fourth of July celebration.[22] Two weeks later the Massachusetts Fifty-Fourth led the charge against the Confederate battery of Fort Wagner, which guarded the southern approach to Charleston harbor. Under relentless fire, a few soldiers managed to gain a foothold in the fort, but only for a moment. In death and defeat—they lost almost half the regiment—the soldiers nonetheless demonstrated a valor which settled the question of whether blacks had the will and skill to fight. By the war's end, 185,000 blacks would become Union soldiers. Mary Walker knew that this was her chance to join the fight.

In late March 1864, Edward Philbrick notified one of the other young plantation superintendents, William Gannett, that several new people would come down on the next ship to the islands. One would be "a Mrs. Walker, a white runaway slave from Cambridge who goes to take temporarily the place of Miss Ware, so she can come home for a visit in summer. She is formerly from Raleigh NC" and "has been a worthy & sensible woman for 12 years past here in Cambridge & now feels much interest in the welfare of *her race,* as she considers the negro to be."[23] "Much interest in the welfare of her race" was surely Mary Walker's phrase. Underlining *"her race"* was Edward Philbrick's emphasis. Clearly, Philbrick was taken aback that so fair a woman, after twelve years in Cambridge, would still consider "the negro to be" *"her race."* Was he conveying even more to the young superintendent? Two years before, Philbrick, the Wares, William Gannett, and other earnest recruits had all come to the Sea Islands with the idea that they too would engage in the holy work of helping the newly freed people. Edward Philbrick and William Gannett both knew by March 1864 that Mary Walker had a lot to learn.

WHAT EDWARD PHILBRICK HELD back from Mary Walker, and what the Wares were reluctant to explain to their sister in Milton, was how much the New Englanders' Sea Islands mission had soured. Starting in mid-1863, Philbrick's young superintendents began to confess their frustrations in journals or letters home—frustrations both with the freedmen they had come to help and with the loss of their own innocence. Cambridge resident and professional "elocutionist" Arthur

Sumner had come to the islands in the first ship, in April 1862, to teach black schoolchildren. Soon assigned to supervise laborers as well, he admitted a year later that "I have lost that liking for them which I had during my first acquaintance." Initially, Sumner had admired their humility and devoutness and was touched by stories of their sufferings under slavery. By June 1863, he found the Sea Islands people absolutely "selfish, ungrateful, deceitful, hypocritical, and licentious."[24] In retrospect, he realized that it "was painful and detrimental to me to be forced to occupy the relation of employer with the negroes. One only sees the mean and hateful side of them." "Almost every planter in the department," no matter how "humane and benevolent" at the outset, had developed "a most rancorous and unamiable spirit of disgust for the negro."[25]

By October 1863, Charles Ware was writing home of his similar disillusionment, though he wasn't yet ready to pronounce the whole enterprise a hopeless failure. Three-fourths of his plantation workers, he claimed, "lie by habit and steal on the least provocation," take "infinite pains to be lazy and shirk," and deceive "even when it is obviously for their own interest to tell the whole truth. 'Wherefore he is called the everlasting Niggah.'" Ware admitted that he was ranting: better to explode in a letter than in the field. "I have had my grumble, and feel better. What I have said 'has truth in it, only distorted.'" After fifteen months, he was more subject to "vexations and annoyances than when the interest was fresh and the work new and untried."[26] In February 1864, twenty-three-year-old William Gannett wrote a similar letter to his father, the renowned Boston Unitarian minister Ezra Stiles Gannett. "Did you know we had long ceased to be philanthropists? We are nothing now but speculators, and the righteous rail against us."[27] Both Charles Ware and William Gannett decided to stay on as supervisors through 1864; both admitted it was less for the welfare of the people than for the money. The salary paid by Edward Philbrick was not small—it was close to $4,000 in 1864.[28]

As Mary Walker would find out, Charles Ware had not confined *all* of his frustration to the letters he wrote home. There was a particular "why and wherefore" behind Harriet Ware's refusal to leave her brother in early 1864, and behind the reticence of both Wares about details. Against the cardinal taboo of Union rule in the Sea Islands, Charles Ware had taken a whip to an ex-slave. For other supervisors who had done so, dismissal was automatic.[29] Everyone understood that physical punishment was absolutely forbidden—Northerners were there to "prove that the blacks will work for other motives than the lash." In fact, the youthful superintendent had not struck a man at all. He had whipped a young pregnant woman for immoral conduct. As she reported it, he had stretched her over a barrel, lifted her skirt over her head, and lashed her exposed bottom. What consequences that act would have were still unclear.[30] Harriet Ware needed to stay with her brother.

It was well that she remained. In the weeks that followed the whipping, anger at her brother fused with the freed people's own disillusionment to stir an unrest that Mary Walker would find still simmering when she arrived in April. For many of the men and women employed by Edward Philbrick, and hundreds more laboring for other Northern planters, the crops they raised and the wages they earned were the means to an end: acquisition of land of their own. Few doubted they had a right to the land confiscated from their former owners. But how could they actually obtain it? Until the second week of February 1864, it appeared that those with money would be able to acquire land by preemption—that ex-slaves on the Sea Islands, like white farmers in the West, would be able to claim and purchase small tracts of government-owned land at nominal prices.[31] But what good was the right of preemption to those who were getting paid so little? So asked Northern abolitionist John Hunn, who had come to the Sea Islands after a twenty-year career as an unrelenting helper of fugitive slaves. At a crowded Sunday church service in late January 1864, Hunn asked:

"What's thirty cents a day in these times for a man who has to maintain himself and his family?" *"That's so, that's so,"* answered the congregation.[32]

Three weeks after John Hunn's address to the church, Harriet Ware reported, there occurred at their Coffin Point Plantation "a thing which has never happened before." The women of the Wares' plantation "came up in a body to complain to Mr. Philbrick about their pay." It "shows the influence of very injudicious outside talk, which has poisoned their minds against their truest friends." What was astonishing was that the "best people were among them, and even old Grace the chief spokeswoman." More than inflammatory outside talk had mobilized the women to confront their employer. Grace, "with the other women, had complained of C. [Charles]," as well. Philbrick may have parried the complaints of the women by saying that the wages he paid were more than fair—and added that if they thought they could do better elsewhere, they could move. More sympathetically, he may have asked them to remember that Charles Ware was normally an easy-going superintendent—and his sister their ministering angel—and urged them to forgive him his trespass. Whatever the reasons, the protesters of Coffin Point pulled back for the time being. As Edward Philbrick was about to depart for the North, Harriet Ware reported on February 14, the people brought eggs and peanuts for him to carry home to his wife. "He told them he could not carry eggs to Miss Helen but would tell her. Then Grace begged his pardon for her bad behavior and complaining the other day, and collecting all the eggs which he had refused, told C. they were for him" and sent them into the house. Harriet Ware saw the gesture as a peace offering.[33]

When Mary Walker arrived at the Sea Islands in the first week of April, an uneasy Coffin Point armistice was still in place.

"THE LONG-LOOKED FOR SCHOONERS have arrived," reported Sea Islands teacher William Allen on April 7, 1864. "We had been tormenting ourselves with fears that they were lost." An older cousin of Harriet and Charles Ware, thirty-four-year-old William Francis Allen had come south along with his wife to teach the freedmen in November 1863; immediately, he began keeping a detailed journal which vividly chronicled life on the islands over the next nine months. The two schooners bound for Port Royal had been just days out of port when the huge winds of "a fearful storm" had roiled the Atlantic. Mercifully, both ships had managed to put into Newport News, Virginia, "during the great storm," and despite "a very rough passage from there," both had made it safely to South Carolina. William Allen and others had feared that the ship captains might be compelled to throw "overboard a good part of their cargoes"—"paper collars, cider, hymn-books and dried apples," and, even worse, to jettison several new rowboats and a "handsome Concord Wagon" (a horse-drawn buggy). But the cargo and all passengers arrived intact, including "a Mrs. Walker (colored) to help Harriet keep house."[34]

Mary Walker was welcomed by Charles Ware, who gathered her things and drove them in his carriage through a natural landscape that stood in stark contrast to the New England she had just left. Jasmines were "now in their perfection" and the season's first strawberries and rosebuds had appeared. Even though the spring weather was uncommonly cold, South Carolina in April always struck every new arrival as magnificently green. "Green beyond description" were the words of Harriet Ware. The palmettos, live oaks, azaleas, and roses dazzled the newcomer's eye, as did the lingering blooms of the peach trees, red camellias, and wild plums that had blossomed the month before.[35]

Perhaps equally striking to Mary Walker's eye was the plantation dwelling they arrived at. The Coffin Point Plantation got its name from its owner, Thomas A. Coffin, and was the largest on St. Helena Island.[36] Prior to the Civil War, Coffin's home had been widely regarded as the most elegant planter's residence on the Sea Islands. Abandoned by its owners at the time of the "Big Gun Shoot," the place quickly fell into disrepair; its furniture was appropriated by ex-slaves, and its upkeep was neglected by the government-hired cotton agent given use of the house in early 1862. When Harriet Ware and Helen Philbrick took over the care of Coffin Point in late April 1862, one observer thought they would find life "pretty rough," entirely devoid of "New England comforts and neatness." A year later, Harriet Ware had transformed Coffin Point into an outpost of home. So reported a twenty-five-year-old Northern visitor in March 1863:

> The house[,] a large old-fashioned one, is beautifully situated on the sea shore. There is a lovely path leading directly thro' the garden down to the beach. Oh it was good to stand upon that beach, feel the cool sea breezes, and listen to the gentle murmur of the waves. I was most unwilling to leave it. The sitting room was the pleasantest I have seen down here, with its books and pictures. And an excellent piano was there—Gilbert's of Boston—which was most refreshing to listen to after the tuneless instruments one hears generally down here. Altogether this is a place I sh'd like to go to for a week, to rest in, thoroughly.[37]

As a housekeeper, Mary Walker would have little difficulty overseeing the New Englanders' establishment at Coffin Point. Far less certain was how she would fit into the world of the newly freed people of the Sea Islands plantations. Mary Walker might consider herself and the islands' ex-slaves as sharing the experience of bondage and African forebears. But is that the way the people would see her?

If the white missionaries' response to her was any indication, she would face doubts and questions. Three days after Mary Walker's arrival on April 7, 1864, the Wares' cousin William Allen "drove to Coffin's . . . in the Concord Wagon" for a Sunday visit. There he met "Mrs. Walker, who used to live with the Wares, [and] came down in the last steamer to relieve Harriet of some of her care. She used to be a slave in

North Carolina, but I never should have suspected her of a drop of negro blood."[38] A month later, Mary Walker met the oldest and best-known teacher on the islands, Laura Towne of Philadelphia. Towne had been converted to abolitionism by the powerful sermons of Philadelphia's Unitarian minister William Furness, and had become acquainted with Susan and Peter Lesley as fellow members of Furness's Philadelphia church. The Wares and Mary Walker had come in a sailboat to make a visit to the Philadelphia teacher; afterward, Laura Towne described the meeting in her journal. "Mrs. Walker seemed to me a very lady-like pretty widow, rather fair and delicate. I should never have guessed her to have been what she is—an escaped slave from North Carolina. She lived with Susie Leslie a long time and for years was her mother's companion."[39]

The Northerners may well have wondered how the Sea Islands people would receive Mary Walker. Would she be regarded simply as the Wares' house-servant, and kept at arm's distance by the people who worked in the fields, just as they had treated house-servants in slavery times? One Northern teacher found herself stunned by the tension between those who lived in the plantation house, favored and sometimes fathered by their owners, and the families who labored in the fields. Would they view Mary Walker with puzzlement? This was how several Coffin Point servants regarded a free man of color from the North, who had been invited to dine at the table with his white hosts. "That stranger man eat up here?" asked the Wares' black servant Rose the next day. "Him free man?" Indeed he was, and educated too. "Yes ma'am," was all the reply Rose could muster. "They don't know what to make of educated blacks," commented Harriet Ware.[40]

Or would the people of the plantation wait to see what temperament and talents Mary Walker had to offer them, as the black folk did with other outsiders? When the well-educated and mixed-race Charlotte Forten arrived in the fall of 1862, she overflowed with excitement. A third-generation free black who had been educated in private academies, and who had been encouraged to come south by none other than the Quaker poet John Greenleaf Whittier, she burst into song on the carriage ride from the wharf to her new residence. "We sang John Brown with a will!" Eager to teach, she found the people perfectly amiable as she walked around to meet them in the quarters. But, clearly, color and caste created distance. "The people on our place are inclined to question a good deal about 'dat brown gal,'" reported reformer Laura Towne. The women who found themselves most welcome were teachers who also had "learnin'"—by which the freed people meant medical knowledge. Charlotte Forten lacked medical knowledge, but overcame distance through music: she played the piano with a will, and soon found that young and old alike were eager to hear her music and teach her their own.[41]

Mary Walker was not a schoolteacher, not a doctoress, not a pianist. How would this "fair and delicate," "lady-like" woman, who had spent sixteen years in the North and twenty years as a Southern house-servant, mingle with the people of the quarters? A few weeks after her arrival, Mary Walker sent a long letter home to her Cambridge friend Catherine Robbins, which "Aunt Kitty" all-too-briefly summarized in a note to her Philadelphia niece, Susan Lesley. "Mary Walker writes that she is very happy. She doesn't have much to do and so spends her time walking about the quarters talking with the people."[42] It is unclear whether Mary Walker conveyed to the people that she had fled slavery; that she was a North Carolinian who knew slave-songs, albeit different ones from theirs; that she was descended from African as well as white forebears; that she was a seamstress with skills to offer them; that she could tell them of life in the North; above all, that her mother and children were still enslaved. Catherine Robbins's report didn't say.

WHAT IS VIRTUALLY CERTAIN IS that Mary Walker sent her letter north before she became an eyewitness to an extraordinary confrontation of freedmen and reformers at Coffin Point. On April 18,

1864, Harriet Ware learned that an agent of the president had arrived in Beaufort to "look into the affairs of our 'concern.'"[43] An agent of the *president?* The freed people of Fripp Point, a plantation adjacent to Coffin Point, had sent a petition to Abraham Lincoln on March 1, asking to be relieved from landowner Edward Philbrick's "oppression"! At one o'clock on April 21, the Wares' servant Robert hastened into the house to tell Harriet Ware and Mary Walker that a huge coach was dashing down the road. Pulled by four white horses, the coach brought four men, including the president's investigator, Judge Austin Smith. On horseback next to the coach rode William Gannett, the superintendent of the alienated Fripp Point people, and Reuben Tomlinson, supervisor of schools on the Sea Islands. All in all, thirteen people had to be served an afternoon meal. With the help of Mary Walker and Coffin Point house-servants Robert and Rose, Harriet Ware flew "about my business" to pull tables and vittles together, and served the men their midday dinner at three o'clock.[44]

The interrogation of the white supervisors began before the meal. The reformers "found Judge Smith to be fair minded, able and clear sighted—not to have dust thrown in his eyes." The judge seemed satisfied that Edward Philbrick was "not a scoundrel" and "all of us aiders and abetters of his iniquities." But Fripp Point supervisor William Gannett knew that the discontented freedmen of his plantation "would never be satisfied" unless they had a personal audience with the president's man. So Gannett rode to get them, and they flocked to Coffin Point so "closely on G's heels" that they almost overtook him. For the next two hours, with the freed people crowding about the door and filling the piazza, the president's emissary conducted a "session of court" in which he took direct testimony from three black leaders at Fripp Point. As Mary Walker served tea to the white guests, she and a large black assembly of "quiet and orderly, but eager listeners" witnessed the exchange between the judge and three ex-slaves.[45]

Outspoken and defiant, the first speaker, John Major, surely reminded Mary Walker of her Boston friend and fellow fugitive slave, Lewis Hayden. Major was the lead signer of the March 1 petition and the acknowledged leader of the Fripp Point people. He had labored on the plantation the year before, as had his wife and children, for around 40 cents a day. But for much of 1863 and 1864, he had taken work at Hilton Head, where white and black soldiers were stationed. There he had earned far more money—$20 to $25 a month—and saved enough to buy two costly horses (*and two watches,* according to his white detractors).

John Major believed that Edward Philbrick had acquired Fripp Point, Coffin Point, and other plantations "under falls pretences." Philbrick purported to buy "their Master's land" with a promise to sell homesteads to its ex-slave occupants at the price he had paid for it: a dollar an acre. He had pledged to reward his workers fairly for their labor. On both counts, he had proved false. After officials had begun the sale of government-owned land on the Sea Islands on February 18, Major asserted, "our brethren" from other places had bought land, planted crops, and built houses, "which they will own forever." But when the Fripp Point people had asked Philbrick "to sell us our land," he had refused. "Not one foot will he sell, and if he does, [he will charge] $10 an acre." Meanwhile, Philbrick's wages were so low that his workers could not pay the inflated cost of goods at his plantation stores: "his stores charge fearful." "If we seek to work for others where we might make something, he turns us out of our houses; we can't live on his place unless we work for him" and "take what he sees fit to pay."[46]

John Major added one more charge, which Mary Walker may have heard about during her walks through the quarters. "We want an agent who will not see wrong, but right done by us[,] one who will deal justly by us. We don't want a Master or Owner. Neither a driver with his Whip. Wee want a Friend." The "driver with his Whip" was Charles Ware, who had punished the young pregnant woman two months before at Coffin Point. Major denounced this as "the worst greavance of all."[47]

From all Mary Walker and other observers could tell, Judge Austin Smith accepted the Northern reformers' characterization of John Major as a "discontented turbulent fellow" whose petition "so overshot the mark that it was palpably absurd to all who knew the facts." Doubtless with her brother's trouble in mind, Harriet Ware took pleasure in "how quickly the judge saw through him, when he has been only a week in the Department and could hardly understand what he said." The judge scolded John Major in front of all those assembled. If the Fripp Point petitioner "thought secesh times were so much better," the United States government "loved him so much it would let him go back to his old master!" The judge told the leader point-blank that he was "a troublesome, mischief-making fellow."[48]

After serving tea, Mary Walker witnessed a more temperate exchange. "Two different men" spoke to the judge, "'Siah and Pompey." In Harriet Ware's opinion, both men were "intelligent, hardworking, honest; Sia was particularly truthful and reliable." Mary Walker may have been as moved as Harriet Ware at the "fine sight" of "these men, two years out of slavery respectfully but decidedly standing up for what they thought their rights in a room full of white people." Though their manners were more respectful, their complaints echoed those of John Major. 'Siah asserted that their wages were too low and they ought to have 50 cents a day instead of 40 cents. Pompey's "great difficulty" was more fundamental. He "considered that Mr. P. [Philbrick] took back his word." Mr. P. had "promised them when he bought the land to sell it to them when the war was over for what he gave for it; now he said $10 an acre."

To Pompey and 'Siah and to the assembled ex-slaves looking for presidential redress, the judge tried to be reassuring. Their houses *did* belong to Edward Philbrick, but the judge thought that, in the course of the year, the government would "probably" make "arrangements so all can buy." As to their getting land, he believed—"though not certain"—that "Mr. Philbrick would sell land to all proper persons, but not to troublesome ones." That evening, the judge privately urged the superintendents to counsel Philbrick to raise wages to 50 cents a day. Harriet Ware and William Gannett knew the people were unsatisfied—"silenced but not convinced"—yet hoped they would be pacified by having had their say with President Lincoln's agent.[49]

Judge Austin Smith never questioned Charles Ware. The investigator had received private assurances from other superintendents that the young supervisor was contrite about the whipping, that the reports of its harshness and the young woman's condition were exaggerated, and that it would never happen again.[50]

"Not a single one of our people came up," Harriet Ware noted the day after the Fripp Point protesters and the president's investigator had left. Doubtless, Mary Walker also noticed that none of the several hundred Coffin Point freed people had joined in the complaints of oppression. Instead, the next day, two men appeared and were most ingratiating when they found out that the confrontation had left "M's Hayyet" with a headache. "Mebbe de confusion make you sick, sorry for dat. Not one of our people come up yere." Harriet Ware was touched. It was "as if they had come up simply to assure me that our people would give no trouble." When it came time to make a contract for the year ahead, Charles Ware had no trouble with his workers.[51]

Whatever hopes Mary Walker may have harbored of being an agent for "the welfare of her race" evaporated in the conflict of April 1864. Her sponsors in the South, who had enlisted black workers in 1862 with promises of fair wages and ultimate landownership, now hedged those pledges with assertions that granting too much too soon would subvert the work ethic at the heart of free labor and spoil the whole enterprise. Even if she'd been so inclined, Mary Walker was hardly in a position to adjudicate the disputes she witnessed.[52] She lived in the Big House with the lapsed liberators. How could she critique them? In the

Africa-infused world of the Sea Islands, she seemed white. Why should black people think her an ally? The responses of the freed people after the April confrontation must have reminded Mary Walker all too painfully of life as it had been when authority belonged to the slaveholder. Rebuffed by the president's man, the Fripp Point dissenters soon turned to subterfuge, while the Coffin Point people presented a face of accommodation. Caught between freedmen she couldn't help and reformers she couldn't challenge, what could Mary Walker do?

"DO PEOPLE EXPECT MUCH OF the negro at Port Royal?" So Charles Ware asked his sisters in the North on July 17, 1864, three months after the confrontation at Coffin Point. "Let them expect. It is amusing to hear Mary Walker. She understands all the peculiarities of affairs down here with wonderful quickness & penetration; I have learned to respect her judgment and opinion. To hear her rail at these people, & slip out sly hints about the conduct of the 'friends of the freedmen' is a treat." As Charles Ware told the tale, Mary Walker, like the reformers who preceded her, had soured on the social experiment and on the Sea Islands people themselves.[53]

To survive the summer, Mary Walker may well have decided to follow the lead of the Coffin Point people and appease her employers.[54] So long as she did not single out particular persons, Mary Walker knew she might rage all she wanted at "these people" without violating the code of the quarters to betray no one. As to her sarcasm about white radicals who encouraged black defiance, it's clear that Mary Walker framed her "sly hints" about the "friends of the freedmen" in ways that Charles Ware never took to mean *him.* Yet Mary Walker's resort to mockery may have had a deeper motive. Charles Ware, in contrast to William Gannett—his earnest and confrontational counterpart at Fripp Point—could let humor defuse what he disliked. Mary Walker had found her own way to mediate at Coffin Point.

The talk of the islands, as Mary Walker was certainly aware, remained the Fripp Point workers. Feeling betrayed by Edward Philbrick and "not satisfied" with the presidential agent's vague assurance that they would "probably" be allowed to buy their homes, they dramatically intensified their subversion of their superintendent, William Gannett. Having started the cotton crop early in 1864, they promptly planted corn between the rows of cotton, claiming this was a customary right allowed them in slavery times. But instead of just a few hills of corn, they planted hundreds. Certain that the corn would cripple the cotton and deny the owner his due, Gannett demanded that the people pull it all up. 'Siah told the supervisor that he might have justice on his side, but he would have *"war"* if he forced the issue. Sure enough, when Gannett persisted, furious women met him in the field, and one of the men—brandishing a revolver—declared he would kill any black man sent to uproot the corn. In short order, Gannett's horse was stolen and injured; his mule suffered a suspicious wound and died; his cashbox was broken into. When Gannett declared his intention to pull up the corn himself, his fellow superintendent Richard Soule—who lived with Mary Walker and the Wares at Coffin Point—urged him to wait and see if the people relented. Even landowner Philbrick declared such unilateral action beneath the dignity of a supervisor. Convinced that the people must "be taught the lesson that they cannot trample on another's right," Gannett started anyhow, promptly fell ill, and had to stop.[55]

Mary Walker saw firsthand the contrasting approach at Coffin Point. The Coffin people had decided it was better to work with Charles Ware than to oppose him—to present themselves as willing, loyal, and worthy workers. The plantation's men seem to have persuaded the women to back off their protest against the whipping of the young girl, perhaps on the grounds that their young manager would make amends by being even more accommodating. Events proved them right. When Coffin Point people planted corn between the rows of cotton, supervisor Ware decided that the amount didn't much exceed the allowance of slavery times, and let it go.[56] Of course, Mary Walker and Charles Ware both knew that he was being taken advantage of, albeit in more subtle ways than William Gannett. "Putting on Massa'" was the inevitable relationship between ruler and ruled on plantations. Yet so long as Ware could rant, have his grumble, and write mischief off as "amusing," he let go of his annoyances.[57] To Mary Walker, young Charley Ware's capacity to laugh at his circumstances was a saving grace—for him, for the people under him, and for her in the summer of 1864. Mirroring the temperament of her household, Mary Walker displayed an irreverence rarely exhibited to her previous employers, keeping "up her spirits well, amusing us with stories of Mrs. Lyman, and joking about every person & thing under the sun."[58]

The reality in the summer of 1864 was that Mary Walker was independent for the first time in her life. She traveled about the islands, taking buggies and skiffs and sailboats to visit reformers at other plantations. She walked at will through the quarters. She went to black baptisms and church services more demonstrative than any that she or the New Englanders had ever seen. In June, having installed Mary Walker as the housekeeper at Coffin Point, Harriet Ware left the Sea Islands to summer in New England. At last, Mary Walker was not "in service"—not at the hourly beck and call—of a white lady whom she was obliged to please. Perceptively, Harriet Ware guessed that her departure would allow Mary Walker to be less inhibited. "I dare say she comes out more now I am away."[59]

Mary Walker was not the only one to "come out." By far the freest spirit in the Coffin Point household was its islands-born young house-servant and cook, Rose, who joined with Mary Walker and Charles Ware in an afternoon of spontaneous parody that highlighted the hunger for humor in the midst of a faltering experiment. Bereft when Harriet Ware departed for the summer, Rose was angry that neither the brother nor Mary Walker seemed to lament her absence. "Mass' Charlie, no one *know* how I miss Miss Hayyut. If my own *mudder* go Nort',

I no miss her mo'."[60] The two women of color were together in the Coffin Point parlor in mid-August when a disgruntled Charles Ware returned from the field after a day of haggling with workers and decided to shake off his blues with banter. "What am I bid for me?" he suddenly asked. Rose was too startled to respond but Mary Walker immediately answered, "One dollar!" When Rose hesitated, Mary Walker upped her bid to "two dollars!" Rose caught on and joined in the blasphemous mock-auction. Acting as both slave and auctioneer, Ware "knocked myself down" to Rose for $5. Ware asked "what work I was to do." Rose didn't hesitate. *"Fetch wauter!"* In a flash, Ware turned the tables, and Rose's "slave" became her *ex*-slave. "I protested that I was sick, and could do no 'straining' work." She "asked with a tone of contempt what kind of work I *could* do?" Charles Ware leapt across the room to the piano bench. "Play the piano," which he "thumped till tea time."[61]

Not to be outspoofed, Rose turned to Mary Walker, whose manners as well as her complexion distanced her from Sea Islands blacks. Rose "held a bread bag before her, like a mantle," reported Charles Ware with much amusement. "See, Miss Waulker, I walk so. Airs & graces." Rose mimicked Mary Walker's parity with the bachelor missionaries of the household, her ability to jest with them, to talk with them about the constellations and planets of the nighttime sky—to regard them momentarily as friends and equals.[62]

UPLIFTING AS THE SEA ISLANDS were for Mary Walker's independence and her health, Charles Ware nonetheless reported that she was "almost sick of this country" and would "no doubt go home with us" at the summer's end.[63] Given that the Wares, Lesleys, and Philbricks were all family friends, the Coffin Point housekeeper could say little in her letters home about what had made her "sick of this country," or whether she thought their way or any way would genuinely free this generation of plantation people.

Mary Walker's actions had to speak her sentiments. She returned to Boston in early September 1864 aboard the schooner that brought Charles Ware and others home for a visit to their families. The Wares invited her to return with them in the fall. There were certainly good reasons to go. In New England, her familiar respiratory cough quickly reappeared, and by winter the cough became "more fearsome than ever." The warmer Sea Islands climate promised improvement for her health. Uncertain job prospects had met her when she returned to Cambridge. For the first time, the gifted Southern seamstress couldn't find work. People went with those who worked the fastest and cheapest, Susan Lesley's aunt reported. The housekeeping post at Coffin Point offered a steady salary. Nonetheless, in the fall of 1864, Mary Walker turned the Wares' offer down flat. Some time later, in a visit with Susan Lesley, her old friend asked Mary Walker point-blank whether she thought Edward Philbrick's experiment had worked for the good of the freedmen. Emphatically, Mary Walker answered: No.[64]

Having seen Reconstruction rehearsed in South Carolina, Mary Walker all the more fervently wanted her children with her in the North. In early 1865, she could do nothing but wait—wait for the Union army to free her family—and hope that liberators would find her mother and children alive and well and willing to leave the plantation South behind. Mary Walker moved into the Cambridge household of Anne Jean Lyman's sister, Catherine Robbins; in sickness and in health, the two women had looked after each other and Anne Jean Lyman for fifteen years. They impatiently followed the war news, first wondering if William Tecumseh Sherman's march through Georgia would ever reach the sea, and then realizing after his conquest of Savannah and Charleston that he had turned his army north toward Mary Walker's native state. In mid-March 1865, a teacher named Mary E. Rice, whom Mary Walker had known from her summer on the Sea Islands, came to visit Cambridge. This friend reported that although Mary Walker had "been kept in the house all winter with a severe cold," she was buoyant. "She is almost wild over the prospect of communication with Raleigh."[65] Once Raleigh was in Union hands, Mary Walker could finally write to her children herself.

She didn't have to write. Less than a month after her friend M. E. Rice visited Mary Walker in Cambridge, the civilian leaders of Raleigh surrendered their city to the advancing troops of Sherman's army. The occupation achieved, a high-ranking officer sought out Mary Walker's children. According to the Lesley family, the officer, a native of Maine, was General Oliver O. Howard—soon to become the head of the Freedman's Bureau. He found twenty-eight-year-old Agnes Walker and twenty-one-year-old Bryant Walker at the Duncan Cameron mansion in Raleigh.[66] He told them that they were free, that their mother was alive, and that she wanted them to come north. Agnes and Bryant wrote at once. Three months later, both arrived in Cambridge.

11 "To Part No More"

Mary Walker was "wild with joy over her son, who is a fine young fellow, good & affectionate & as rejoiced to find her, as she him. Her daughter with her husband will arrive the last of the week." So Catherine Robbins reported from Cambridge on July 3, 1865, the eve of the first Independence Day after slavery's end.[1] Surely echoing for Mary Walker was the refrain from the song sung in secret by her mother in olden days.

Their union shall be sweet
At their dear Redeemer's feet,
And they meet to part no more,
Who have loved, who have loved.

Mary Walker had lived to see the day—the reunion of her family, a new life for her children. How much of a new life was possible, her son would put to the test.

THE STORY OF THE WALKER family's reunion unfolds largely in the pages of Catherine Robbins's journal and through her letters to Susan Lesley. Catherine was in Philadelphia in April 1865 when she first learned that Mary Walker had heard from her children. "I know she must be in a terribly excited state and felt sorry not to be there."[2] Catherine had come to Philadelphia to be with her niece Susan, who was ill from another miscarriage and a bout with diphtheria. The journal-keeper's capacity for celebration was numbed by the jolting events of the month. First she and the Lesleys had rejoiced at the Northern victory at Appomattox, only to be shattered days later by the assassination of the president. "Why need it have been so?" she agonized in her journal. When the funeral train and Abraham Lincoln's coffin arrived for viewing at Independence Hall, she and her niece went to witness the melancholy nighttime scene, illuminated by the "weird light of torches" and accompanied by the doleful sound of muffled drums. The murder of the president overshadowed all the reports that followed—the death of the assassin, the final Confederate surrender in North Carolina, Mary Walker's news of her children. "None of these things affect us as they used to, & the impression of the great tragedy is still stronger than anything else."[3]

While Mary Walker waited in Cambridge for further word from the South, Catherine Robbins remained in Philadelphia with her ailing niece, where they both contemplated the Walker family's future in a solemn frame of mind. "I know that she will want to come on here very much & am sorry S. does not feel able to have her."[4] Apparently, Mary Walker had expressed a hope of returning to Philadelphia and going into service there for Susan Lesley. Whether this was a first preference or simply a possibility she wanted to explore isn't clear. By letter, she had kept up some Philadelphia connections, and may have seen advantages for herself and her children in its larger black community and in reattachment to the Lesleys. Whether or not Mary Walker actually asked Catherine Robbins to raise the question, Catherine did so, and for Susan Lesley the answer was no. Neither she nor her husband felt well. She was still recovering from the taxing pregnancy and stillbirth that had set her back physically and spiritually. Peter Lesley, strained by the demands of his work and the difficulty of sustaining an income during the war, had suffered a nervous breakdown in 1863, and despite a restorative trip abroad, "P's health . . . seems greatly undermined & his nervous tendency increased."[5] To be sure, the Lesleys did need the help of a domestic worker. But their memories of Mary Walker were splotched with recollections of her chronic consumption and periods in which her employer had to care for *her.* There could be no assurance that Mary Walker would ever again enjoy robust good health.

But worries over Mary Walker's future went deeper than health concerns. Both the Lesleys and Catherine Robbins had doubts that the relocation of her children to the North would be a cure-all. Peter Lesley had expressed reservations in 1859, at the very time he wrote the appeal to Mildred Cameron to let Mary Walker buy her own children. To his wife, he confessed that he was not sure what success would bring. If Mildred Cameron did release the children, then what? They would come north and need work. Who would provide it? Peter Lesley wondered if Mary Walker's Southern-born children were hardened enough to make it in the North. Susan Lesley and her aunt found their happiness for Mary Walker dampened by concern about her children's prospects. They could not "see at all how she will provide for her daughter or be able to keep her with her." Catherine Robbins, sensing that her own bleakness might make things harder for her friend, reflected: "Perhaps it is well that she should get through this without me."

THE LETTER THAT MARY WALKER had received from her children in mid-April had contained both welcome and painful news. Her children were well, but her mother, Silla, was dead—and this knowledge was "a great grief." Both the twenty-five-year-old Agnes and the twenty-one-year-old Bryant were married. Placing four adults, as well as finding work for herself, in uncertain and inflationary times would be no easy task. But in contrast to the fears of her friends, Mary Walker's response was determined and unhesitating. She wanted all to come north as soon as they could.

Then, for almost six weeks, there was only silence. Mary Walker wondered what had happened. Had they had a change of heart? Had their former owners stepped in, either to block their way or to entice them to stay? Had those they had married in slavery objected to moving north? Desperate in the face of silence, she and Catherine Robbins, who had returned in May from Philadelphia, sought out a man in nearby Newton who was going south, to see if he would detour to Raleigh and learn what was happening. They missed him. "It seems as if every effort failed, about that business," the diarist recorded on June 7. "No wonder she is depressed."[6]

Was there a chance the Walker children might have chosen to remain in Raleigh as paid domestic servants in the white household they had grown up in? The daughters of Duncan Cameron had kept the Walker children and their grandmother together, despite pressure from their brother Paul to sell off the family of fugitives as *"ungrateful pets."* The postwar white family still required servants to meet its needs—to cook and clean, cut wood and make fires, care for horses and drive coaches, and of course look after Mildred Cameron, who remained an invalid. A gardener was indispensable for keeping up the grounds of the Raleigh estate, whose elegance dazzled an Ohio soldier in May 1865 with its "ample yards and gardens, adorned with flowers and shrubbery."[7] Had Agnes and Bryant Walker wished to stay, they most certainly would have found Margaret Cameron Mordecai and her husband, George Mordecai, willing to pay them to remain.

It may well be that the silence Mary Walker encountered was occasioned by the need to work out the choices for four people, both her children and their spouses. What might freedom be like in Raleigh and in North Carolina if they stayed? What might it be like in the North if they left? Agnes and Bryant Walker were literate and could now freely read newspapers published in Raleigh after its occupation by Union troops. They may have been startled to see that debate persisted in the local press about whether the Emancipation Proclamation, and the Thirteenth Amendment passed by the wartime Congress, did in fact end bondage in the state. Raleigh editors thought so and said so, but they continued to publish letters and speeches by those who insisted that only each sovereign state had the right to abolish slavery. The Union military commander in Raleigh found it necessary to reiterate that Emancipation "is no longer an open Question."[8]

News about Northerners was mixed. There was plenty of local testimony about depredations by Union soldiers as they foraged around Raleigh, wantonly destroyed livestock, burned crops and barns, and assaulted black women and men. What kind of people *were* these Yankees? On the other hand, the Raleigh *Unionist Standard* published in full an address by Massachusetts abolitionist Wendell Phillips, which may have swayed the Walker children. Wendell Phillips argued that any reconstruction of the South that fell short of giving full voting rights to the freedmen would be worthless: black suffrage was the only thing that could guarantee "absolute equality with the white man." If Agnes, Bryant, and their spouses read the account, they surely would have noted that this advocate of "absolute equality with the white man" was addressing a supportive audience in Boston—the city to which their mother beckoned them.[9]

If Mary Walker's daughter and son did give thought to staying in service to the Mordecai and Cameron families, they would have been among the few to do so. Within weeks, most of the servants in both households had left their former mistresses and masters. A particularly dramatic parting revealed the fictions that had sustained servitude and the anger that Emancipation released. In the late 1850s, Paul and Anne Cameron had moved from their magnificent plantation dwelling at Fairntosh to a capacious mansion in the town of Hillsboro, fifteen miles away. There, they continued to have a dozen servants who looked after their home and grounds and attended the family during the Civil War. Just weeks after the war's end, words passed between the Camerons and their cook. She took off her apron, looked the Camerons' daughter Maggie in the eye, and said "her skin was nearly as white as hers—that her hair was nearly as straight—& that she was quite as free!"[10] Within days, the Hillsboro servants of all complexions had left. When Cameron sought replacements among the hundreds of former slaves who remained on the grounds at Fairntosh and at his other nearby plantation quarters, only one man volunteered. Cameron canvassed family and friends from Raleigh to Petersburg, Virginia, to see if he could find willing workers, black or white. Few came; none stayed. At the Mordecai-Cameron household in Raleigh, the ex-slaves likewise departed. Two months after the city's surrender, only a handful remained, out of a contingent of almost two dozen who had labored there in bondage.[11]

LETTERS FINALLY CAME IN mid-June reaffirming the children's intent to come north. Bryant arrived in Cambridge on June 28, 1865—the "event she has so long looked & hoped for, & despaired of." The son came alone; the bride he had wed in slavery had decided not to leave. Mary Walker was overcome with joy. Catherine Robbins found herself pleased with Bryant Walker's appearance and carriage. He was a "fine looking youth of one & twenty, seems intelligent & amiable & good in every way." She gave no description of him—nothing about whether he resembled his mother, nothing about his height or the color of his eyes and hair, nothing about whether his skin was dark or fair. She simply registered her delight that he seemed a thoroughly winning young man, and her astonishment—even though she had known Mary Walker for fifteen years—that he'd come through bondage so poised and skilled: if "slavery trains people to be as he appears, it does better than our institutions for his race."[12] Newspaper reports from the South prompted profound gratitude that Mary Walker's reunion was almost complete. President Andrew Johnson was beginning to appease white Southerners; Union soldiers were mistreating emancipated people; the fortunes of freedmen were plummeting. No wonder Catherine Robbins recorded on July 14 that the "event of the week" was the arrival—at last—of Agnes and her husband, James Burgwyn.[13]

The long-sought reunion of the Walker family overwhelmed Catherine Robbins as much as Mary Walker herself. "And now she has all the remnant of her family with her, a wonderful thing after so many years of separation, & leaving them children, to find them at this period matured persons, & so satisfactory & good as they appear to be. A great cause of thanksgiving indeed."[14]

SEVENTEEN YEARS AFTER Mary Walker had left her owners and her family, fifteen years after she had arrived in Massachusetts as a refugee, it was time to celebrate. Happily, Susan and Peter Lesley were on vacation in nearby Brookline, visiting friends and recuperating from illness and fatigue. On the afternoon of Monday, July 17, the Lesleys came to Cambridge. "We had a reunion of colored friends, Mary & all her family," recorded Catherine Robbins. Peter Lesley, whose once-expansive diary entries had atrophied to brief notations, wrote simply: "Drove Susan over to see Aunt Kitty. Mary Walker with her daughter Alice [*sic*] & her husband & Bryant Mary's son, were all there; have just arrived from Raleigh. Great enthusiasm."[15] Neither chronicler described Mary Walker's appearance, nor that of the two young people whom all had labored to rescue in slavery days. They made no mention of songs, toasts, thanks, or testimonials; nor did either diarist elaborate a list of the people there. The one named guest of color was Anne Reason, who had also cared for Anne Jean Lyman in the early 1850s and whom Mary Walker had seen through perilous pregnancies and hard times in the years since. And Lewis Hayden—the great black leader of the Boston Vigilance Committee who had led daring rescue efforts of captured fugitives and who had met with the Philadelphia carpenter commissioned to rescue Mary Walker's children in 1854—was he there for the occasion? Did the guests include Phillis Gault, Mary Walker's friend and fellow fugitive, the two of them both aided by the same Underground Railroad friends in Philadelphia and Boston? Did her "colored friends" embrace some of the fourteen Cambridge fugitive slaves who had come together at the invitation of Susan Hillard the previous November, to celebrate the nation's first Thanksgiving Day at her Boston home?[16]

If the forty-seven-year-old Mary Walker could have summoned all those who over the years had supported the quest for her children, the room would have been crowded: Lewis Hayden, Frederick Douglass, Harriet Beecher Stowe, and General Oliver O. Howard; the Garden Street household of Anne Jean Lyman, including housekeeper Mary Cashman and family friend Chauncey Wright; minister William Pryor of the Old Cambridge Baptist Church; Irish domestic servants in Milton and Cambridge who had become treasured friends; Philadelphia allies with whom she had kept up over time and distance; even James Price, the would-be rescuer thwarted in Raleigh. Catherine Robbins captured the miracle of the moment when she confided to her journal that the gathering, though "most fitting and natural," was "a thing I hardly expected ever to see."[17]

"It is a wonderful thing for her. I hope she will [realize] the blessing and be wise in her management." With that mixture of hope and anxiety for Mary Walker, Catherine Robbins left Cambridge for the summer of 1865 to journey for two months through the mountains of northern New England. Mary Walker managed well. Word of the family's progress came in a remarkable letter from Agnes Walker Burgwyn to none other than her former owner, Margaret Cameron Mordecai. "I have often thought of sending a letter to you," Agnes wrote in October 1865, "as you were kind enough to wish to hear from me." Her mother had found lodging for the family that summer, and "We are now all living together at housekeeping, very happily." Her mother, during her years in Cambridge, had acquired a large circle of friends—as a skilled dressmaker, as a devoted caregiver, as a faithful churchgoer, as a lady of genteel bearing. Those friends now helped to find employment for her family. "My mother does work as a Seamstress in different families, & gets work for me when I am able to do it. She has many friends here, & more work than she can do." Bryant, who had tended the beautiful grounds of the Cameron estate in Raleigh, obtained a job at Harvard "in the College Garden." James Burgwyn, who had mastered carpentry as a bondsman, found "constant work at his trade."[18]

The migrants had more than just their mother's connections to ease their way into Mary Walker's Cambridge world. They each came able to read and write. Favored within the families that had enslaved them, they also came with life-long experience in the diplomacy of dealing with white folks. That deftness was evident in Agnes Burgwyn's letter to her former owner. Like her mother and grandmother, Agnes knew how to comport herself in a manner that was refined and correct. After giving news of their move to the North, she added a request. "I want to ask the favor of Mr. Mordecai to go to my Minister, Mr. Pell, & ask him to send me a letter of recommendation to a Methodist church here. I have not joined any, & am desirous to have a letter from my minister to show, before I do so." She had so far attended the "flourishing Baptist Church here, of which my mother is a member." But "I would like to get a letter to the Methodist." Agnes Walker Burgwyn planned to start off properly in a church of her own denomination. She closed her letter with the wish "to know how all my friends are, particularly Miss Mildred. Please remember me kindly to her. Please give my love to all my friends & companions who may inquire for me." Despite her literacy, handwriting did not come easily, so she gave the letter to an amanuensis, who prepared the final draft in elegant script. Discreet in form and content, everything about the letter conveyed

Agnes Burgwyn's wish to cultivate connections—with those she'd left behind, as well as with new friends in Cambridge.[19]

THOUGH MARY WALKER REGULARLY found "work as a Seamstress in different families" and had "more work than she could do," one of her many friends, Mary Stearns, had not forgotten her feats as a caregiver. In the summer of 1866, she sought Mary Walker's help on behalf of Wendell Phillips, the renowned abolitionist.

Mary Stearns was an enthusiast. She had rightfully earned a place as the zealous helpmeet of her husband, industrialist George Stearns, and of their friends among Boston's antislavery leaders. She and George had repeatedly welcomed the most radical of those leaders, Wendell Phillips and William Lloyd Garrison, to the Stearns mansion in Medford, "The Evergreens." She had wholeheartedly endorsed her husband's financial backing of John Brown, and, after Brown's execution, George's fundraising to support Brown's widow. Mary Stearns had cheered her husband when he dedicated himself and their fortune to the cause of raising black regiments for battle in the Civil War. She had met Mary Walker several times. The Stearnses had visited Anne Jean Lyman in Cambridge in the 1850s; when Susan Lesley hoped Agnes Walker might be ransomed, she had taken Mary Walker to Medford to see if the Stearnses would be good employers for her daughter.

Mary Stearns liked to do good works, and the good she had in mind in early June 1866 was to find a caregiver to look after Wendell Phillips's long-incapacitated wife, Ann Terry Greene Phillips, when the couple left Boston for their summer vacation at the shore. Mary Stearns had arranged for her own servant Vesta to accompany the Phillips family for the summer, when Vesta backed out to get married. Only half in jest, Stearns apologized to her friend Wendell Phillips, the "dear confiding, long suffering friend of humanity and woman rights in particular," for engendering in "your trusting heart that there should be a girl, a servant girl, that had the remotest idea in her damned little head of ever keeping her d. word." "O Lord, what's the use of being a Reformer, trying to make these creatures better? I'm going to give it all up—sail for Europe—turn Conservative, and Aristocrat, and believe in the divine right of Kings, and enjoy myself generally. There!"[20]

The next morning, exasperation and the urge to escape gave way to a better idea. "Almost the first thought that daylight brought to my mind was 'Why not try for Mary Walker?' You know the handsome *white* African, who took care of *unfortunate* Mrs. Lyman, so many years!" Always candid to a fault, Mary Stearns herself brought up the issue of color: Might there be objections from other vacationers at the seashore? "As for her *Race,* nobody but the *right minded* would ever know that she was not 'just as good as white folks.' So there could be no hitch about *color.*" Mary Stearns decided to give it a try. After breakfast, she "took the carriage and drove to Cambridge. Found Mary, told her I wanted her to go with Mrs. Phillips to the seashore. She liked the proposition," and promised to meet Wendell Phillips the next Saturday to talk it over. There *was* a "hitch." The "house they [the Walkers] now occupy is sold over her head, and this week is to be taken hunting a home for them. Hence the delay in seeing you. She *knows* how to do every thing you mentioned and a good deal more beside. Is a perfect lady in Manners. Kind, and considerate. Worships *you,* as the sleepless friend of her Race—*both* of them—for we must claim relationships. So much for this string to your bow."[21]

It's not known whether Mary Walker went to the seashore with the famed abolitionist and his wife in June 1866, or whether the search for new Cambridge lodgings for her mixed-race family was so time-consuming that she was unable to oblige "the sleepless friend of her Race." What is clear is that Mary Walker still considered herself a person of color, even though others perceived her as a "*white* African." Mary Stearns, with characteristic forthrightness, gave voice to the duality of identities that she thought Mary Walker was entitled to claim, and that Mary Stearns—as a woman of privilege—would clearly have expressed in her stead: "her race—*both* of them—for we must claim relationships." Neither Mary Walker nor her daughter ever made that claim.

Bryant Walker did.

BRYANT WALKER WAS EAGER to break free of the limits on life he'd known in the South. By the summer of 1866, he'd obtained work as a coachman, perhaps to supplement his work as a gardener, perhaps in lieu of it.[22] Most likely driving for others (given the cost of a coach and horse), he ventured into a more mobile and remunerative job than gardening. Northern coachmen were an independent lot. Brusque, expensive, not above a trick or two, they were far different from the liveried servants of the South. If Bryant Walker brought even a touch of Southern deference and a splash of his great-uncle Luke's skill with horses to his Boston coachman's role, he would please, assuming he could master the crazy-quilt topography of the city. For the twenty-two-year-old migrant from Raleigh, a position as coachman was a promising start toward life in a wider world.

His job gave him mobility, and somewhere in his travels he met a woman from Ireland named Annie Gorey. Born around 1837, Annie, along with her parents, Edward and Catherine Gorey, had migrated from Ireland in 1860. The census of that year listed two Annie Goreys. One was a textile-mill worker in Lowell, Massachusetts, who labored alongside a Catherine Gorey, presumably her sister. Both lived in a factory dormitory with other young women workers. The other was an Ann Gorey living in Boston, employed as a domestic servant. It's not clear where or when the twenty-two-year-old Bryant Walker met the twenty-nine-year-old immigrant from County Kildare. What is clear is that they became lovers, and that by the summer of 1866 she was pregnant with their child. On July 23, 1866, Bryant Walker and Annie Gorey were married by a justice of the peace in Lynn, Massachusetts, home of the bride's parents.[23]

Cambridge had never been a site for the sporadic strife among Irish Catholics, black Americans, and native-born Protestants that had marked Boston and other Northern cities. Harvard librarian and diarist James Sibley, guardian of the college's gentility, took a dim view of the fact that immigration and high birthrates would inevitably make Irish of humble origins the majority in Cambridge. From the perspective of the Emerald Isle, it appeared to Daniel O'Connell—the great Irish liberation leader of the 1820s and 1830s—that there should be grounds for an alliance between the American Irish struggling for acceptance and American blacks struggling for freedom. But most of his countrymen in America rejected his call. Competing with African Americans for jobs, neighborhoods, status, and sometimes women, and suffering from comparisons which depicted the Irish as racially akin to blacks, most Irishmen rejected both alliance and comparison. In the words of historian Noel Ignatiev, the Irish in America took every step they could to "become white."[24] When Civil War conscriptions in July 1863 obliged Irishmen as well as native-born Americans to serve in an army now fighting for slave-emancipation, brutal draft riots pitting Irish against blacks broke out in New York City and on a smaller scale in Boston.

Such hostilities did not prevail everywhere. When Mary Walker came north, she was free of Yankee assumptions about the Irish; two Irish domestic servants would become her closest friends. Bryant Walker, too, arrived in the North bearing no animosity toward the Irish. Annie Gorey, had she grown up as an Irish-American woman in the United States, might well have looked askance at people of color. But she had lived twenty years in Ireland before emigrating in 1860. She could make up her own mind. When the two immigrants met in 1866, they were both from places they were happy to leave behind. Well into her twenties, Annie Gorey, still a single woman, was looking at the possibility of lifelong employment as a domestic or a factory worker. The handsome young coachman from the South, whose carriage and bearing so impressed Catherine Robbins, was also starting a new life in a new world. Bryant and Annie were not alone. In Boston, by the 1870s, fully 38 percent of all men designated as "mulatto" by the federal census had married women designated as "white."[25] In becoming lovers and then marrying, the two descendants of different pasts were among many who were gambling that they could advance beyond histories which had heretofore dictated that Irish and people of color must be adversaries in America.

Could Bryant and Annie Walker and their children forge identities that transcended the rules of the past? Mary Walker, for her part, was not sanguine. As always, she confided her doubts to Catherine Robbins. The marriage was a "misalliance."[26] The Irish domestics that Mary Walker had esteemed in the 1850s, Mary Cashman and Mary Moore, were educated, refined, and devoted. Neither had worked in a factory. The sixty-six-year-old Catherine Robbins, always circumspect when it came to sexual matters, did not record whether Mary Walker objected to her daughter-in-law's background, religion, or color, or to the circumstances of the marriage. Whatever the reasons, Bryant's choice left her heartsick.

The marriage may have created new difficulties for keeping the family in one household. In October 1866, Catherine Robbins reported that Mary Walker again was on the lookout for lodgings—for "some of her family." Temporarily, Mary Walker had to move back into the dwelling with Catherine Robbins on Garden Street.[27] Had tensions over the marriage erupted between Bryant Walker and the Burgwyns? Had their Cambridge landlord decided he didn't want a pregnant Irishwoman and her mixed-race husband on his property? When family members found new housing, they split up.

In most ways, the new quarters that Bryant Walker found for himself and his wife could not have been better. He became the gardener on the extensive grounds of the Cambridge house of proofreader John Owen, and lived in Owen's home just a block and a half off of Brattle

Square.[28] An 1827 graduate of Bowdoin College, John Owen had become the publisher of the poems of a young Bowdoin professor named Henry Wadsworth Longfellow, who had moved to Cambridge in the 1830s. When Owen's publishing house failed in 1846, he became a full-time proofreader, and continued in that role for Longfellow, whose literary fame and marriage to heiress Fanny Appleton enabled the poet to acquire the most magnificent residence on Brattle Street, George Washington's headquarters during the American Revolution. John Owen became, as well, a lifelong admirer of Charles Sumner, the outspoken Republican senator from Massachusetts, for whom he likewise worked as a proofreader. Sumner, before his election to the Senate in 1851, had been a vocal supporter of people of color in Boston, and he continued to be their advocate for the rest of his life. Owen was as passionate as Charles Sumner on the subject of the "Equal Rights of All." He filled his house with books which reflected his convictions, and he expressed his beliefs vigorously, at home and in encounters with Longfellow on Brattle Street. Probably no landlord in Cambridge could have made Bryant and Annie Walker—and the future they were trying to forge—feel more accepted.[29]

Mary Walker's first grandchild was born on February 22, 1867. The names that the parents gave to their new son, and to the children that followed, suggested that they saw their family as a hybrid—connected with their Irish and African-American lineages, and linked as well to the emancipators who had made their union possible. They named their first child Edward, after Annie Gorey's father, and perhaps after Bryant's brother Edward, who died when he was eight and Bryant was four; their second child Frederick, after Bryant Walker's father; their third child John. The children who came later were named Carrie, after Annie Gorey's mother, Catherine; Mary Agnes, after Bryant's mother, Mary, and his sister, Agnes; Hannah Frances, after Bryant's brother Frank; and James, after Bryant's brother-in-law, James Burgwyn. But it was the *middle* names of the first three children that suggested the association the couple felt with the great liberators of their day. Edward Walker was Edward *Lincoln* Walker. Frederick Walker was Frederick *Gray* Walker, after antislavery lawyer Ellis Gray Loring, who had assembled documents in 1850 to protect Mary Walker from recapture. John Walker was *John Andrew* Walker, named for the wartime governor of Massachusetts, who had been the first governor in the country to call for black troops to fight in the Civil War, and who had commissioned the Fifty-Fourth Massachusetts Colored Regiment that had so distinguished itself at the battle of Fort Wagner in July 1863.[30] These children of freedom had many forebears, and their parents wanted them to know it.

Mary Walker had seen newly emancipated folk test the frontiers of freedom on the Sea Islands in 1864. Now it was her son in the North who was pushing the boundaries. She did all she could to help look after her infant grandchildren, especially when they were sick. But apprehension marked her outlook for their future. The people of the Sea Islands had also been optimistic at the outset of freedom, only to find that they and their liberators soon parted company. What reason was there to think that her son and grandchildren would achieve the aspirations that their names pointed toward?

In fact, Bryant Walker was not alone in thinking that he lived in a time and place where he might script a future different from the past. Unbeknownst to Mary Walker when she was on the Sea Islands in 1864, a similar choice was considered by Charlotte Forten, the young mixed-race woman who had also come from Massachusetts to help the South Carolina freedmen. Living and working with white teachers, the twenty-six-year-old Charlotte had found herself attracted to several of the male reformers. She tried to stifle her feelings. "I like Mr. T."—David Thorpe, a Brown University student and plantation supervisor. "Report says that he more than likes me. But I know it is not so. . . . Although he is very good and liberal he is still an American, and w'd of course never be so insane as to love one of the prescribed [i.e., proscribed] race."[31] Caught between desire and doubt, she ceased writing in her journal. But secretly she became engaged to Charles F. Williams, "a thoroughly good abolitionist . . . very intelligent, gentlemanly and pleasant." The couple planned a marriage in Boston in 1865—or so Charlotte thought. In fact, Charles Williams never revealed the engagement to his well-to-do antislavery parents. When they learned of the plans, Charles's father begged her to wait, writing that he and his wife feared their son was too weak to withstand the difficulties that would follow crossing the color line in marriage.[32] Charlotte Forten ended the engagement, and thirteen years later married the Reverend Francis Grimke, the mixed-race son of a Charleston planter and the nephew of Sarah and Angelina Grimke, the planter's sisters, who had moved north and become the nation's leading female abolitionists in the 1830s.

Other New Englanders of the 1860s also imagined a future in which marriage offered a path beyond racial divides. The leading advocate of this view was none other than antislavery writer Lydia Maria Child—the old sparring partner of Anne Jean Lyman from their Northampton days together, the lifelong correspondent of Susan and Peter Lesley, and the editor who had helped with the publication of Harriet Jacobs's *Incidents in the Life of a Slave Girl.* In 1867, Child wrote and published *A Romance of the Republic,* a novel which plotted the marriage of two fair-skinned mixed-race women to two white men—and which ended happily for all. Earlier writings, including her own, had portrayed such liaisons as destined for heartbreak, especially for "the tragic mulatto." In the postwar world, Child visualized the creation of new identities and even national reconciliation through marriage and miscegenation. Her imagined ending was characteristic of reformers in the Age of Emancipation. People of color would move toward white skin, embrace white civilization, and thereby assimilate and ascend. Child neither doomed mixed-race unions, as had her predecessors, nor condemned them, as would writers later in the century, who viewed them either as desecrations of white purity or as betrayals of black solidarity.[33] In 1867, Maria Child and Bryant Walker sensed the same currents of possibility.

To Maria Child's vision, the response came quickly. Almost no readers embraced her book. When she sent *A Romance of the Republic* to the mother of Robert Gould Shaw, the martyred young colonel who had led the Massachusetts Fifty-Fourth Colored Regiment and had died at Fort Wagner, the response was curt: "very clever." Another acquaintance wrote forthrightly, "I don't like the subject." From others, silence. The "apathy of my friends took all the life out of me," Maria Child confessed.[34] She never wrote another novel.

Would Bryant Walker's children be able to "claim relationships"—to draw on all their heritages to navigate their future? The answer remained uncertain. Mary Walker and Annie Gorey Walker stepped in to ensure that the generation born in Cambridge would have choices about the course of their lives.

BRYANT AND ANNIE WALKER MADE no decision about the religion of their first child, Edward. But after the birth of their second son, Frederick Gray Walker, exactly a year later, he and Edward were baptized together at Saint Mary of the Annunciation, a small Catholic church near Central Square in Cambridge. Thereafter, all of the Walker children followed the faith of their mother.[35]

Catholicism was the faith that had sustained Annie Gorey and her family through their trials in the County Kildare of her upbringing—seven years of famine, from 1845 to 1852, and before that years of occupation by British soldiers and rule by British landlords.[36] Through it all, the family had stood by the Catholic Church, and the Church by them. Annie Gorey Walker may have felt that her children would need no less of a bastion in America, and that for them, as for her, the Church would prove a sanctuary and a source of strength. For the baptism of her first two children, she chose the Catholic congregation that was the smallest and the most distant from their lodging off Brattle

Street. Did she wish to avoid questions—questions about their father's background—from persons living closer to the family's home? In fact, the Catholic hierarchy of New England after 1865 was sending a clear message to followers: religion overrode racial heritage. Whether priest or parishioner, an individual baptized and brought up Catholic was a Catholic first.[37] The next two Walker children were christened at Saint Peter's Church, just a few blocks west of the family's dwelling. Not only was Annie Walker's church now closer; so were her friends. Those who signed as sponsors of the baptized Walker infants—and thereby agreed to become their godparents—were Catholics who lived nearby. The Walker children's hybrid of heritages now included the Cambridge Catholic community.

Meanwhile, Mary Walker focused on securing more work for her son-in-law and her son. James Burgwyn had come north as a carpenter trained in bondage. His skill was such that even in Cambridge, with more than three dozen white carpenters listed in the classified section of the City Directory, he promptly found "constant work at his trade." But it became clear that James Burgwyn had arrived with talents and ambitions beyond carpentry. He was one of the few enslaved servants brought to Raleigh by the Burgwyn family of eastern North Carolina in 1863, when it fled its 4,000-acre plantation to avoid marauding Union troops.[38] There had been no need to bring a carpenter to a rented dwelling in Raleigh. More likely, he had come as the personal servant of the patriarch of the family, John Fanning Burgwyn, who at the time was eighty and in poor health. Born in 1783 in Britain, where his American father had pursued the export-import trade, John Fanning Burgwyn had lived in Britain until he was eighteen, when he came to America and doubled the family fortune through his work as a merchant, landowner, and planter—and through marriage to one of North Carolina's wealthiest heiresses.[39] He was a widower with two children at the time of James Burgwyn's birth in the early 1840s. To the census-taker of 1880, who asked not only each person's race but the birthplace of his or her parents, James Burgwyn responded that his race was "mulatto," his mother had been born in North Carolina—and his father had been born in Britain.[40]

American and British, black and white, carpenter and valet, James Burgwyn would find in the Anglophile professors and students of Harvard a natural clientele. Entrée to that clientele was almost certainly provided by Mary Walker. Her fifteen years in Cambridge had led to acquaintanceships with numerous Harvard professors and students. It was easy for Mary Walker to recommend her able son-in-law for work of all types. As needed, James Burgwyn served his patrons as a handyman, valet, or steward. A photograph taken of "Jim Burgwyn" in the 1870s shows a man of poise and confidence, who clearly thrived in his roles.[41]

Mary Walker used her connections as well to find a second job for her son Bryant. By the spring of 1869, Annie Gorey Walker had given birth to two children in two years, and a third was on its way. For help, Mary Walker turned to Tracy Howe, a member of the family she had known since coming to Cambridge in 1853 to care for the Howes' aunt, Anne Jean Lyman. The Howes and their younger aunt, Catherine Robbins, were members of the First Parish Church in Cambridge. Founded in 1636, the year that Harvard had been established, and located just across the street from the college and only a few doors from the clustered residences of the Howe family, First Parish had become a Unitarian Fellowship by 1830. In 1869, the church needed a new sexton. A sexton was a caretaker who lived near his church; his role was to be available at all times as needed by its members. He held down that job in addition to his regular work: Cambridge sextons were clerks, undertakers, custodians, and gardeners. No doubt the job was a plum, both respectable and remunerative. Tracy Howe, treasurer of the First Parish Church, proposed Bryant Walker for sexton, and in mid-May the Parish Committee—of which Howe was a member—appointed Bryant Walker "Sexton with a salary of Two hundred Dollars per annum dat-ing from Jan 1 '69." Tracy Howe was named to "superintend the Sexton's duties."[42] There is no indication that the Unitarians had raised qualms about Bryant Walker's color or his children's Catholicism. He was Mary Walker's son, handsome, able, winning in his ways; he kept proofreader John Owen's landscape pleasing to behold; the church treasurer vouched for him.

In their different ways, Mary Walker and Annie Gorey Walker had found anchors for the family.

DESPITE THE WALKER FAMILY'S achievements by 1870, uncertainties clouded the future. Bryant Walker's employer, John Owen, was living on a shoestring of intermittent commissions from the celebrated Bostonians who employed him as their proofreader; his life was increasingly in disarray. Soon his two daughters were trying to force the sale of his home; the dwelling fell into such disrepair that when it rained he "literally sleeps—or tries to sleep, with a bathing tub and an umbrella on his bed."[43] Mary Walker lived just a few blocks away, with the childless Burgwyns. On visits to her grandchildren, it surely became evident that her son and his wife would soon have to move again. Next time, they might not be lucky enough to find a landlord who believed in the "Equal Rights of All," especially one near enough the First Parish Church to allow Bryant Walker to continue as sexton. As for Mary Walker herself, she and Agnes and James Burgwyn rented adequate housing at School Court (now Farwell Place), a one-block street perpendicular to Brattle Street. Mary Walker lived no more than two blocks from the homes of Cambridge friends she had known and served since 1853: Anne Jean Lyman, Catherine Robbins, and the Howes. Nonetheless, she knew that her children and grandchildren were vulnerable. Twice in the 1860s the mixed-race families had been compelled to find new lodgings. What was to keep that from happening again, perhaps forcing them away from the people and places that consistently employed them?

In the spring of 1870, fortune smiled on Mary Walker. A house on Brattle Street came up for sale. Mary Walker would have been among the first to know, since the house was directly opposite the School Court dwelling in which she lived with her daughter and son-in-law. She had savings, but hardly enough to purchase a $4,500 home. Even if she could muster a down payment, would that persuade a real estate agent or Cambridge banker to sell a Brattle Street house—three blocks from the mansion of Henry Wadsworth Longfellow—to a woman of color? What Mary Walker did have on her side, yet again, was the family she had served, in sickness and in health, for twenty years. James Murray Howe and Estes Howe were the sons of Sarah Robbins Howe, whom Mary Walker had nursed in the spring of 1862, during Sarah's last months of life. Half-brothers of Tracy Howe, they were also nephews of Anne Jean Lyman, whom Mary Walker had steadfastly cared for during Mrs. Lyman's painful declining years. Both men were living in Cambridge in 1870; James was a successful Boston broker, and Estes was the treasurer of the Cambridge Gas Light Company. Mary Walker may have needed to say no more to the Howes than that a home of her own would bring long-sought security to her family and ease her anxieties about their future. She surely promised to pay them, over time. They may have replied that, in many ways, she already had. They would set no timetable.

On the first day of June 1870, James Murray Howe purchased a dwelling at 54 Brattle Street from Annie Louise Pratt Smith of Northampton, Massachusetts, and her husband, George Smith. The next day, James Murray Howe deeded ownership of the house to Mary Walker.[44] At last she might hope that those "who have loved, who have loved," could dwell in security, "to part no more."

THE HOUSE ON BRATTLE STREET that became the property of Mary Walker was a conditional acquisition. On June 1, James Murray

Howe paid $4,500 for the dwelling: $2,000 in cash and $2,500 through a mortgage with the Cambridge Savings Bank. The next day, he deeded the property to Mary Walker—provisionally. But the proviso bound *him,* not Mary Walker.

In the legalistic language of the deed, Howe bound himself and his heirs to hold "said real estate" for "the following uses, purposes, and trusts," and "for no other interests, uses, purposes, or object or right whatsoever": "To permit Mrs. Mary Walker" and her family to occupy and hold the dwelling "whenever and so long as she or they may choose free from any charge." She and her family could sell the residence "whenever and at such price as she or they may request"; they could "lease the same always paying all sums received as purchase money or rent to her or them." If the house was sold by Mary Walker or her heirs, the Howes were to be reimbursed for the interest they had paid on the $2,500 mortgage. Otherwise, James Murray Howe reiterated in the deed, he had "no interest in said real estate except as such Trustee."[45]

This remarkable arrangement secured for Mary Walker a no less remarkable house. Number 54 Brattle Street was a two-story wooden structure with enough rooms to accommodate all of her family. It was set perpendicular to Brattle Street, rather than fronting on it. Mary Walker, along with Agnes and James Burgwyn, dwelt in the half of the house closest to the street. Bryant and Annie Walker resided in the rear half of the dwelling with their three young sons, ages one, two, and three—and with their new daughter, Mary Agnes, born in August 1870.[46] Plain on the outside and worn on the inside, 54 Brattle Street was nonetheless no ordinary Cambridge house. Its former owner, Annie Louise Pratt Smith, had grown up there and was the daughter of Dexter Pratt—the village blacksmith of Cambridge. Adjacent to the house had stood his blacksmith's shop, and in front of the house and shop was a towering chestnut tree. Three blocks up on Brattle Street lived Henry Wadsworth Longfellow. It was on one of his walks down Brattle that Longfellow was inspired to compose the poem that would immortalize the owner of the house now belonging to Mary Walker.

Under a spreading chestnut tree,
  The village smithy stands;
The smith, a mighty man is he,
  With large and sinewy hands;
. . . . .
His hair is crisp, and black, and long,
  His face is like the tan;
His brow is wet with honest sweat,
  He earns whate'er he can,
And looks the whole world in the face,
  For he owes not any man.

By the time the Walkers moved in, Dexter Pratt had died and his shop was no more. But the "spreading chestnut tree" survived until 1876, and the village blacksmith's house—the Dexter Pratt family house from 1827 to 1858 and the Walker family home from 1870 to 1912—remains to this day a historic landmark.[47] Though surrounded now by urban Cambridge, the house, in the Walkers' time, nestled among residences occupied by a mix of working people, students and professors, and families that took in lodgers to make ends meet. Perhaps every other family had a servant girl, usually an unmarried young woman who had migrated from Ireland or Nova Scotia. Besides the Walkers, few residents of Brattle Street were people of color. Most African Americans lived a mile or more east of the Walkers, concentrated in Cambridgeport and living near Central Square.

For more than a year, all went well for the Brattle Street residents. Mary Walker continued her work as a seamstress and dressmaker, usually going to the homes of her patrons to fit their garments, though the needlework took a toll on her eyesight. Always she stood ready to look after Catherine Robbins, her friend of twenty years, whose fearful illness the year before had kept Mary Walker at her bedside for more than a week.[48] When another longtime Cambridge friend, Chauncey Wright, sprained his ankle, Mary Walker "came to the rescue," and saw the now-corpulent Harvard mathematics instructor through to recovery. At home, she showered a grandmother's care on her four young grandchildren, who traded ailments with one another and with her in the process.[49] Meanwhile, son-in-law James Burgwyn kept at his carpentry, finding work through all but the coldest months of winter, and otherwise burnished his skills as a steward for Harvard students. Bryant held down his two jobs, gardening for John Owen and others during the week and tending to his sexton's duties on Sunday. After the day's work, in the privacy of their home, Mary Walker surely shared some of the stories that had so amused her friends on the Sea Islands in 1864, and lightened the evenings with spicy new tales as well.

Then something happened.

NO DOUBT THE HOWE FAMILY and Mary Walker herself had considered it a boon when Bryant was hired in January 1869 for $200 a year as the sexton of the First Parish Church, the oldest house of worship in Cambridge. The responsibilities of the sexton were second only to the minister's, so much so that in Cambridge city directories, the sexton's name was listed immediately after the pastor's—along with the home addresses of both. If anything went wrong, church members knew immediately where to find one man or the other.

Just how responsible the sexton's role was came out in a discussion in the *Cambridge Chronicle* in May 1865, a month before Bryant arrived in the North. An anonymous letter to the editor, expounding on the "Duty of Sextons," declared that the sexton was "next to the minister in begetting and sustaining the interest of a congregation," and itemized the demands of the job. He should be "a man of taste, neat in his personal appearance and winning in his manners." His duty should be to sweep the house of God, certainly once a week—on Saturday and not on Sunday morning, as many do. He should keep the church well ventilated, dust from top to bottom in every hole and corner. "Not a pew, or seat, or rail should be neglected." Ensuring warmth and light in the church, before services, was his responsibility. Who can enjoy church "if the house be dark, or cold or overheated?" If the temperature needed changing during the service, the sexton should do so in a "manner as not to disturb an eye or an ear in the congregation." He was not to permit persons to "stand round the doors or in the entry talking, laughing, eyeing and making remarks upon those that are passing." If a boy or girl got boisterous in church, the sexton should restore order with a "nod, a look, a wink"—not "with loud rapping against a pew door or the church floor." When strangers came into the house of the Lord, a sexton must discreetly know where to place them—never in the reserved pews, even if vacant. "People that own or hire pews wish to control them." Finally, "a sexton should always be willing to be instructed in things pertaining to his office, *without taking offence.*" The letter-writer signed himself "An Humble Worshipper."[50]

Bryant Walker may have wondered, as did a reader of the newspaper in a letter to the editor two weeks after the "Duty of Sextons" appeared, just what kind of person "would come up to his standard of what a sexton should be?" "I fear it would be a long search" to find such a person, "if confined to mortals on earth." If the idealized sexton had "only this one individual to please, he might by giving his *whole* time and attention" perform his duties well. But how could he pacify "several hundred different persons"? Temperature control highlighted the hopelessness of asking a sexton to please everyone at once. "If the sexton lowers a window to cool an overheated churchman, he 'meets with rebuke' from another." Regarding the discreet placement of visitors in a way that didn't upset owners of pews with empty spaces, the writer wondered how the sexton could achieve such discretion and still seat eighteen to twenty strangers likely to turn up each Sabbath. As for the sexton's duty to receive criticism *"without taking offense,"* there was the more fundamental issue of how the congregation treated the sexton in the first place. Paying him "MONEY" was a start, but only a start. There was the further matter of respect. The sexton "should be treated as a gentleman" if parishioners expected him to act as one. Too often the treatment was just the opposite. *"[B]ecause he is a sexton,"* persons regarded "him as the one for every body to vent their displeasure upon, or talk to, or treat him, as they choose." If anything like the perfect sexton could be found, the responder concluded, "he would be worth considerably more than the paltry sum of two or three hundred dollars—which is now given."[51]

As Catherine Robbins was returning from worship at the First Parish Church on the second Sunday of January 1872, she stopped by to visit Mary Walker at her Brattle Street residence. There, as the church bell tolled, she found Bryant in the house. He had lost his job as sexton. Drinking was the cause of his dismissal. Drink had undermined the conduct expected of the First Parish sexton—deference to church members, diligence as church custodian, punctuality in opening the church and in ringing the bell. Catherine Robbins found Mary Walker and the Brattle household enveloped in gloom. As Agnes said to Catherine, "nobody could tell how dreadfully they felt when they heard the Church bell ring & Bryant moping at home."[52] As the bell tolled, Catherine Robbins must have realized that it was her nephew Tracy Howe —the First Parish treasurer who had persuaded the church to employ Bryant Walker in 1869 and was made his supervisor—who had discharged Mary Walker's son.

What drove Bryant Walker to drink? One can only speculate. It is certainly possible that he took liquor as one of his prerogatives as a free man, just like many other free men who frequented the dozens of saloons that flourished in Cambridge. Perhaps household tensions led him to take to the bottle: four children in four years; a dapper brother-in-law who so easily charmed the Harvard crowd with his ways as a valet. One can only guess at the goads. Like thousands of others who began with a drink now and then, he could not have foreseen that he would become an alcoholic, and that he would shame his mother and family by incurring not only loss of salary but "loss of standing, as everybody knew the cause."[53]

Still, it seems worthwhile to consider whether his turn to liquor was rooted in the demands of the sexton's job. Had one too many persons vented "their displeasure" upon him or talked to him "as they chose"? Had someone said, "Bryant, you're just a servant here, just a guest in our church and our city, just a man of color who'd best mind his place"? In the South he might have been defiant, as was the ex-slave who quit the Camerons' service in 1865 with the declaration that her skin was nearly as white as theirs and "that she was quite as free!" But defiance was complicated in Cambridge, for he surely knew he'd gotten the job in part as a favor—to his mother, to his "race," to the cause of black freedom. To whom could he protest? Even his mother's friend Peter Lesley confessed impatience in 1871 with the increasing assertiveness by blacks in the North, whom the one-time abolitionist now labeled "our querulous northern tribe."[54] The migrant from North Carolina, who had named his Cambridge sons after emancipators, may have discovered by 1871 that self-assertion was "querulous." Drink might have allowed him to blot out—or act out—what couldn't be spoken.

MARY WALKER HAD DEALT with descent before. She had cared for her employer Anne Jean Lyman for ten years as Mrs. Lyman succumbed to dementia. She had coped with her own plunge into depression in the mid-1850s. Now she had her son's disillusionment to deal with. What could Mary Walker do? Her son's dismissal, his loss of $200 a year in income, and perhaps the erratic performance of his gardening work meant foremost that Mary Walker had to continue—and perhaps redouble—her labors as dressmaker and seamstress, while her son-in-law continued his carpentry, her daughter took in lodgers, and her daughter-in-law took in laundry, to make up the difference. Not surprisingly, as Catherine Robbins later reported, discord came to plague the Brattle Street household. How "could it come to anything else"? Mary Walker, though she sought to keep her spirits up, appeared even more worn out than she had the year before. She not only had to work without respite; she had to mediate among family members as well.[55]

Mary Walker tried to settle her son as best she could. Had it been up to Catherine, Bryant would have received a stern talking-to and been strictly superintended until he came to his senses. To the New Englander, leniency simply fed dissipation. But Mary Walker may have sensed how hard it would be to manage either her son's conduct or his distress. For she surely guessed what self-discipline it had taken for him *not* to addict himself before he "went to the bad by drink."

Mary Walker knew that in the Raleigh household of Bryant Walker's upbringing, whiskey was regarded as an expected failing of the enslaved male servants.[56] One can only wonder if Silla had drilled into her grandson that he could not afford to go the way of the other men. His mother and his brother Frank were runaways. It would hardly have been surprising for Silla to remind Bryant that one more infraction could get them all sold.[57] In Cambridge, he was living in a city with saloons on every block. Yet no evidence indicates that drink became a problem with him before 1871. Mary Walker may have understood all too well what it had taken for her son to refrain from drinking, in bondage and in freedom, while others secretly or openly indulged. If so, she also fathomed the depth of disillusionment that had led to his surrender. All that Mary Walker could do was convey to her son, whom she had once left behind in slavery, that she would never abandon him again.

MARY WALKER HAD NO WAY of knowing that slights which may have unsettled her son were omens of a great reversal in the Atlantic world, whereby millions who had hoped to assimilate would find themselves mocked and marginalized once more.[58] In Europe, in the Americas, in Africa, persons convinced they could win full privileges and social acceptance encountered barriers, rising racism, and rejection. What Mary Walker did know was that she had to protect Agnes and her grandchildren from the harm that her son's drinking might bring. What if his habit got him into debt? He might try to borrow against the house. He might even, in the grip of debt or drink or anger, try to sell the house. Mary Walker had seen how exposed people of color were in the economy of Boston and Cambridge—and how their vulnerability was magnified when they didn't possess the home they lived in. They periodically had to find new locations, pay high rents, shift to less desirable neighborhoods. They had to face exacerbated family tensions and fears. If unemployment accompanied or followed the move, family breakup often came in its wake. In this scenario of uncertainty and worry, drink could complete the dissolution—and often did.

Mary Walker wanted her children and her grandchildren to have the Brattle Street house as their sanctuary, come what may. In July 1872 she again turned to trusted members of the Howe family to help her achieve that goal. James Murray Howe, who in 1870 had helped Mary Walker to acquire the Cambridge dwelling by purchasing it and then holding it in trust for her benefit, drew up a will to safeguard the home for the next generation. Once again he committed himself and his family to be the trustees and executors of Mary Walker's wishes. Her last will and testament bequeathed "unto James Murray Howe and Archibald Murray Howe" and their heirs "all my estate . . . In trust." The

Howes were to oversee Mary Walker's estate—a small savings account and the Brattle Street residence—"for the use of my beloved daughter Agnes Burgwyn . . . during the term of her natural life." After her daughter's death, the Howes were to hold the property for the benefit of "each and every child then living of my son Bryant Walker and of my daughter Agnes" (in the event she had children). When "the youngest of such children shall reach the age of twenty-one years," Mary Walker's grandchildren were to inherit her estate "in equal amounts." Mary Walker's will bypassed her son and her son-in-law. Through the guardianship of the Howes, the will allowed Mary Walker to keep the house in the family—and her family in the house—until her youngest grandchild turned twenty-one. With a young Harvard Latin professor and his wife (lodgers in a home owned by James Murray Howe) serving as witnesses, Mary Walker signed her will. The date was July 4, 1872.[59]

In his poem of 1839, Henry Wadsworth Longfellow had imagined the village blacksmith of Brattle Street as a neighbor who "looks the whole world in the face, / For he owes not any man." The world that Mary Walker faced, from her 1848 escape from bondage to the will she signed almost a quarter-century later, allowed her no such bravado. From the moment she left slavery, she'd had to rely on others—first for refuge and work, then for assistance in recovering her children. She turned to friends again in order to protect the Brattle Street sanctuary for her grandchildren. But the debts went both ways. The family members that obliged Mary Walker were reciprocating for their many years of reliance on her.

More than her son's troubles had prompted Mary Walker to arrange her will in July 1872. Worry, work, and anxiety about money had exacted their toll on her health. For the first time in her life, she had to take time off from her labors and responsibilities.[60] After signing the will, she left Cambridge for the summer. When she came back at the end of August, she was visited by Harvard professor Ephraim Gurney, a mutual friend of Chauncey Wright and of Susan and Peter Lesley. The versatile professor, who became the beloved first dean of Harvard College, had worried a good deal about Mary Walker before she "went away in the summer." But after "she returned, & she represented herself as so much better," he "felt much less concerned about her." Busied with Harvard students in the fall, Gurney did not call on Mary Walker after September.[61] Others who normally looked in on Mary Walker every week or so—and might have noticed a change in her health as colder weather came on—were away from Cambridge. Chauncey Wright, who had lost his teaching post at Harvard, took the advice of friends and traveled to Europe to renew his spirits. Catherine Robbins, visiting the old family homestead in nearby Milton, was felled by illness in early November. Sleepless at night and wretched all day, she made arrangements to go home to Cambridge, but found herself too feeble to start the trip. Neither of Mary Walker's oldest Cambridge friends was in the city when she became ill with pneumonia on November 3.[62]

Both Mary Walker and Catherine Robbins spent the week of November 3, 1872, battling illness, Mary in Cambridge with pneumonia and Catherine in Milton with debilitating rheumatism. The physician attending Mary Walker examined her at the end of the week and "pronounced [her] better." Catherine Robbins hoped soon to regain sufficient strength to get home to Cambridge. Time dragged on until Friday night, November 8, when Catherine glanced out the window and was startled. Looking from Milton toward Boston, she caught sight of "a fire in the north, very bright & continuous. At midnight I looked out & it was larger & brighter than before." On Sunday, November 10, viewing Boston and Cambridge, she "saw a dense smoke all the time, but heard nothing about it till about 4." Then she learned the cause. "There was the most fearful and disastrous fire ever known in Boston, destroying the most valuable business part of the city" and reducing "thousands to want. How terrible that such things can be all in a single night."

Eager but still too fatigued to depart, Catherine Robbins was still in Milton on November 12, when the evening paper arrived—and with it, another shock. "I saw the death of my poor Mary Walker."[63]

The next day, Susan Lesley received a full report from family member Mary Howe. Though the doctor had thought Mary Walker improved from her pneumonia, over the smoke-plagued weekend "suddenly both lungs became affected, her strength failed utterly, and on Sunday last—Nov 10th—about three o'clock, she ceased to breathe. She had been perfectly conscious & had spoken within a few moments of her death."[64] Mary Walker was fifty-four years old.

CATHERINE ROBBINS RUSHED TO Cambridge on the morning of November 13 and made it to Mary Walker's house on Brattle Street in time to be with the family and view the body before the funeral. She described the scene in her journal. Her friend "was arranged for her last rest, dressed as in life & unchanged in appearance. She looked as if asleep, as if she might wake & speak to you." Beautiful flowers surrounded her; there was "every mark of respect and thoughtfulness." Her "friends white and colored" were there, perhaps Harriet Jacobs among them. Agnes Burgwyn's Methodist minister was at the house, and led everyone in prayer. Then the mourners followed the casket to the Old Cambridge Baptist Church, where Mary Walker had worshiped as a member since her baptism in 1855. After the funeral service in the church, the cortège proceeded the final half-mile to "her last home," in Cambridge's beautiful Mount Auburn Cemetery.[65] By the time of the afternoon burial at Mount Auburn, the smoky haze of the previous week had lifted. "A soft Indian Summer day," Brattle Street neighbor Henry Wadsworth Longfellow recorded in his diary. "All peaceful, at last."[66]

As Mary Walker's longtime Cambridge friends reflected on her death and her life, lamentation mixed with relief. It fell to Susan Lesley to write to Chauncey Wright, still abroad in Europe. First she explained why she had not written for many months. Last "year was a hard year with us, a constant strain of one kind and another." Caring for Philadelphia in-laws (a sister-in-law dying, a brother-in-law bankrupt) "absorbed our time & strength" and thoughts, though never "to the exclusion of many whom we were forced to neglect, and of this number you always stand in the front rank." Finally she got to the painful point of her letter.

> I have written two pages already, dreading to come to the sad news of dear Mary Walker's death, which reached me yesterday in a note from Mary Howe, and which I know will affect you deeply. . . . I did not receive the letter till yesterday, Wednesday PM about the hour of her funeral. Poor Soul! Her sad chequered life, so full of sorrow & disappointment—is ended at last. We ought not to feel sorry that it has, for she had little to look forward to but weariness & disability, had it been prolonged. [I regret] that I had not seen her these last two years, and that I had no way of making her life easier. It was always on my mind & heart to do so, but I could not accomplish it. But I feel thankful for all the good she did receive from others, if not from me. I am so glad you were able to be so constant and true a friend to her, all these years.[67]

Susan Lesley sent her letter to one of Chauncey Wright's Cambridge colleagues, Harvard professor Ephraim Gurney, and asked that he forward the letter to their mutual friend in Europe. Replying that he would gladly do so, Ephraim Gurney added his own thoughts about Mary Walker. "For her I can not but feel a sense of relief, but for those she leaves behind . . ." His sentence trailed off. "You know how much concern she has felt for the last year about Bryant's—her son's—habits, & what a struggle it has been on her part to keep him from going to the bad by drink. This with her anxiety about Chauncey & pecuniary worry, as she felt her own health failing, & her ability to work have been almost too much even for her stout heart." Her cares "must have shortened her days, which, if not few, were certainly evil."[68]

"MY POOR MARY WALKER . . ." Catherine Robbins had known Mary Walker ever since her flight to Massachusetts in late 1850 to escape the reach of the Fugitive Slave Law. Over the years, in sickness and in health, the two women had cared for each other, for Anne Jean Lyman, and for Susan Lesley. Catherine Robbins had shared Mary Walker's anguish at the repeated failures to recover her children before 1860, and her ecstasy at the arrival of her son and daughter in Cambridge in 1865. But by 1872, Catherine Robbins, too, thought that bleakness had overtaken Mary Walker's life. "What a hard suffering life she has had & never harder than the last year, with Bryant's failure & her own impaired health. . . . I shall miss her much," Catherine confessed in her journal, "but it is well with her. There were many trials & discords still for her, though outwardly so well situated, & though I shall often miss her I ought not to regret the change for her." The journal gave voice to the shared sentiment of all. "Poor soul it is all over now, her trials are at an end. . . . I trust she sees clearer than she could here of the meaning & end of it all."[69]

Weeks after Mary Walker's death, Catherine Robbins herself tried to see "the meaning & end of it all." Just before Christmas, she looked in on Agnes, and was distressed to find that "she is poorly & the family in poor condition." The disarray reawakened the foreboding Mary Walker's friend had felt even at the moment of Bryant's joyous arrival in Cambridge in June 1865: "I hope she will [realize] the blessing and be wise in her management." In December 1872, the New Englander couldn't help wondering if Mary Walker had provided too much and guided too little. "Poor Mary, she could do many things to get along, but was most unwise in her influence over them."[70]

On New Year's Day, 1873, Catherine Robbins reviewed the previous year in her Cambridge journal. "A year full of the most tragical events, public & private, many of which might & ought to have been prevented by human foresight, but many others without their reach."[71] Perhaps she was ready to allow that a mother who'd left her son for seventeen years could not just manage him at will. For Susan Lesley in Philadelphia, a year's distance from Mary Walker's passing renewed her faith in the uses of "sorrows & disappointment." To her daughter, she wrote that all the "goodness and beauty you see on earth today" was "brought about by ages of suffering and misery." Martyrs "have made the earth a better place for me and you to live in."[72]

Mary Walker was no seer. But from her decade in Anne Jean Lyman's household, from her months on the Sea Islands in 1864, from the year of her son's fall in 1872, she had surely learned that the fruits of freedom would not be gained in a single generation. What she could do, and what she did do, was to provide a haven so that her grandchildren would have options when they came of age. As long as her family lived in the Brattle Street house, they would have one of the good houses of Cambridge. They would have around them people who knew who they were, who knew of Mary Walker's story and strivings, who were ready to help. They would have security and resources greater than she or her children had ever known. Thanks to her, they would have greater choices as well.

Home and haven, the Brattle Street house remained in Mary Walker's family until 1912.

EPILOGUE

"Their Works Do Follow Them"

Forced to leave her mother and three children behind in bondage, Mary Walker found sanctuary with a couple who gave her refuge and made her family's recovery their antislavery mission. Trust in Susan and Peter Lesley led Mary Walker to share her feelings and her history, her hopes and frustrations, her triumphs and setbacks. The Lesleys, along with their relatives and friends, became chroniclers of her efforts and theirs to free her family. And in journal entries and hundreds of letters written over a period of twenty-two years, they cast a unique light on the life of a woman refugee from slavery.

Mary Walker's experience mirrored that of thousands. Everyone who escaped bondage left family members behind. If they tried to make contact, as did Mary Walker's son Frank in 1853, they risked revealing their location and hazarded recapture. Mary Walker's story reveals what many had to deal with: anxiety, remorse, obsession to free those still captive. But Mary Walker's life does more than illustrate ways in which, for the self-emancipated, freedom was never complete. Her "silent heartbreak" gave voice as well to the feelings of women and men who remained in bondage. Attachments of the heart led most to endure what they had to, if it allowed them to keep their families together.

For the Lesleys, and for their relatives and friends, "fugitives" such as Mary Walker served as a living message. She read, wrote, prayed; she was a gifted seamstress and devoted caretaker. She was a woman so fair she could be taken for white. Still, by law she was a slave. No doubt her color and cultivation made it easier for Northern whites to regard her with empathy. Yet her appearance and carriage confronted all who knew her with the utter arbitrariness of slavery in America. But for the grace of birth or fate, they too might be property, bodies which could be owned, bought, subjected, and sold. Northerners like the Lesleys were transformed into abolitionists by the Mary Walkers in their midst. Exiles brought slavery home.

In Mary Walker's story, large events of the Civil War era unfolded on an intimate human scale. Resistance to the "Slave Power" induced Northern states—Pennsylvania and Massachusetts among them—to pass personal-liberty laws which granted freedom to enslaved persons brought into a free state voluntarily and which forbade officials from aiding the recapture of fugitive slaves. When Mary Walker left her owners in Philadelphia in 1848, she believed she was free and safe. Anger, and fear that such laws would incite still more slaves to desert, led Southern leaders to demand a new federal Fugitive Slave Law. Its passage in 1850 forced Mary Walker to flee farther north. During the 1850s, increasing boldness on the part of those who sought the further expansion of slavery and those who sought to contain it inspired bolder private actions to recover Mary Walker's children. The most extreme of the decade's confrontations—John Brown's 1859 raid on Harpers Ferry and his subsequent trial and execution—cast the country on Brown's course to "purge this land with blood" and ended the era of quests to release individuals from bondage one by one. The coming of war radicalized Mary Walker. By 1863, she stood ready to have her children rise up and die if need be, in order to hasten freedom for their people. In 1864, invited to join reformers who were schooling and supervising emancipated blacks on the Sea Islands of South Carolina—rehearsing

Reconstruction—Mary Walker witnessed firsthand the mutual disillusionment of freedmen and reformers.

Every event of those momentous decades had an impact on Mary Walker and found its way into the writings of her antislavery friends. Catherine Robbins reflected: "When I have read in history long ago of wars & revolutions, battles and bloodshed, they filled me with horror. I felt that life would be of no value in the midst of such events, I felt that we were far removed from them, that they would never come to us. But now . . . all the fearful scenes of which we have read are enacted in our own country, upon a larger scale than was ever known." Catherine Robbins was always alert to the consequences of events for her longtime friend from the South, and vocal about how they buoyed or dampened hopes for her family. By 1865, however, the fearful scenes of war and harsh personal experience had steeled Mary Walker. Her tenacious determination was now shared by millions. For her children, for herself, for her people, she wanted one thing only: deliverance.

IN MOUNT AUBURN CEMETERY TODAY, at the gravesite for Mary Walker, one finds a striking marker. It is a seven-foot-tall white obelisk, on top of which is a winged dove. The dove's wings are outspread, as if it has just landed, or is about to take flight. Inscriptions are on three sides of the obelisk. One is "Mary Walker, Born in Orange County, North Carolina, Died in Cambridge, November 10, 1872, Aged 54 years." On another side of the marker is her son's information: "Bryant Walker, Born in Raleigh, North Carolina, Died in Cambridge, Aged 50." On the third side are the following lines:

Blessed are the dead
Who die in the Lord
They rest from their labor
And their works do follow them.

It was Mary Walker's daughter, Agnes, who chose the monument and the inscriptions, and who had the marker placed in Mount Auburn Cemetery in 1895. The year before, her brother Bryant had died, ending a life buffeted by expansive hopes and deep disappointments.[1] Twenty years before his death in 1894, Bryant Walker apparently steadied himself after the turn to drink that brought his dismissal as church sexton. Reconciling with his brother-in-law, he named a son born in 1876—destined to live only three months—in honor of James Burgwyn.[2] He resumed his work as gardener, placed his name in the classified listings of the Cambridge City Directory of 1878, and retained that occupation for the remainder of his life. Private gardens all over Cambridge showcased the skill he had in his hands, and Bryant conveyed both his knowledge and the aspirations of his younger self to his four sons. In the 1890s, each began as a laborer, took up a trade, and within a decade rose a further step up the occupational ladder. Edward Walker moved from painter to artist, John Walker from laborer to coachman, Frederick Walker from plumber to gas inspector, William Walker from laborer to clerk and finally to proprietor of a lunch counter in Cambridge.[3] In July 1890, Bryant's oldest daughter, nineteen-year-old Mary Agnes Walker, married a twenty-three-year-old French-Canadian confectioner at St. Paul's Catholic Church and soon gave her parents a grandson and a granddaughter.[4] Four years later, on the night of November 4, 1894, Bryant Walker died.[5]

During Bryant's lifetime, Agnes had supported her brother and his family in many ways, as Mary Walker hoped her daughter would do. Part of her care was to make the Brattle Street house pay dividends for them all. Year in and year out, Agnes Burgwyn took in lodgers. Mary Walker's old friend Chauncey Wright boarded in the house in 1875, where Wright and his peer Henry James enjoyed conversations in the parlor. Herself childless, Agnes instructed her nieces—Mary Agnes born in 1870 and Hannah Frances born in 1874—in the skills of fine sewing, skills passed on to her by her grandmother Silla and her mother, Mary. By the time the nieces came of age, both were earning an income as dressmakers in Cambridge.[6]

Though Agnes could not ward off her brother's disappointment, she recognized that in his better moments Bryant channeled his talents into the plants he tended. One of his small landscapes was the Mount Auburn burial plot of his mother. When Agnes had the obelisk erected on the family gravesite in 1895, she realized that the installation would require uprooting the plants her brother had placed there. She asked the supervisor to put them back exactly where her brother had planted them.[7]

Perhaps Agnes Burgwyn chose the unusual cemetery obelisk—with the dove on top—as a symbol for Mary Walker and Bryant Walker both. The biblical dove traditionally represented a visitation of the heavenly spirit, a visitation that came for Mary Walker at the moment of her redemptive baptism at the Old Cambridge Baptist Church in 1855, when she'd "thanked her savior for giving her a seat in his kingdom, for sending his spirit like a dove, and for clothing her in a robe of righteousness." Its wings outspread, the dove atop the obelisk may also have symbolized Bryant Walker's spirit, at last taking flight from the snares of the world.

Agnes Walker Burgwyn lived into the first decade of the twentieth century, and, as had her mother before her, she earned many admirers as a genteel woman of cultivation and intelligence. Like her mother, she worked hard at self-improvement. The clearest symbol of her success was her handwriting. When she came out of slavery in 1865, her script was so crabbed that she employed an amanuensis to compose her letter to the Cameron sisters back in North Carolina, reporting on her arrival and resettlement in Cambridge. Her signature on documents in the early 1870s was a labored scrawl. By 1895, the year of her letter to the supervisor at Mount Auburn Cemetery, her handwriting was elegant, her grammar good, and her punctuation impeccable.[8] Those who knew of Mary Walker recognized in her daughter a fitting successor to the Cambridge refugee of half a century before. When the *Cambridge Tribune* reported the death of Agnes Burgwyn on December 8, 1907, it revealed how she was regarded by descendants of the families that had known her mother. She "was the daughter of Mary Walker, a fugitive to the North in anti-slavery days, who through her superior qualities and interesting personality won the friendship of many of the foremost abolitionists." Mary Walker's daughter "was a woman of refinement and intelligence, whose wise counsel and sympathy endeared her to many friends." Obliquely, the obituary also acknowledged the fidelity of the sister to her troubled brother. Agnes Burgwyn was "faithful and devoted in all the relations of life."[9]

THE OPTIONS OPEN TO THE next generation of Mary Walker's descendants in Cambridge were suggested by the life of her grandson Frederick Walker. In 1894 he married dressmaker Edith Ham, the white Protestant daughter of Daniel and Ellen Ham. During the 1890s, step by step, he moved up the occupational ladder. A laborer when he started work, he was listed as a plumber in the Cambridge City Directory of 1894 and a gas inspector four years later. But the career that Frederick Walker wanted most was quite different from laborer, plumber, or gas inspector: he wanted a job delivering mail for the Cambridge Post Office. Cambridge-born and Catholic-reared Frederick Walker bided his time, let his interest and his character be known, kept on the alert for an opening, and, when the opportunity came in 1896, seized the chance to become a substitute carrier. For five years, as a "sub-carrier," he took the routes of others whenever needed, and his reward came on February 14, 1901, when at the age of thirty-three he became a regular mail carrier at the Harvard Square Post Office. Frederick Walker, the grandson of a fugitive slave who could never risk sending a letter to the South, served as a Cambridge letter carrier for the next twenty-five years of his life.[10]

The Brattle Street house was the means through which Mary Walker's guardianship extended into the twentieth century. All of Mary Walker's grandchildren were able to grow up at 54 Brattle; Frederick Walker and his sister Hannah Walker remained in the house into adulthood. Both were present at the passing of their mother, seventy-one-year-old Annie Gorey Walker, in 1911. A year later, with the consent of all the living Walker children and of the last Howe family descendant to serve as trustee for the house, Hannah and Frederick Walker sold 54 Brattle Street to a next-door neighbor. With proceeds from the sale, Frederick Walker and his wife, Edith, bought a home a block away and invited his aged uncle James Burgwyn to move in with them.[11] When James Burgwyn died in 1916, he left his life savings of $5,791.53 to his nephew Frederick.[12] Frederick Walker, in turn, named *his* nephew as the executor of his will and stipulated that after Edith Walker died, the nephew would inherit all of his savings and property.[13]

Mary Walker's house—as a residence, as a rent-free home, and as the source of equity for descendants to buy their own homes—proved to be a sustaining legacy.

IN THE 1940S, THE Brattle Street house came full circle. A haven to Mary Walker, her children, and her grandchildren from 1870 to 1912, 54 Brattle Street became the "Window Shop" in 1946. A sanctuary for refugees fleeing oppression and war in Europe, the Window Shop had been founded in 1939 by Harvard faculty wives and moved to Brattle Street after the war's end. Women refugees ran the store in front of the house, stocked it with European baked goods and pastries, and also sold hand-sewn blouses, frocks, and skirts. Brought from slave-labor camps to Boston, "depressed and bewildered," they needed housing and jobs. The Window Shop on Brattle Street provided a paying outlet for their skills and a "meeting place in a strange land." In the words of one refugee, it was a "shelter for those who could not find their way," a "place to turn in times of woe," a lifeline to "hope and renewal."

Having heard of the good work done there, Eleanor Roosevelt paid the Window Shop a visit in May 1950. "So many happy faces greeted me," she wrote in her newspaper column of May 30. "Women who had been in concentration camps or had spent long years waiting to find themselves [were] able to begin life again in a new country." There was no way for the former First Lady to have known of the links between her husband's family and that of Mary Walker. Franklin Delano Roosevelt's great-grandmother was Anne Jean Lyman, whom Mary Walker had cared for throughout the 1850s. Nor could Eleanor Roosevelt have known that this was the second era in its lifetime that the Brattle Street dwelling had served as a refuge and a place to start again.[14]

STARTING AGAIN FOR MARY WALKER had occurred many times. She began a new life when she walked away from her owner in Philadelphia in August 1848, rather than be sent into exile as punishment for what he deemed her impudence. She most certainly started again when she succeeded in 1865 in reuniting her family in Cambridge. But in many ways, a crucial turning point in her life had come in Milton, Massachusetts, in June 1852, at the moment when she felt able to put her complete trust in Susan Lesley as her protector and advocate. It was after that breakthrough that Mary Walker began to reveal the details of her life in bondage—details that Susan Lesley divulged to no one but her husband for forty years. Once her stories began to flow, Mary Walker recited songs her mother sang at midnight prayer meetings in bondage. She recalled one song especially that required maximum secrecy, for punishment was certain if whites overheard it.

Our bondage it shall end
With our threescore years & ten
And to Canaan we'll return
By & Bye, by & bye . . .
There friends shall meet again,

Who have loved, who have loved.
Their union shall be sweet
At their dear Redeemer's feet,
And they meet to part no more,
Who have loved, who have loved.

A century and a half after Mary Walker had sung this song for Susan Lesley, descendants of each woman met for the first time. Andrea Kenney House, the descendant of Mary Walker, met Mary Ames Wolff, the descendant of Susan Lesley, in Denver in June 2008. By then, they knew in full the stories of their forebears—of Mary Walker's relentless struggle to recover her children, of the long-lasting ties between their ancestors, of those who had joined together to free a family.

They were as friends who met again.

Notes

1. Reluctant Runaway

1. Deposition of William Johnson, City of Philadelphia, December 20, 1850, in the Ellis Gray Loring Papers, Schlesinger Library, Harvard University (hereafter Loring Papers, Schlesinger Library). Four acquaintances of Mary Walker gave depositions about her in December 1850 and January 1851; the depositions were placed in the keeping of Massachusetts attorney Ellis Gray Loring, a leading antislavery lawyer. For the reasons, see Chapter 2. There were twenty one William Johnsons in the Philadelphia City Directory of 1846. I concluded that the waiter William Johnson who lived at 10 Currant Alley, just four blocks from the lodgings of the Camerons on Sansom and Seventh, was the most likely to have encountered Mary Walker "almost every day."

2. Deposition of William Johnson, December 20, 1850, in Loring Papers, Schlesinger Library. Duncan Cameron was a judge on the North Carolina Superior Court from 1814 to 1817.

3. Julie Winch, *Philadelphia's Black Elite: Activism, Accommodation, and the Struggle for Autonomy, 1787–1848* (Philadelphia: Temple University Press, 1988), pp. 85–89, 146; Julie Winch, ed., *The Elite of Our People: Joseph Willson's Sketches of Black Upper-Class Life in Antebellum Philadelphia* (University Park: Pennsylvania State University Press, 2000), p. 20. Joseph Borome, "The Vigilant Committee of Philadelphia," *Pennsylvania Magazine of History and Biography* 92 (July 1968), 323–325.

4. Borome, "Vigilant Committee," 325–328; Winch, ed., *Elite of Our People*, p. 30; Winch, *Philadelphia's Black Elite*, pp. 146–151.

5. Deposition of James McCrummill, City of Philadelphia, January 16, 1851,

in Loring Papers, Schlesinger Library. In the deposition, McCrummill stated that he himself "heard Judge Campbell refer to Mary" as "[my servant] who would not leave me." Subsequently, the notary scratched through that part of the deposition. The claim of overhearing Cameron's statement may have come from another party, been related by McCrummill, and then been withdrawn as secondhand rather than firsthand testimony.

6. Deposition of Nicholas Boston, December 27, 1850; Deposition of Annie E. Hall, December 26, 1850, in Loring Papers, Schlesinger Library. Nicholas Boston's occupation of laborer is found in the 1850 United States Federal Census Record for Philadelphia, microfilm roll M432–819, p. 284, image 433. Ann E. Hall was listed as a dressmaker in the 1848 Philadelphia City Directory; she lived on Currant Alley, as did fellow deponent William Johnson.

7. Deposition of Annie E. Hall, December 26, 1850, Loring Papers, Schlesinger Library.

8. Mary Walker was listed with four children in the 1845 inventory of slaves dwelling in the Raleigh household of Duncan Cameron. Their ages were computed from other slave-lists. Slave-inventories from 1777 to 1864 can be found in the Cameron Family Papers at the Southern Historical Collection, University of North Carolina at Chapel Hill (hereafter Cameron Papers, SHC). For tax and other purposes, such inventories were usually done every year. Inventories of taxable slaves included only persons from age twelve to age fifty. The slave-lists in the Cameron Papers are not complete; there are no inventories from 1846 through 1848. By 1848, Mary Walker's son Edward had died.

9. Jean Bradley Anderson, *Piedmont Plantation: The Bennehan-Cameron Family and Lands in North Carolina* (Durham, N.C.: Historic Preservation Society of Durham, 1985), pp. 5, 160. At least half of the slaves came from Richard Bennehan's brother-in-law, Thomas Amis, Jr., in eastern North Carolina; Amis had given up farming, moved from Halifax to the port town of Edenton, and relinquished the use of twenty slaves to Richard, the husband of his sister, Mary Amis. Most of the Amis slaves were subsequently bequeathed to the Bennehans' daughter Rebecca, and became her dowry when she married Duncan Cameron in 1803. The Bennehan slave inventory of 1803–1804 in the Cameron Papers lists Aggy's age as twenty-three in 1804: hence the birth year of 1781. Herbert Gutman superbly charted the genealogies of the "Bennehan-Cameron Plantation Slave Families," organizing them by family groups, then giving the names of each set of parents and the birthdates of their children. See Herbert Gutman, *The Black*

Family in Slavery and Freedom, 1750–1925 (New York: Pantheon, 1976), p. 172 (Table 24).

10. Ira Berlin, "Time, Space, and the Evolution of Afro-American Society on British Mainland North America," *American Historical Review* 85 (February 1980): 44–78.

11. Thomas Amis, Jr., to Thomas D. Bennehan, February 9, 1797, September 22, 1805, February 22, 1807, March 2, 1807, Cameron Papers, SHC.

12. Rebecca Bennehan Cameron to Duncan Cameron, April 26, 1815; Duncan Cameron to Rebecca Bennehan Cameron, April 27, 1815; Thomas D. Bennehan to Margaret B. Cameron, August 7, 1830, Cameron Papers, SHC; Anderson, *Piedmont Plantation,* pp. 15–16.

13. The birth of Aggy's child in October 1796 was noted on a Miscellaneous Slave List in the Cameron Papers, where the name appears as "Pracilla"; the handwriting and spelling were those of an overseer. "Silla" (variously spelled later as "Sillar" or "Sylla") was listed as seven years old in the annual slave inventory of 1803–1804. Aggy's "derangement" was noted in Rebecca Bennehan Cameron to Duncan Cameron, June 14 and June 25, 1804, Cameron Papers, SHC.

14. Rebecca Bennehan Cameron to Duncan Cameron, March 27, 1816; Duncan Cameron to Paul Cameron, February 1, 1841; Mildred Cameron to Paul Cameron, April 27, 1845; George W. Mordecai to Margaret Cameron Mordecai, February 4, 1856, Cameron Papers, SHC. While unusual, it was not always illegal for enslaved persons—most often skilled or household servants—to be taught to read and write, that they might better serve their owners. African Americans, in turn, taught each other, with or without permission. Such instruction (by both whites and blacks) was widely outlawed in the wake of the appearance in the South of copies of free black David Walker's 1829 *Appeal to the Colored Citizens of the World,* which bitterly denounced slavery and called for armed resistance to it. North Carolina's response to Walker's incendiary pamphlet came in 1830: "any free person, who shall hereafter teach, or attempt to teach, any slave within this State to read or write . . . shall be liable to indictment," fines between $100 to $200, and imprisonment. Free blacks who gave instruction would be whipped publicly; slaves would receive thirty-nine lashes. The law was not universally enforced; the Camerons appeared to ignore it as they saw fit. See Heather Andrea Williams, *Self-Taught: African American Education in Slavery and Freedom* (Chapel Hill: University of North Carolina Press, 2005), pp. 14–15, 203–206.

15. Anderson, *Piedmont Plantation,* pp. 17–23; P. Browne to William Duffy, n.d.,

William Duffy Papers, North Carolina State Archives, Raleigh, North Carolina.

16. Anderson, *Piedmont Plantation,* p. 27; Duncan Cameron to Rebecca Cameron, April 27, 1815, Cameron Papers, SHC.

17. For the definition of a cord of wood, see the *Oxford English Dictionary.* See Ledger of credits and purchases by blacks at the Bennehan store, 1809–1811, Cameron Papers, SHC. For the role and rewards of Luke as Duncan Cameron's right-hand servant, see Thomas Bennehan to Duncan Cameron, July 8, 1811; Rebecca Cameron to Duncan Cameron, October 3, 1813, October 19, 1814; Duncan Cameron to James Webb, May 25, 1814; and letters throughout the Cameron Papers from the 1820s through the 1850s. For Luke's kinship link to his sister Aggy and niece Silla, see Gutman, *Black Family,* p. 172. Michael Tadman develops the concept of "Key Slaves" in his new introduction to the paperback edition of Tadman, *Speculators and Slaves: Masters, Traders, and Slaves in the Old South* (Madison: University of Wisconsin Press, 1996), pp. xxxi–xxxvii.

18. I arrived at Mary Walker's date of birth by working backward from her age at the time of her death on November 10, 1872. Her age at death was reported as fifty-four years, two months, and twenty-three days. See the *Cambridge Chronicle,* November 23, 1872. The conjecture that Duncan Cameron was Mary Walker's father can be found in James Lesley to Peter Lesley, November 9, 1850, in the Ames Family Historical Collection, private collection (hereafter AFC). The second source is the coroner's report filled out after Mary Walker's death in 1872, where "—— Taylor" was provided as the surname of her father. The correspondence of Peter and Susan Lesley is part of the Ames Family Historical Collection. The papers are in the possession of Mary Wolff and her daughter Linda Cowan, descendants of Peter and Susan Lesley, who have spent decades organizing and perfecting a guide to the correspondence. Spanning three centuries, encompassing thousands of letters, the collection is thought to be the largest of its kind still in private hands. For an illuminating article on the family and on the collection as window to American social history, see Kirk Johnson, "In 200 Years of Family Letters, a Nation's Story," *New York Times,* January 29, 2006.

19. Silla was listed continuously as a household servant of the Camerons from 1804 to 1864. See the slave inventories in the Cameron Papers and also those in a separate collection of papers, at the Southern Historical Collection, of Margaret Bain Cameron Mordecai, Duncan Cameron's married daughter. The 1872

report is that of the Cambridge coroner, who listed "—— Taylor" as Mary Walker's father. Dr. William Taylor was among several physicians who attended Silla from 1816 on; he was on call if her "case is dangerous." Taylor also looked after Duncan Cameron. See Rebecca Cameron to Duncan Cameron, March 27, 1816; Dr. James Webb's account with Duncan Cameron, December 1816; William Taylor to Thomas Bennehan, February 13, 1821, Cameron Papers, SHC.

20. Anderson, *Piedmont Plantation,* pp. 27–29.

21. Frank was first listed in the slave inventory of 1834 as "Frank, son of Mary," age two. His description came in an 1853 affidavit in the Cameron Papers, and is quoted in Anderson, *Piedmont Plantation,* p. 98.

22. The "sickliness" of the plantation compelled several overseers to leave their posts well before the crop came in. See Thomas Bennehan to Duncan Cameron, February 13, 1830, Cameron Papers, SHC. Malaria and its relationship to mosquitoes had yet to be understood, but the Camerons had a growing awareness of the relationship between low-lying wet grounds and slave illnesses. See Anderson, *Piedmont Plantation,* pp. 106–108.

23. Fabius Haywood to Duncan Cameron, February 5, 1828; J. G. Stanly to George E. Badger, March 10, 1831, Cameron Papers, SHC. Alice Eley Jones interviewed the Cameron plantation black descendants in the 1990s and was told that the Camerons had been slave-owners who "stole your labor" but kept your folks together. Her illuminating interviews are on file at the Stagville Historic Preservation Center in Durham, North Carolina.

24. William Kirkland to Duncan Cameron, July 14, 1823; Dr. Lueco Mitchell to Duncan Cameron, July 23, 1826; William Anderson to Duncan Cameron, December 12, 1828, Cameron Papers, SHC.

25. Anderson, *Piedmont Plantation,* pp. 46–47; Paul Cameron to Thomas Ruffin, July 21, 1833, Cameron Papers, SHC.

26. See Paul Cameron's record of slave deaths and their causes, 1837–1844. Cameron began the inventory on April 1, 1837, and continued it. When nursing his workers, Paul Cameron categorized them as "sick," "very sick," and "seriously ill." The sick and very sick he treated in their own dwellings; dangerous cases were brought to Fairntosh and placed in the "kitchen," where a doctor could be called to treat them. The illness and deaths of the Cameron sisters are recounted in Anderson, *Piedmont Plantation,* p. 45.

27. Rebecca Cameron to Paul Cameron, November 25, 1839, Cameron Papers, SHC; Anderson, *Piedmont Plantation,* p. 45.

28. Susan Lyman Lesley to Peter Lesley, June 20, [1852], AFC.

29. Ibid. For a description of Anne Owen Cameron's death, see Frederick Nash to wife, n.d., 1840, Frederick Nash Papers, North Carolina State Archives, Raleigh.

30. Journal of Mildred Cameron, May 30, 1840, Cameron Papers, SHC; Anderson, *Piedmont Plantation*, p. 45.

31. Susan Lesley to Peter Lesley, June 13, 1852, AFC. For the context of Mary Walker's revelations about the midnight prayer meetings, her mother, and herself, see Chapter 3.

32. In 1845, Paul Cameron made a comprehensive list, organized by quarters, of all the enslaved persons owned by the Camerons. The inventory of Raleigh household servants listed Mary Walker and her children; all were recorded with full first names. Agnes Walker's middle name, Priscilla, was provided in her burial record. See the record for Agnes P. Burgwyn, Lot No. 4312, Kalmia Path, Mount Auburn Cemetery, Cambridge, Massachusetts.

33. Susan Lesley to Peter Lesley, June 13, 1852, AFC. Silla's use of the term "bought ye"—which Susan Lesley rendered in dialect as "bot ye"—refers to the belief found in traditional song and parable that the blood of Jesus Christ, shed as he perished at the Crucifixion, bought the salvation of believers.

34. Margaret Cameron to Anne Ruffin Cameron, no date, found in Undated Correspondence File (Box 77), George W. Mordecai Papers, Southern Historical Collection, University of North Carolina. The Margaret Bain Cameron Mordecai letters are a subset of the George W. Mordecai Collection.

35. Thomas D. Morris, *Free Men All: The Personal Liberty Laws of the North, 1780–1861* (Baltimore: Johns Hopkins University Press, 1974), ch. 6 and pp. 107–119. For the impact of James K. Polk and the Mexican War, see Michael F. Holt, *The Fate of Their Country: Politicians, Slavery Extension, and the Coming of the Civil War* (New York: Hill and Wang, 2004), chs. 1 and 2.

36. Morris, *Free Men All*, p. 118. The 1788 law had been passed for the benefit of Southern representatives who brought enslaved servants to Philadelphia when the city was the country's capital.

37. For reports on Mildred Cameron's condition, see Duncan Cameron to Paul Cameron, June 15, June 17, July 1, July 18, July 25, 1848, Cameron Papers, SHC. It was Cameron's old friend Frederick Nash who reported to his wife that Cameron's sense of command was gone. Frederick Nash to wife, [n.d.], 1848, Frederick Nash Papers, North Carolina State Archives, Raleigh. Duncan Cameron himself revealed his debilitating condition and resignation in letters to his

son, starting on November 2, 1848, and concluding in December (Cameron Papers, SHC).

38. Duncan Cameron to Paul Cameron, July 5, 1848, Cameron Papers, SHC; Deposition of Nicholas Boston, December 27, 1850, Loring Papers, Schlesinger Library.

39. Margaret Cameron to Paul Cameron, M[ay] 28, [1850], Cameron Papers, SHC.

40. Edward S. Philbrick to William C. Gannett, March 24, 1864, William C. Gannett Papers, Rush Rhees Library, University of Rochester. Philbrick likely received this explanation from members of a Massachusetts family that knew Mary Walker well; see Chapter 9.

41. Sydney Nathans, "Fortress without Walls: A Black Community after Slavery," in *Holding On to the Land and the Lord,* ed. Robert L. Hall and Carol B. Stack (Athens: University of Georgia Press, 1982), pp. 55–65.

42. Paul Cameron to Duncan Cameron, December 2, 1845, Cameron Papers, SHC.

43. Paul Cameron to Duncan Cameron, November 18, December 2, 1845; Duncan Cameron to Paul Cameron, November 27, 1845, Cameron Papers, SHC.

44. Sydney Nathans, "'Gotta Mind to Move, a Mind to Settle Down': Afro-Americans on the Plantation Frontier," in *A Master's Due: Essays in Honor of David Herbert Donald,* ed. William J. Cooper, Michael F. Holt, and John McCardell (Baton Rouge: Louisiana State University Press, 1985), pp. 204–206. Duncan Cameron to Paul Cameron, December 1848, Cameron Papers, SHC. Paul Cameron revealed his plans to Virgil P. M. Bennehan, the personal servant of Cameron's late uncle, Thomas Bennehan. In his will, Thomas Bennehan freed Virgil and provided the means for his former slave to go to Liberia. In April 1848, Cameron accompanied Virgil and his family to Baltimore, where the former slaves departed to Africa by ship. Virgil Bennehan wrote Cameron after his arrival, and asked his "Dear young master & friend" to "write me who you have sent To The South." Virgil P. M. Bennehan to P. C. Cameron, May 29, 1848, in *Slaves No More: Letters from Liberia, 1833–1869,* ed. Bell I. Wiley (Lexington: University of Kentucky Press, 1980), pp. 260–261. The original letter is in the Cameron Papers, SHC. Most certainly Virgil Bennehan did not communicate Paul Cameron's plan to Mary Walker. But others may have guessed Cameron's intention from the white family's conversations or correspondence.

45. In his deposition, James McCrummill mentioned that Mary Walker had

received a letter from her mother while Mary was with the Camerons in Philadelphia. Deposition of James McCrummill, January 16, 1851, Loring Papers, Schlesinger Library.

46. Two years later, confronted with a case of "insolence" in the "language and deportment" of his Raleigh house-servant John Sears, Cameron "felt it my duty to punish him, which I did with great reluctance. I told him then, that I would send him away. . . . It is much to be regretted that he is so insolent & unmanageable." Duncan Cameron to Paul Cameron, August 27, 1850, Cameron Papers, SHC. Paul Cameron temporarily relocated John Sears from Raleigh to Fairntosh—not to Alabama.

47. Duncan Cameron gave August 9 as the day of their planned departure to North Carolina. Duncan Cameron to Paul Cameron, August 8, 1848, Cameron Papers, SHC. In his 1850 deposition, Nicholas Boston stated that Mary Walker left her owners one day before they departed. Deposition of Nicholas Boston, December 27, 1850, Loring Papers, Schlesinger Library.

2. *Sanctuary*

1. The story of the woman who voluntarily returned to bondage originally appeared in the New York *Herald Tribune,* and was reprinted in the *Pennsylvania Freeman.* The *Freeman* editor critiqued her case as unrepresentative. *Pennsylvania Freeman,* August 27, 1846. Deposition of James McCrummill about Mary Walker, January 16, 1851, in the Ellis Gray Loring Papers, Schlesinger Library, Harvard University.

2. In 1847, the Philadelphia Society of Friends commissioned a "Statistical Inquiry into the Condition of the People of Color of the City and Districts of Philadelphia," which it based on a census of five thousand households in the city. That 1847 manuscript census has been digitized as the "Philadelphia African-American Census" by the Friends Historical Library of Swarthmore College (hereafter "digitized 1847 Census"), under the direction of Curator Christopher Densmore. An invaluable source, the digitized collection gives the name of each head of household listed, the household address, his or her occupation, the occupation of others in the household; it also states if members of the household were born slaves and if so, whether they were manumitted or bought their freedom. Household heads can be found by name. The record for *William Still* revealed that he lived at the rear of 22 Washington Street, that he was a clerk, that his wife was a dressmaker, and that both were born free. See William Still entry, digitized 1847 Census. Still was also listed as a clerk at

22 Washington Street in the Philadelphia City Directory of 1848. His wife's name, Letitia, was given in the 1860 U.S. Federal Census, Philadelphia Ward 4 West Division, Philadelphia, roll M653_1154, p. 991, image 492, available on Ancestry.com.

3. In the digitized 1847 Census, James Fells's address was given as 11 Washington Street and his occupation as carpenter. His employees were listed in the 1850 U.S. Census and property given in the 1870 U.S. Federal Census. See the 1850 U.S. Census, Philadelphia Spruce Ward, roll M432_813, p. 348, image 164; and 1870 U.S. Census, Philadelphia Ward 7 District 18, roll M593_1392, p. 313, image 177, both found on Ancestry.com. For information on the involvement of James and Eliza Fells and of James McCrummill in the American Baptist Missionary Association, see the annual reports of the American Baptist Missionary Conventions, 1849, 1852–54, and 1857/58–59, available on microfilm from the Southern Baptist Theological Seminary Library, Louisville, Kentucky.

4. James Fells entry, digitized 1847 Census.

5. The *Pennsylvania Freeman* of August 22, 1850, first reported William Still's surprise encounter with the man he discovered to be his brother—one of the young sons left by their mother.

6. William Still, *The Underground Railroad* (1871; repr., Chicago: Johnson Publishing Company, 1970), pp. 104, 339.

7. *Pennsylvania Freeman,* October 5, October 12, October 26, 1848.

8. *Pennsylvania Freeman,* November 9, 1848.

9. Sean Wilentz, *The Rise of American Democracy: Jefferson to Lincoln* (New York: W. W. Norton, 2005), pp. 645–646.

10. Wilentz, *Rise of American Democracy,* pp. 645–646, 650; *Pennsylvania Freeman,* July 5, 1849.

11. Susan Lyman Lesley to Margaret White Harding, November 12, 1850, Ames Family Historical Collection, private collection (hereafter AFC).

12. Thirty-year-old Sarah Elbert was listed as a member of the Philadelphia household of twenty-six-year-old James Lesley in the 1850 U.S. Federal Census, Philadelphia High Street Ward, roll M432_816, p. 195, image 391, available at Ancestry.com. James Lesley, Sr., had lived in Harrisburg in the 1830s and 1840s, but by 1850 was living in Chambersburg, Pennsylvania, with his wife Ellen and their mulatto servant, whose name was recorded as Mary Albert. See the 1850 U.S. Census for Chambersburg, Franklin, Pennsylvania, roll M432_781, p. 244, image 492, available at Ancestry.com. By 1860, the senior Lesleys had moved to Philadelphia and Sarah Elbert had become a domestic servant in their house-

hold. 1860 U.S. Federal Census, Philadelphia Ward 24, Precinct 6, roll M653_1175, p. 835, image 323, available at Ancestry.com. The address of James Lesley, Jr. (243 High Street) was given in Philadelphia city directories starting in 1849. High Street was changed to Market around midcentury; Lesley's address was 243 Market in the 1855 City Directory.

13. Mary Lesley Ames, ed., *Life and Letters of Peter and Susan Lesley,* 2 vols. (New York: G. P. Putnam's Sons, 1909), vol. 1, p. 13; Peter Lesley to Stepmother, November 30, 1850, AFC.

14. Peter Lesley to Susan Lesley, June 24, 1852; Susan Lesley to Peter Lesley, [June 28, 1852], AFC.

15. *Pennsylvania Freeman,* October 21, 1847.

16. *Pennsylvania Freeman,* January 17, 1850.

17. *Pennsylvania Freeman,* March 14, April 4, 1850.

18. *Pennsylvania Freeman,* June 6, 1850.

19. *Pennsylvania Freeman,* September 5, September 12, September 19, 1850.

20. *Pennsylvania Freeman,* October 3, October 17, October 31, 1850.

21. Margaret Cameron to Anne Ruffin Cameron, [August 1848?], found in Undated Files, George W. Mordecai Papers, Southern Historical Collection, University of North Carolina at Chapel Hill; Medical Report on Mildred Cameron by Dr. Louis Bauer, Brooklyn Orthopedic Institute, May 13, 1856, pp. 4–5, found in Cameron Family Papers, Southern Historical Collection, University of North Carolina at Chapel Hill (hereafter Cameron Papers, SHC).

22. Paul Cameron addressed 1849 and early 1850 letters to his sisters at 2 Dugan Row, Spruce above Twelfth Street (Paul Cameron to Sisters, November 29, 1849, February 20, 1850); and to Duncan Cameron at that address (May 18, 1850). Autumn 1850 letters from Paul Cameron to his father were addressed to the Corner of Broad and Brighton (Paul Cameron to Duncan Cameron, October 15, November 14, 1850, Cameron Papers, SHC).

23. Duncan Cameron to Paul Cameron, May 29, 1850, Cameron Papers, SHC.

24. Anne Ruffin Cameron to Paul Cameron, November 6, [1849], Cameron Papers, SHC.

25. Duncan Cameron to Paul Cameron, October 11, November 12, November 23, 1850; Paul Cameron to Duncan Cameron, November 14, November 23, 1850, Cameron Papers, SHC.

26. James Lesley to Peter Lesley, November 9, 1850, AFC. James Lesley wrote: "Her master came on here the week after she left—and returned home without his prey." Duncan Cameron had been in Philadelphia continuously since *August*

1850 and did not return to North Carolina until the *end* of November. James Lesley's claim therefore seems mistaken on both counts—unless "came on here" referred to James Lesley's High Street address (where Mary Walker had lodged and worked) and "home" to the Camerons' Philadelphia boardinghouse at Broad and Brighton. Independently, William Johnson asserted in his deposition of December 20 that Mary Walker "is now claimed as a slave" by Duncan Cameron. See the Deposition of William Johnson about Mary Walker, December 20, 1850, in the Ellis Gray Loring Papers, Schlesinger Library, Harvard University.

27. James Lesley to Peter Lesley, November 9, 1850, AFC.

28. Ames, *Life and Letters,* vol. 1, pp. 2–9, 16–17.

29. Ames, *Life and Letters,* vol. 1, pp. 18–19.

30. Peter Lesley to Sister, April 25, 1839; Peter Lesley to Father, July 24, 1841, in *Life and Letters,* ed. Ames, vol. 1, pp. 24, 35.

31. Peter Lesley to Father, March 13, 1843, in *Life and Letters,* ed. Ames, vol. 1, p. 45.

32. Ames, *Life and Letters,* vol. 1, pp. 134–141.

33. Peter Lesley, Sr., to Peter Lesley, February 18, 1847; Peter Lesley to Father, March 14, 1847, in *Life and Letters,* ed. Ames, vol. 1, pp. 146–147.

34. Ames, *Life and Letters,* vol. 1, pp. 149–161.

35. Letters detailing Lesley's conflict with the clergy over his religious views can be found in *Life and Letters,* ed. Ames, vol. 1, pp. 163–168, 195–207.

36. Peter Lesley to Susan Lyman, December 26, 1848, in *Life and Letters,* ed. Ames, vol. 1, p. 204.

37. J. P. Lesley, "An Address to the Suffolk North Association of Congregational Ministers" (Boston: Wm. Crosby and H. P. Nichols, 1849), pp. 1–9, 12–13, 17, 22–23, 31–33, 52–54.

38. James Lesley to Peter Lesley, August 18, 1849, AFC.

39. For the characterization of Wendell Phillips, see James Brewer Stewart, *Wendell Phillips: Liberty's Hero* (Baton Rouge: Louisiana State University Press, 1986), pp. 130–131. Peter Lesley to Stepmother, September 3, 1847; Peter Lesley to Allen Lesley, February 13, 1848; Peter Lesley to [Susan Lyman], November 25, 1848; Peter Lesley to Father, December 15, 1848, in *Life and Letters,* ed. Ames, vol. 1, pp. 157, 162, 198, 203.

40. Peter Lesley to Sister, June 18, 1839, in *Life and Letters,* ed. Ames, vol. 1, pp. 27–28.

41. Peter Lesley to Stepmother, June 21, 1847, in *Life and Letters,* ed. Ames, vol. 1, pp. 150–151.

42. "Speech of Wendell Phillips," Franklin Hall, May 12, 1848, reported in the *Pennsylvania Freeman,* June 8, 1848; Peter Lesley to Susan Lyman Lesley, May 1849, in *Life and Letters,* ed. Ames, vol. 1, pp. 220–221.

43. Allen Lesley to Peter Lesley, October 9, 1849, AFC; Peter Lesley to Father, March 13, 1852, in *Life and Letters,* ed. Ames, vol. 1, pp. 260–261.

44. Peter Lesley to Allen Lesley, December 23, 1848, December 16, 1849, AFC. For a brief overview of Peter Lesley's views on slavery, race, and the South from the 1850s to Reconstruction, see Lester D. Stephens, "'Forget Their Color': J. Peter Lesley on Slavery and the South," *New England Quarterly* 53 (June 1980): 212–221.

45. Peter Lesley to Stepmother, October 18, 1848, in *Life and Letters,* ed. Ames, vol. 1, p. 195; Peter Lesley to Susan Lyman, [October 18, 1848], AFC.

46. Peter Lesley to Father, October 2, 1850, in *Life and Letters,* ed. Ames, vol. 1, pp. 232–233; Susan Lyman Lesley to Margaret E. White, October 6, 1850, AFC.

47. Peter Lesley to James Freeman Clarke, November 3, 1850, in *Life and Letters,* ed. Ames, vol. 1, p. 233–234.

48. When Mary Walker left Philadelphia for refuge in Massachusetts, James Lesley sent with her a letter explaining the circumstances of her flight. She mislaid the letter. Peter Lesley notified his cousin by mail of the missing letter and on November 9, 1850, James Lesley wrote: "I hasten to reply immediately to your letter just received." My conclusion is that James Lesley had communicated with his cousin in late October, prior to Mary Walker's arrival, and that she had arrived (but mislaid the letter) at the end of October or the beginning of November. Hence my inference that when Peter Lesley gave his sermon, Mary Walker was in the household or known to be en route. James Lesley to Peter Lesley, November 9, 1850, AFC.

49. "The Fugitive Slave Bill: A Sermon Delivered in Milton, (Mass.), October 30, 1850," by J. P. Lesley, in the *Liberator,* November 1, 1850. My speculation is that for the October 30 sermon to be published in the November 1 issue of the *Liberator,* editor William Lloyd Garrison must have received an advance copy from Peter Lesley.

3. "In the Midst of Friends"

1. Susan Lyman Lesley to Margaret Harding White, November 12, 1850, Ames Family Historical Collection, private collection (hereafter AFC).

2. Anne Jean Robbins Lyman to daughter Anne ("Annie") Jean Lyman, No-

vember 15, 1829, in Susan I. Lesley, *Recollections of My Mother* (Boston: Press of Geo. H. Ellis, 1886), pp. 250–251.

3. Anne Jean Lyman to Abby Greene, July 14, 1833, in Lesley, *Recollections,* pp. 275–276.

4. Correspondence and remembrances collected in Lesley, *Recollections,* chronicle the illness and death of Annie Lyman. Her mother's grief poured out in letters to family and friends. See Anne Jean Lyman to [Edward Lyman], December 11, 1836; Anne Jean Lyman to Dr. Austin Flint, February 1, 1837; Anne Jean Lyman to Abby Greene, February 20, 1837, all in Lesley, *Recollections,* pp. 301–326. Susan Lyman wrote of her sister's deathbed advice in a letter to her closest aunt, Catherine Robbins. Susan Lyman to Catherine Robbins, February 29 [*sic*], 1837, in AFC. For the statement of the pledge that united Susan forever to her sister, see Susan Lyman to Peter Lesley, October 5, 1848, AFC.

5. Lesley, *Recollections,* pp. 259–260, 350–351, 455–463.

6. Susan Lyman to [Margaret E. Harding?], May 6, 1842, in Mary Lesley Ames, ed., *Life and Letters of Peter and Susan Lesley,* 2 vols. (New York: G. P. Putnam's Sons, Knickerbocker Press, 1909), vol. 1, p. 183.

7. Lesley, *Recollections,* pp. 338–339, 491–492. Commenting in 1848 on the life and recent death of John Quincy Adams, who had defiantly confronted Southern slave-holders in his post-presidential years as a Massachusetts congressman, Anne Jean Lyman praised Adams but characteristically hoped that there would be enough virtue on both sides to keep the peace while she lived. "I mean to keep in my narrow sphere by treating all God's children (of whatever caste or colour . . .) as well as I know how, and as I wish to be treated myself." Anne Jean Lyman to Susan Lyman, March 10, 1848, AFC.

8. Susan Lyman to Catherine Robbins, October 3, 1846, AFC.

9. Susan Lyman to Peter Lesley, October 31, 1848, AFC.

10. Susan Lyman to Anne Jean Lyman, December 26, 1846, AFC.

11. Carolyn L. Karcher, *The First Woman in the Republic: A Cultural Biography of Lydia Maria Child* (Durham, N.C.: Duke University Press, 1994), pp. 173–175, 180–184, 190–193.

12. Karcher, *First Woman,* ch. 12, pp. 309–312.

13. Karcher, *First Woman,* pp. 269–299; Fergus M. Bordewich, *Bound for Canaan: The Epic Story of the Underground Railroad, America's First Civil Rights Movement* (New York: Amistad/Harper Collins, 2005), ch. 3, pp. 133–134.

14. Karcher, *First Woman,* pp. 314, 366; Susan Lyman to Anne Jean Lyman, January 24, February 12, 1847, AFC.

15. Susan Lyman to Catherine Robbins, June 29, 1847, AFC.
16. Susan Lyman to Peter Lesley, October 31, 1848, AFC.
17. Karcher, *First Woman,* ch. 12.
18. Susan Lyman to Anne Jean Lyman, March 19, 1848; Susan Lyman to Peter Lesley, October 23, 1848, AFC.
19. References to the failed romance came in correspondence between Susan Lyman and her trusted aunt, Catherine Robbins. The letters from "Aunt Kitty" to Susan, addressed to "Dearly Beloved" or "My Dear Child," gave the month and day but not the year they were sent. See Catherine Robbins to Susan Lyman, September 7, October 24, October 30, and November 6, in the Undated Files of the Catherine Robbins box of letters in the Ames Family Collection. Letters from Susan Lyman to her Aunt Kitty suggest that her suitor—referred to only as "E" or "Edmund"—ended the courtship in 1847. See Susan Lyman to Catherine Robbins, February 27, 1847 (in which she says she will steer clear of Boston to avoid "E"), and undated letters (with neither dates nor years given), also in the Catherine Robbins Undated Files, AFC. A letter of January 29, 1847, from Susan Lyman to Catherine Robbins, may also have touched on the romance. It is the only letter in the entire Ames Family Historical Collection with a paragraph physically cut out of it.
20. Lesley, *Recollections,* p. 396; Susan Lyman to Anne Jean Lyman, November 13, 1843, AFC.
21. Susan Lyman to Catherine Robbins, June 17, July 7, 1848, AFC.
22. Susan Lyman to Peter Lesley, October 5, October 23, 1848, AFC.
23. I infer that Susan Lyman knew of Peter Lesley from a letter sent to her by her aunt. Catherine Robbins to Susan Lyman, May 28, 1848, AFC. Her aunt wrote of a May visit from a "worn-out" Mr. Lesley to her residence in Cambridge.
24. Peter Lesley to Susan Lyman, [October 1848], AFC. In this October letter to Susan Lyman, Peter Lesley is quoting back to her what she had reported to him about their first meeting in July 1848.
25. Susan Lyman to Peter Lesley, October 5, 1848; Peter Lesley to Susan Lyman, October 14, 1848; Susan Lyman to Margaret Harding White, October 20, 1848, AFC.
26. Peter Lesley to Susan Lyman, [October 18, 1848]; Susan Lyman to Margaret Harding White, November 29, 1848, AFC.
27. Susan Lyman to Margaret Harding White, October 3, 1848, AFC.

28. Susan Lyman to Peter Lesley, October 5, 1848, AFC.

29. Susan Lyman to Margaret Harding White, November 29, 1848, AFC.

30. Journal of Peter Lesley, entries for April 4, July 5, September 28, 1850, AFC.

31. James Lesley to Peter Lesley, November 9, 1850, January 29, 1851, AFC.

32. Susan Lesley to Margaret Harding White, November 12, 1850; Margaret Harding White to Susan Lesley, December 5, 1850, AFC.

33. Louisa Loring to Susan Lesley, December 19, 1850, J. Peter Lesley Papers, American Philosophical Society, Philadelphia (hereafter Lesley Papers, APS).

34. Ames, *Life and Letters,* vol. 1, pp. 214, 236–237, 252.

35. The four depositions, discussed in Chapter 1, are in the Mary Walker File of the Ellis Gray Loring Papers, Schlesinger Library, Harvard University. James Lesley to Peter Lesley, January 29, 1851, AFC.

36. The Supreme Court's 1857 decision in the Dred Scott case confirmed Loring's foresight.

37. Ellis Gray Loring to Peter Lesley, April 22, 1851, Lesley Papers, APS. Loring had written to friends in Philadelphia for their opinion and awaited their reply. "In the mean time, I will retain the affidavits, as they may be of great value to Mary, & I think it best not to trust them to the mail." Loring's decision to safeguard the depositions led to their placement in the Loring Papers at the Schlesinger Library.

38. Catherine Robbins to Susan Lesley, August 27, September 11, 1851; Susan Lesley to Peter Lesley, June 22, 1852, AFC; Ames, *Life and Letters,* vol. 1, p. 265.

39. Catherine Robbins to Susan Lesley, November 12, [1851]; Susan Lesley to Margaret Harding White, May 29, [1851], April 19, 1852; Peter Lesley to Susan Lesley, May 5, 1852, AFC; William S. Thayer to Peter Lesley, April 15, June 17, 1852, Lesley Papers, APS; Ames, *Life and Letters,* vol. 1, pp. 262–268.

40. Lesley, *Recollections,* pp. 191–192, 336–359, 413–451, 455–463, 490–493. New Northampton neighbors in 1838, Maria Child and Anne Jean Lyman immediately crossed swords over "whether slave-holding was or was not sin." Child wrote that "Mrs. Lyman seems determined that she will get acquainted with me, though she is the very embodiment of aristocracy. Hates republics, hates democracy in every form, and of course hates reforms of all sorts. . . . But she is a fine looking woman (anything but a drooping and twining vine) of noble impulses, and a brave, imprudent frankness; and I like her, notwithstanding her distorted views of men and things. If she can manage to like me, antislavery

rights of woman and all, it must be because she respects the daring freedom of speech which she practices." Lydia Maria Child to Ellis Gray Loring, July 10, 1838, Loring Papers, Schlesinger Library.

41. Susan Lesley to Peter Lesley, May 17, 1852, AFC.

42. Peter Lesley to Susan Lesley, April 5, 1852, AFC. Only expurgated versions of the letters about the painful breakup with Henry Rogers were published in *Life and Letters,* ed. Ames, vol. 1, pp. 262–266.

43. Susan Lesley to Peter Lesley, April 15, 1852; Peter Lesley to Susan Lesley, April 20, 1852, AFC.

44. Peter Lesley to Susan Lesley, April 20, 1852, AFC.

45. Susan Lesley to Peter Lesley, [April 13, 1852], May 2, May 9, 1852; Susan Lesley to Margaret Harding White, April 19, 1852, AFC.

46. Susan Lesley to Peter Lesley, April 28, 1852, AFC.

47. Ibid.

48. Peter Lesley to Susan Lesley, May 5, May 9, May 16, 1852, AFC.

49. The undated statement to Sarah Forbes, explaining Mary Walker's dilemma and refusal, was dictated by Susan Lesley to her aunt Catherine Robbins, and recorded in Catherine Robbins's handwriting. I infer that Susan Lesley asked her aunt to convey the explanation to the Forbes family. Susan Lesley was deeply upset with her cousin, whom she felt had "selfishly pounced" on Mary Walker without regard for the refugee's needs. See the undated Catherine Robbins letters in Box 61 of the Ames Family Historical Collection.

50. Susan Lesley to Peter Lesley, May 15, May 21, 1852, AFC. The plight of the refugee is distilled in Gerda Lerner, *Fireweed: A Political Autobiography* (Philadelphia: Temple University Press, 2002), p. 122. Refugees were expected to be "excessively polite and try to make themselves unobtrusively useful. Like poor relatives, they anticipate the wishes of their hosts, who expect, at the very least, sincere and frequent expressions of gratitude." The compliant role repelled Gerda Lerner when she became a refugee from fascist Vienna in 1938. Not "able or willing to offer any of this as I should have," she instead "offered my cheerful, optimistic activism as a way of showing my appreciation. . . . That's another way of being a refugee and it was one more suited to my personality and inclinations."

51. Susan Lesley to Peter Lesley, May 17, 1852, AFC.

52. Susan Lesley to Peter Lesley, May 21, May 25, 1852, AFC.

53. Susan Lesley to Peter Lesley, May 27, 1852, AFC.

54. Anonymous to Miss Margaret Cameron, n.d., in Undated Correspon-

dence, Box 80, Cameron Family Papers, Southern Historical Collection, University of North Carolina at Chapel Hill. My thanks to Jean Bradley Anderson for pointing me to this anonymous "poison-pen" letter in the Cameron Papers.

55. Susan Lesley to Peter Lesley, June 8, 1852, AFC.

56. Peter Lesley to Susan Lesley, June 27, 1853, AFC.

57. Susan Lesley to Peter Lesley, June 13, June 20, 1852, AFC. These stories are detailed in Chapter 1.

58. Susan Lesley to Peter Lesley, June 24, June 29, 1852; Susan Lesley to Catherine Robbins, September [n.d.], 1852, AFC.

59. Catherine Robbins to Susan Lesley, September 13, September 30, October 19, 1852, AFC.

60. Catherine Robbins to Susan Lesley, October 25, November 16, 1852; Susan Lesley to Anne Jean Lyman, November 25, 1852, AFC. Anne Jean Lyman had written to her daughter of "my soul's desolation, weariness of life." Responding, Susan Lesley asked her mother to think more positively. She was neither poor nor dependent; her children's marriages and departures were in the nature of things; their homes were open to her; Susan would visit each summer. "Must I think of my dear mother whom I love so truly as . . . unable to make a quiet and peaceful home for herself? Give my love to all, particularly to Mary Walker."

61. M.E.W. to Susan Lesley, January [5 and 6], 1853, Lesley Papers, APS. The Guide to the Lesley Papers at the American Philosophical Society in Philadelphia mistakenly credits this letter, signed with the initials M.E.W., to a Lesley family friend, Mary Elizabeth Ware. Mary E. Walker had the same initials. The handwriting, occasional phonetic spelling, and content of the letter make it clear that the letter is from Mary Walker. For Anne Jean Lyman's mention of sewing for and reading to Mary Walker, see the journal entries of November 25 and December 25, 1852, and those of January 9, January 17, January 30, and February 20, 1853, in the Journal of Anne Jean Lyman, AFC.

62. Catherine Robbins to Susan Lesley, December 31, 1852; January 9, January 16, February 9, February 24, April 25, April 27, [1853], AFC; Lesley, *Recollections*, pp. 467–469.

4. "Never Reject the Claims of the Fugitive"

1. Catherine Robbins to Susan Lesley, [February 24, 1853], Ames Family Historical Collection, private collection (hereafter AFC).

2. James McKim, editor of the Philadelphia antislavery newspaper, the *Penn-*

sylvania Freeman, and employer of William Still, the clerk in the newspaper's office, kept in touch with Mary Walker through the Lesleys. In June 1851 he wrote that he doubted that a slave-catcher would come after her in Boston, but urged her to remain on guard. He promised to be on the lookout for information about her children. By the end of 1851, having heard nothing, Mary Walker gave up hope of hearing from her children. Susan Lesley to Catherine Robbins, June 10, 1851; Susan Lesley to Margaret Harding White, December 15, 1851, AFC.

3. Catherine Robbins to Susan Lesley, [February 24, 1853], AFC.

4. Susan Lesley to Catherine Robbins, March 9, 1853, AFC.

5. Paul Cameron to Duncan Cameron, January 30, 1835, Cameron Family Papers, Southern Historical Collection, University of North Carolina at Chapel Hill (hereafter Cameron Papers, SHC); Jean Bradley Anderson, *Piedmont Plantation: The Bennehan-Cameron Family and Lands in North Carolina* (Durham, N.C.: Historic Preservation Society of Durham, 1985), pp. 96, 105–106, 109–110.

6. Thomas Ruffin to Paul Cameron, January 24, 1834, Cameron Papers, SHC. Anderson, *Piedmont Plantation,* pp. 44–45, 49–52.

7. Paul Cameron to Sister, February 17, 1829, Cameron Papers, SHC; Anderson, *Piedmont Plantation,* pp. 33–34.

8. Paul Cameron to Duncan Cameron, April 26, 1835, Cameron Papers, SHC. Anderson, *Piedmont Plantation,* p. 97.

9. Paul Cameron to Duncan Cameron, May 20, 1835, Cameron Papers, SHC.

10. Paul Cameron to Duncan Cameron, June 10, 1835, March 25 [1846], Cameron Papers, SHC. The story was passed on in the "Narrative of James Curry," in *Slave Testimony: Two Centuries of Letters, Speeches, Interviews, and Autobiographies,* ed. John Blassingame (Baton Rouge: Louisiana State University Press, 1977), p. 149.

11. Sydney Nathans, "'Fortress without Walls': A Black Community after Slavery," in *Holding On to the Land and the Lord,* ed. Robert L. Hall and Carol B. Stack (Athens: University of Georgia Press, 1982), pp. 55–58.

12. Susan Lesley to Peter Lesley, June 6, 1853, AFC.

13. Susan Lesley to Margaret Harding White, April 19, 1852, January 18, 1853; Susan Lesley to Catherine Robbins, March 9, 1853, AFC.

14. Susan Lesley to Peter Lesley, June 6, 1853, AFC.

15. Susan Lesley to Peter Lesley, June 19, 1853, AFC. Mary Walker may have had good reason to be startled by the Lorings' rejection of her request for help. In January 1853, Peter Still, the brother of William, had come to Boston to raise money to buy his wife and children, enslaved in Alabama. Ellis Gray Loring was one of seven signers of a public letter that commended the case of "PETER

STILL to the benevolent," and stated that "Any contribution for the object above named may be forwarded to any of us." The letter was published in the *Liberator,* January 21, 1853. *Liberator* editor William Lloyd Garrison did not sign the letter, but privately sympathized with the fundraising effort by Peter Still, though he found the slave-holder's ransom demand "revolting." Abolitionists debated and divided over whether efforts to purchase individual slaves were tolerable or harmful. Garrison, for example, defended the purchase of Frederick Douglass's freedom by British friends. To Garrison, contends biographer Henry Mayer, ransom "epitomized not complicity with evil but the 'extortionate power' of slaveholders. To liberate a loved one under coercion, as many black families found themselves obliged to do, was very different from a policy that legitimized the slaveholders' property right." See Henry Mayer, *All on Fire: William Lloyd Garrison and the Abolition of Slavery* (New York: St. Martin's Press, 1998), p. 372. On the other hand, the editor of the *Pennsylvania Freeman,* where William Still worked as a clerk, declared ransom an act of "mistaken philanthropy" which sacrificed "the general to the individual good." *Pennsylvania Freeman,* February 20, 1851. A letter writer to the *Freeman* in early 1853 distilled the dilemma. "What would I not do if my wife was still in bondage, like that in which Peter Still's wife is pining away? Nevertheless, I believe great evil is growing out of this practice of purchasing slaves for freedom. What vast sums have been expended to emancipate a few among the millions, when the same money otherwise expended might do much toward hastening universal emancipation?" N. R. Johnston to the *Pennsylvania Freeman,* letter reprinted in the *Liberator,* April 8, 1853. The debate continues in the twenty-first century. See Kwame Anthony Appiah and Martin Bunzl, eds., *Buying Freedom: The Ethics and Economics of Slave Redemption* (Princeton: Princeton University Press, 2007), especially the essays by Kevin Bales, Margaret M. R. Kellow, and John Stauffer.

16. Mary Walker to Catherine Robbins, April 18, 1853; Susan Lesley to Peter Lesley, June 19, 1853, AFC.

17. Susan Lesley to Peter Lesley, June 19, 1853, AFC.

18. Ibid.; Peter Lesley to Susan Lesley, June 24, June 27, 1853, AFC. Peter Still, the brother of the head of the Philadelphia Vigilance Committee, William Still, was also trying to "obtain the ransom" for his enslaved family from sympathetic New Englanders. William Lloyd Garrison found Peter Still "as modest as he is untiring, and as patient and hopeful as he is affectionate and upright." Garrison felt "fire in all my veins to think of such a man being robbed of his wife and family . . . as though he were a mere beast, and they were literally but pieces of

merchandise." He hoped that Still's "uphill work" would "not be in vain." Garrison did not state whether he contributed to the ransom. William Lloyd Garrison to Samuel J. May, May 31, 1853, in Garrison Papers, Antislavery Collection, Boston Public Library.

19. Susan Lesley to Peter Lesley, June 19, 1853, AFC.

20. Ibid.

5. The Rescue Plot

1. Peter Lesley to Susan Lesley, June 24, 1853, Ames Family Historical Collection, private collection (hereafter AFC).

2. Ibid.

3. T[homas] V[erner] Moore to Peter Lesley, July 2, 1853, J. Peter Lesley Papers, American Philosophical Society, Philadelphia (hereafter Lesley Papers, APS).

4. T. V. Moore to Peter Lesley, July 14, 1853, Lesley Papers, APS; Peter Lesley to Susan Lesley, July 16, 1853, AFC.

5. Susan Lesley to Peter Lesley, July 18, 1853, AFC.

6. Peter Lesley to Susan Lesley, July 16, July 27, July 31, 1853, AFC.

7. Peter Lesley to Susan Lesley, July 31, 1853, AFC.

8. Ibid.

9. See Harriet A. Jacobs, *Incidents in the Life of a Slave Girl, Written by Herself* (1861), ed. Jean Fagan Yellin (Cambridge, Mass.: Harvard University Press, 1987), xv, chs. 5–7, 9–10; and Jean Fagan Yellin, *Harriet Jacobs: A Life* (New York: Basic Civitas Books, 2004), ch. 2.

10. Peter Lesley to Susan Lesley, July 31, 1853, AFC.

11. Susan Lesley to Peter Lesley, August 6, August 14, 1853, AFC.

12. Susan Lesley to Peter Lesley, August 14, 1853, AFC.

13. Paul Cameron to Sisters, n.d. [March 8, 1853], Cameron Family Papers, Southern Historical Collection, University of North Carolina at Chapel Hill (hereafter Cameron Papers, SHC). For information on Archy Drake as a grogshop owner, see Elizabeth Reid Murray, *Wake: Capital County of North Carolina,* vol. 1 (Raleigh: Capital County Publishing Company, 1983), p. 399. See also the entry for Archy Drake in the U.S. Federal Census for 1850 for Raleigh, Wake County, roll M432–647, p. 286, image 571. All census information was accessed through Ancestry.com.

14. Paul Cameron to Sisters [March 8, 1853], Cameron Papers, SHC.

15. Ibid.

16. Paul Cameron to Sisters, [March 8], March 10, March 17, [1853], Cameron Papers, SHC.

17. Margaret Cameron to Paul Cameron, March 15, [1853]; Paul Cameron to Margaret Cameron, March 17, [1853], Cameron Papers, SHC.

18. George E. Badger to the Honorable Mr. Stockton, March 13, 1853, Cameron Papers, SHC. See the Cameron Affidavit "For Mr. Jas. Woods" in the following note.

19. Cameron Affidavit "For Mr. Jas. Woods," from the Cameron Papers, SHC; see also Jean Bradley Anderson, *Piedmont Plantation: The Bennehan-Cameron Family and Lands in North Carolina* (Durham, N.C.: Historic Preservation Society of Durham, 1985), pp. 98–99. A *copy* of the Cameron Affidavit, describing Frank Walker and designated "For James Woods," can be found at the Stagville Historic Preservation Center in Durham, a North Carolina Historic Site. My thanks to former Stagville site manager Jennifer Farley for supplying me with a photocopy and a typed transcription. I have not been able to locate the original affidavit in the Cameron Papers at the Southern Historical Collection, either in the run of letters about Frank Walker during March 1853, or in the Undated Correspondence under the name of Jas. Wood.

20. Paul Cameron to Sister, n.d., [1853], Cameron Papers, SHC.

21. Cameron to Sister, n.d., [1853]; William Anderson to Paul Cameron, March 23, March 26, 1853, Cameron Papers, SHC.

22. In the 1850 Federal Census for Raleigh, A. G. Drake had no occupation listed next to his name. By 1860, he was listed as a merchant, with real estate valued at $2,500 and personal property of $500. The 1850 listing is on roll M432–647, p. 286, image 571; the 1860 listing is roll M653–916, p. 0, image 319. The 1870 census listed a forty-five-year-old "Arch Drake," born in North Carolina, as a black farmer living in Henderson, Tennessee. See roll 593–1537, p. 76, image 146, all available at Ancestry.com. Margaret Cameron informed her brother: "Your agent Mr. Woods made no secret of his business." Margaret Cameron to Paul Cameron, March 15, [1853], Cameron Papers, SHC.

23. Emily Bingham, *Mordecai: An Early American Family* (New York: Hill and Wang, 2003). Throughout the 1840s, the correspondence between George Mordecai and Duncan Cameron was cordial and straightforward.

24. See the 1852–1853 anguished "billet-doux" correspondence—secret notes between the lovers forbidden to court—in the George W. Mordecai Papers,

Southern Historical Collection, University of North Carolina at Chapel Hill. George Mordecai's family also wrote of the ban, attributing it to Duncan Cameron. Bingham, *Mordecai,* p. 234, n. 26.

25. Paul Cameron to Margaret Cameron, April 21, 1853; Thomas Ruffin to Paul Cameron, May 9, 1853; Margaret Cameron to Paul Cameron, May 23, 1853; Paul Cameron to Margaret Cameron, May 24, 1853, all in Cameron Papers, SHC.

26. Susan Lesley to Peter Lesley, September 25, 1853, AFC.

27. Margaret Harding White to Peter Lesley, August 19, 1853, AFC.

28. Rosa [Hopper] to Susan and Peter Lesley, December 29, 1853, AFC.

29. Peter Lesley to Catherine Robbins, [October 26, 1853]. The name "Mary," given to the Lesleys' daughter, paid homage to many women—Peter Lesley's mother, Susan Lesley's sister, an aunt, a cousin, and a friend. Explaining to her skeptical mother why they'd picked the name "Mary," Susan Lesley stated that she hoped her daughter would "be half so good as any one of these. I hope to find time to write a letter to Mary Walker." Susan Lesley to Anne Jean Lyman, December 22, 1853, AFC. In an 1854 letter, Susan Lesley wrote to Mary Walker that they would always associate their daughter's name with her. Susan Lesley to Catherine Robbins, n.d. [December 1854], AFC.

30. Susan Lesley to Peter Lesley, July 24, 1853; Peter Lesley to Susan Lesley, July 27, 1853, AFC.

31. Anderson, *Piedmont Plantation,* p. 38.

32. For the 1870 and 1880 U.S. Census listings of Lucy Stephens in Caswell County, N.C., see the 1870 Census, roll M593–1128, p. 396, image 221, and 1880 Census, roll T9–956; Family History Film 1254956; for Stephen Stephens in 1870, see roll M593–1128, p. 419, image 267, accessed through Ancestry.com. For the identification of Stephen Stephens as a former "slave in the Mordecai-Cameron family," see Murray, *Wake,* vol. 1, p. 496.

33. Lucy Stephens would have been the conduit for the letter to Mildred Cameron, rather than its recipient. In the censuses of both 1870 and 1880, she was listed as unable to read or write.

34. Catherine Robbins to Susan Lesley, April 9, [1854], AFC.

35. Susan Lesley to Margaret Harding White, March 23, 1854, AFC.

36. Catherine Robbins to Susan Lesley, May 30, June 6, [1854], AFC.

37. Susan Lesley to Peter Lesley, June 4, June 6, July 24, 1854, AFC.

38. Peter Lesley to Susan Lesley, July 27, 1854, AFC.

39. Peter Lesley to Susan Lesley, July 27, 1853, AFC.

40. Peter Lesley to Susan Lesley, July 29, 1854, AFC.

41. Ibid.

42. Peter Lesley to Susan Lesley, August 4, August 6, 1854, AFC.

43. Peter Lesley to Susan Lesley, August 8, 1854, AFC.

44. Peter Lesley to Susan Lesley, August 4–13, 1854, AFC.

45. Stanley J. Robboy and Anita W. Robboy, "Lewis Hayden: From Fugitive Slave to Statesman," *New England Quarterly* 46 (December 1973): 591–603; Gary Collison, *Shadrach Minkins: From Fugitive Slave to Citizen* (Cambridge, Mass.: Harvard University Press, 1997), chs. 7–8.

46. For the listing of James M. Price in the 1850 U.S. Census for Philadelphia, see roll M432–817, p. 303, image 197, available at Ancestry.com.

47. Peter Lesley to Susan Lesley, August 8, 1854, AFC. The letter of August 8 was the most comprehensive of five separate letters sent to Susan Lesley about the Price mission, from August 6 to August 13, 1854.

48. Peter Lesley to Susan Lesley, August 8, 1854, AFC.

49. Ibid.

50. Susan Lesley to Peter Lesley, August 10, 1854, AFC.

51. Susan Lesley to Peter Lesley, August 13, 1854, AFC.

52. Ibid.

53. Peter Lesley to Susan Lesley, August 20, 1854, AFC.

54. Ibid.

6. *"A Spirit Like a Dove"*

1. Susan Lesley to Margaret Harding White, July 4, 1854, Ames Family Historical Collection, private collection (hereafter AFC).

2. Ibid.; Susan Lesley to Peter Lesley, August 6, 1854, AFC.

3. Susan Lesley to Peter Lesley, July 11, 1854, AFC.

4. Susan Lesley to Peter Lesley, July 24, 1854, AFC.

5. Susan Lesley to Peter Lesley, August 16, August 25, 1854, AFC.

6. Susan Lesley to Peter Lesley, September 10, 185[4], AFC.

7. Ibid.; Peter Lesley to Susan Lesley, September 17, 1854, AFC.

8. Susan Lesley to Peter Lesley, October 16, October 21, 1854, AFC.

9. Susan Lesley to Anne Jean Lyman, October 8, 1854; Susan Lesley to Margaret Harding White, December 24, 1854, AFC.

10. Susan Lesley to Margaret Harding White, December 24, 1854, AFC.

11. In June 1855, Susan Lesley accidentally revealed the name of Mary Walker's Albany friend to her aunt, Catherine Robbins. Her aunt was startled. Though she promised "never to show the slightest consciousness of her knowledge,"

Catherine Robbins's "great surprise" suggests that the person was a man of some note. It's my conjecture that his prominence—and his connection with Mary Walker—may have come from involvement with Albany's Underground Railroad. I've been unable to establish who the man was. Susan Lesley to Peter Lesley, June 28, 1855, AFC.

12. Susan Lesley to Peter Lesley, October 8, 1854, AFC.

13. Susan Lesley to Peter Lesley, October 21, 1854, AFC.

14. Susan Lesley to Margaret Harding White, December 24, 1854, AFC.

15. Susan Lesley to Catherine Robbins, Friday, n.d. [December 1854]. During December 1854, Susan Lesley and her aunt Catherine Robbins corresponded continually about Mary Walker's illness. The Ames Family Historical Collection contains only Susan Lesley's letters to her aunt. They came in rapid succession and were dated only by day of the week, rather than by month, day, and year. Here, I have noted them all as being sent in December 1854.

16. Susan Lesley to Catherine Robbins, Friday, [December 1854], AFC. My thanks to Darla McCarley-Celentano of Plum Creek Forensic Laboratory for her attempt to detect the scratched-out names through the use of a video spectral comparator. Mary Walker asked that the letters from her friend in Albany be returned to him. Though not destroyed by Susan Lesley in 1854–1855, the correspondence of Mary Walker has not been found.

17. Susan Lesley to Catherine Robbins, Wednesday, [December 1854]; Susan Lesley to Margaret Harding White, December 24, 1854, AFC.

18. Susan Lesley to Anne Jean Lyman, January 14, 1855; Susan Lesley to Margaret Harding White, February 21, 1854, AFC.

19. Anne Jean Lyman to Susan Lesley, January 21, 1855, AFC.

20. Ibid.

21. Susan Lesley to Catherine Robbins, [January 29, 1855], AFC.

22. Susan Lesley to Catherine Robbins, [February 20, 1855], AFC.

23. Diary of Anne Jean Lyman, December 1854, AFC.

24. Susan Lesley to Catherine Robbins, January 29, [1855], AFC.

25. Susan Lesley to Catherine Robbins, Friday evening, [December 1854], December 26, [1854], AFC.

26. Susan Lesley to Peter Lesley, August 25, 1854; Susan Lesley to Catherine Robbins, Wednesday, [December 1854], AFC.

27. Susan Lesley to Peter Lesley, May 17, May 24, May 29, 1855, AFC.

28. Susan Lesley to Peter Lesley, June 24, 1855, AFC.

29. Ibid. For the record of Mary Walker's baptism, see the Minutes of the Old

Cambridge Baptist Church for June 23, 1855, housed in the office of the minister. My thanks to the Reverend Irv Cummins for permitting me to view the church records.

30. Susan Lesley to Peter Lesley, July 7, 1855, AFC.

31. Susan Lesley to Peter Lesley, July 15, [1855], AFC.

7. A Season of Silence

1. Peter Lesley to Susan Lesley, September 8, 1855, Ames Family Historical Collection, private collection (hereafter AFC).

2. Susan Lesley to Peter Lesley, August 24, [1854], AFC.

3. Peter Lesley to Susan Lesley, August 28, 1854, AFC.

4. William Still, *The Underground Railroad* (Philadelphia: Porter and Coates, 1872; repr. New York: Arno and New York Times, 1968), p. 188. There are two different reprint editions of William Still's book. The two editions, unfortunately, have different paginations. I have used both editions.

5. Elizabeth Reid Murray, *Wake: Capital County of North Carolina,* vol. 1 (Raleigh: Capital County Publishing Company, 1983).

6. "Lunsford Lane: An Interesting Fact" (1842), in *Slave Testimony: Two Centuries of Letters, Speeches, Interviews, and Autobiographies,* ed. John Blassingame (Baton Rouge: Louisiana State Press, 1977), pp. 145–150. The most recent complete edition of Lunsford Lane's narrative is found in B. Eugene McCarthy and Thomas L. Doughton, eds., *From Bondage to Belonging: The Worcester Slave Narratives* (Amherst: University of Massachusetts Press, 2007).

7. Peter Lesley to Susan Lesley, September 21, 1855, AFC.

8. Susan Lesley to Peter Lesley, [July 30, 1855], AFC.

9. Susan Lesley to Peter Lesley, September 12, September 22, 1854, AFC.

10. Susan Lesley to Peter Lesley, September 22, 1855; Peter Lesley to Susan Lesley, [September 26, 1855], AFC.

11. Susan Lesley to Catherine Robbins, January 1856, March 2, 1856, AFC.

12. Susan Lesley to Catherine Robbins, March 8, 1856, AFC.

13. Chauncey Wright to Professor Lesley, March 25, 1856, in *Letters of Chauncey Wright, with Some Account of His Life,* ed. James Bradley Thayer (Cambridge, 1878; repr. New York: Burt Publishing Company, 1971), pp. 38–39. The bracketed sentence is in the original letter.

14. Elizabeth Reid Murray's comprehensive study of Raleigh and Wake County makes brief mention of the Reverend Drury Lacy and of two of the trustworthy men of color that Mary Walker named: Glasgow Saunders and Wil-

lis Haywood. See Murray, *Wake,* pp. 476 and 606 (Drury Lacy), pp. 541 and 568n. (Willis Haywood), and p. 253 (Glasgow Saunders). The Drury Lacy Papers at the Southern Historical Collection, University of North Carolina at Chapel Hill, contained no information about "Uncle Zack" or other persons named in Mary Walker's instructions.

15. Susan Lesley to Peter Lesley, June 28, 1855, AFC.

16. Frederick Douglass to Susan Lesley, September 6, 1856, J. Peter Lesley Papers, American Philosophical Society, Philadelphia.

17. Susan Lesley to Peter Lesley, July 18, 1856, AFC.

18. Susan Lesley to Peter Lesley, July 24, July 27, August 1, 1856, AFC.

19. Susan Lesley to Peter Lesley, September 2, 1856, AFC.

20. Peter Lesley to Susan Lesley, September 22, 1856, AFC.

21. Susan Lesley to Peter Lesley, October 3, 1856, AFC.

22. Ibid.

23. Peter Lesley to Susan Lesley, July 19, 1856, in *Life and Letters of Peter and Susan Lesley,* ed. Mary Lesley Ames, 2 vols. (New York: G. P. Putnam's Sons, 1909), vol. 1, p. 332–333.

24. Peter Lesley to Susan Lesley, July 19, 1856; Susan Lesley to Peter Lesley, July 24, 1856, AFC.

25. Peter Lesley to Susan Lesley, July 31, 1856; Susan Lesley to Peter Lesley, September 11, 1856, in *Life and Letters,* ed. Ames, vol. 1, pp. 337–339.

26. Susan Lesley to [Margaret Harding White], October 19, October 23, November 2, November 12, 1856, AFC.

27. Susan Lesley to [Margaret Harding White], November 12, 1856, AFC.

28. Ibid.

29. Ames, *Life and Letters,* vol. 1, pp. 350–353, 363–364.

30. Mary Walker to Catherine Robbins, November 4, 1858, AFC.

8. "A Case of Heart Breaking Distress"

1. Susan Lesley to Peter Lesley, July 21, 1859, Ames Family Historical Collection, private collection (hereafter AFC).

2. James Freeman Clarke, *Anti-Slavery Days* (New York: John W. Lovell, 1884), pp. 82–83; William Still, *The Underground Railroad* (Philadelphia: Porter and Coates, 1872). For this chapter, I have used the edition reprinted in 1970 by the Johnson Publishing Company of Chicago. See pp. 373–374. For evidence of Hillard's outspokenness against slavery in the 1830s, see Deborah Weston to

Mary Weston, February 23, 1835, and Anne [Weston] to Deborah Weston, January 1, 1837, in Weston Papers (Antislavery Collection), Boston Public Library.

3. In *The Underground Railroad,* William Still reported several instances in which the Lesleys befriended fugitive slaves in Philadelphia and arranged for them to receive sanctuary in the Boston safe house of Susan Hillard, Susan Lesley's cousin. See Still, *Underground Railroad,* pp. 559, 565. For the account of Phillis Gault's escape from Norfolk, see Still, *Underground Railroad,* pp. 168 and 171–172.

4. The handwritten entry in William Still's journal was made on November 29, 1855. "Journal C. of the Underground Railroad in Philadelphia, Kept by William Still: Containing Notices of Arrivals of Fugitive Slaves in Philadelphia . . . , 1852–57," Pennsylvania Abolition Society Papers, available on microfilm at the Historical Society of Pennsylvania, Philadelphia. William Still elaborated and updated his portrayal of Phillis Gault in his 1872 book. Still, *Underground Railroad,* pp. 171–172.

5. Gary Collison, *Shadrach Minkins: From Fugitive Slave to Citizen* (Cambridge, Mass.: Harvard University Press, 1997), pp. 45–51. Still, *Underground Railroad,* pp. 164–172.

6. On William Bagnal, see the 1860 United States Manuscript Federal Census for Norfolk, Virginia, roll M653_1366, p. 344, image 349, available at Ancestry.com. William Bagnal, who was fifty-six in 1860, had real and personal property valued at $18,500.

7. Thomas F. Page to William Still, February 25, 1857, printed in Still, *Underground Railroad,* p. 333.

8. Still, *Underground Railroad,* p. 565. The 1860 United States Census listed Florence Gault and Richard Page as members of the household of George and Susan Hillard. See the microfilmed 1860 Federal Census for Boston, roll M653_521, p. 709, image 710, accessed through Ancestry.com.

9. Mrs. Flarece P. Gayult to William Still, March 22, 1858, printed in Still, *Underground Railroad,* pp. 171–172. For the listing of the free black Philadelphia dentist Harry Lundy, see the microfilmed 1860 Federal Census for Philadelphia, roll M653_1153, p. 317, image 320, available at Ancestry.com.

10. Susan Lesley to Peter Lesley, July 21, 1859, AFC.

11. Ibid.

12. Peter Lesley to Susan Lesley, July 26, 1859, AFC.

13. Peter Lesley to Mildred Cameron, September 4, 1859, Cameron Family Papers, Southern Historical Collection, University of North Carolina at Cha-

pel Hill. The published version of this letter, excerpted from the original, first drew my attention to Mary Walker. See Herbert Gutman, *The Black Family in Slavery and Freedom, 1750–1925* (New York: Pantheon, 1976), pp. 183–184. The interpretation that follows is based on the manuscript of the September 4, 1859, letter, found in the Cameron Papers.

14. Peter Lesley to Susan Lesley, September 4, 1859, AFC.

15. Susan Lesley to [Catherine Robbins], November 27, 1859, AFC.

16. Ibid.

17. Excerpts from William Furness's sermons quoted in Still, *The Underground Railroad,* pp. 663–664.

18. Susan Lesley to Joseph [Lyman], December 2, 1859, AFC.

9. *If They Die for Their Freedom, Amen*

1. Catherine Robbins to Susan Lesley, January 4, 1863, Ames Family Historical Collection, private collection (hereafter AFC).

2. Susan Lesley to Joseph Lyman, August 9, 1860, AFC.

3. Susan Lesley to Joseph Lyman, August 14, 1860, AFC.

4. Entries for November 13, December 1, 1860, [August 17, 1861], Journal of Catherine Robbins, AFC. Catherine Robbins sometimes gave full dates for the entries in her journal. Other times, after entering the *date* for a Sunday entry, she noted simply the *day* for subsequent entries of the week. In the latter cases, I have extrapolated the full date and placed it in brackets.

5. Entries for [November 5, November 6, 1860], Journal of Catherine Robbins, AFC. In November 1859, when Susan Lesley met John Brown's wife in Philadelphia, she described Mary Brown "as like Mary Cashman. . . . An immensely large, strong looking woman." Susan Lesley to Catherine Robbins, November 27, 1859, AFC.

6. Entry for [December 6, 1860], Journal of Catherine Robbins, AFC.

7. Entry for [November 14, 1860], Journal of Catherine Robbins, AFC.

8. Entries for [November 26, November 27, December 3, December 22, 1860], Journal of Catherine Robbins, AFC.

9. Entry for [January 29, 1861], Journal of Catherine Robbins, AFC.

10. Entries for [January 25, January 26, February 22, 1861], Journal of Catherine Robbins, AFC.

11. Lydia Maria Child to Peter and Susan Lesley, February 8, 1861, J. Peter Lesley Papers, American Philosophical Society, Philadelphia (hereafter Lesley Papers, APS).

12. Jean Fagan Yellin, *Harriet Jacobs: A Life* (New York: Basic Civitas Books, 2004), chs. 2–3.

13. Harriet Jacobs lived in Boston for a time in the late 1840s but left to live in New York before Mary Walker arrived in Massachusetts in November 1850. However, Jacobs's daughter Louisa continued to work in Cambridge and Boston after that. Harriet Jacobs intermittently returned to see her daughter and their antislavery friends during the 1850s. Yellin, *Harriet Jacobs,* pp. 75–100, 130–134. Letters from Boston abolitionist William Nell noted Harriet Jacobs's visits to Boston in 1853, 1854, 1857, and 1860. See *William Cooper Nell: Selected Writings, 1832–1874,* ed. Dorothy Porter Wesley and Constance Porter Uzelac (Baltimore: Black Classic Press, 2002), pp. 354, 397, 488, 494, 594–596.

14. Harriet Jacobs to Amy Post, May 18–June 8, 1857, quoted in Yellin, *Harriet Jacobs,* pp. 134–135. William Cooper Nell arranged the meeting between Maria Child and Harriet Jacobs which resulted in Child's decision to introduce and champion the manuscript. Yellin, *Harriet Jacobs,* pp. 141–143.

15. Harriet Jacobs to Amy Post, May 18–June 8, 1857, quoted in Yellin, *Harriet Jacobs,* p. 135.

16. Peter Lesley to Susan Lesley, June 28, 1861, in *Life and Letters of Peter and Susan Lesley,* ed. Mary Lesley Ames, 2 vols. (New York: G. P. Putnam's Sons, 1909), vol. 1, pp. 399–400.

17. Entries for [April 28, April 29, 1861], Journal of Catherine Robbins, AFC.

18. Entry for [January 26, 1861], Journal of Catherine Robbins, AFC.

19. Susan Lesley to Catherine Robbins, March 26, 1861, in *Life and Letters,* ed. Ames, vol. 1, p. 293.

20. Susan Lesley to Catherine Robbins, July 1, 1861, AFC.

21. Entries for [July 3, July 6, 1861], Journal of Catherine Robbins, AFC.

22. Entries for [July 23, July 26, 1861], Journal of Catherine Robbins, AFC.

23. Entries for [July 23, August 18, 1861], Journal of Catherine Robbins, AFC.

24. Susan Lesley to Peter Lesley, [September 1861] and October 10, 1861, AFC.

25. Susan Lesley to Peter Lesley, October 10, 1861, AFC. Anne Jean Lyman died at the McLean Asylum in 1867, with Mary Walker at her side.

26. Susan Lesley to Catherine Robbins, November 3, 1861, AFC.

27. Catherine Robbins to Susan Lesley, December 1, 1861, AFC.

28. Entries for [November 19, November 23, December 3, 1860; January 21, January 26, 1861], Journal of Catherine Robbins, AFC.

29. Stanley J. Robboy and Anita W. Robboy, "Lewis Hayden: From Fugitive to Statesman," *New England Quarterly* 46 (December 1973): 591–613.

30. Mary Millburn of Norfolk, Virginia, escaped bondage to Philadelphia and by 1858 was living at Susan Hillard's safe house in Boston. Writing under the pseudonym "Louisa F. Jones," she was the one who reported seeing so many acquaintances at the house on Pinckney Street; Louisa F. Jones to William Still, May 15, 1858, published in William Still, *The Underground Railroad* (Philadelphia: Porter and Coates, 1872; repr. New York: Arno and New York Times, 1968), p. 559.

31. *Liberator,* September 6, 1861, cited in *Nell: Selected Writings,* ed. Wesley and Uzelac, p. 613.

32. Entry for January 1, 1862, Journal of Catherine Robbins, AFC.

33. William Marvel, *Burnside* (Chapel Hill: University of North Carolina Press, 1991), pp. 66–77.

34. *Letters of Chauncey Wright,* ed. James Bradley Thayer (Cambridge, Mass.: J. Wilson, 1878), p. 13.

35. Chauncey Wright to Frederick Wright, April 29, 1862, in *Letters of Chauncey Wright,* ed. Thayer, pp. 49–50.

36. Adelaide M. Cromwell, "The Black Presence in the West End of Boston, 1800–1864: A Demographic Map," in *Courage and Conscience: Black and White Abolitionists in Boston,* ed. Donald M. Jacobs (Bloomington: Indiana University Press, 1993), p. 182.

37. Robboy and Robboy, "Lewis Hayden," p. 609; Address of William Nell at the Emancipation Day Meeting at Tremont Temple, Boston, January 1, 1863, printed in *Nell: Selected Writings,* ed. Wesley and Uzelac, p. 634.

38. James Oliver Horton and Lois E. Horton, "The Affirmation of Manhood: Black Garrisonians in Antebellum Boston," in *Courage and Conscience,* ed. Jacobs, pp. 132–133, 143–144, 146.

39. James Brewer Stewart, "Boston, Abolition, and the Atlantic World, 1820–1861," in *Courage and Conscience,* ed. Jacobs, p. 117. For a full account of Charles Redmond's argument in the 1858 debate, see *Nell: Selected Writings,* ed. Wesley and Uzelac, pp. 526–527.

40. Peter Lesley to Leo Lesquereux, February 10, 1862, Letter Press Copy, Lesley Papers, APS.

41. Susan Lesley to Peter Lesley, February 28, 1862; Peter Lesley to Susan Lesley, May 18, 1862, in *Life and Letters,* ed. Ames, vol. 1, pp. 409–411.

42. Peter Lesley to Catherine Robbins, September 10, 1862; Peter Lesley to Susan Lesley, September 18 and September 25, 1862, in *Life and Letters,* ed. Ames, vol. 1, pp. 415–416.

43. Entry for December 31, 1862, in Journal of Catherine Robbins, AFC.

44. *Liberator,* January 9, 1863.

45. Catherine Robbins to Susan Lesley, January 4, 1863, AFC; *Liberator,* January 9, 1863.

46. *Liberator,* January 9, 1863.

47. Catherine Robbins to Susan Lesley, January 4, 1863, AFC.

48. Ibid.

10. *"The Welfare of Her Race"*

1. Willie Lee Rose, *Rehearsal for Reconstruction: The Port Royal Experiment* (New York: Oxford University Press, 1964).

2. Mary Elizabeth Ware to Harriet Ware, May 15, 1863, Annie Ware Winsor Allen Papers, Schlesinger Library, Harvard University (hereafter Annie Ware Winsor Allen Papers, Schlesinger Library).

3. Mary Elizabeth Ware to Harriet Ware, April 27, May 4, 1862, Annie Ware Winsor Allen Papers, Schlesinger Library.

4. Susan Lesley to Catherine Robbins, February 1, 1863, Ames Family Historical Collection, private collection (hereafter AFC).

5. Rose, *Rehearsal for Reconstruction,* ch. 1.

6. On the partnership of Edward S. Philbrick, civil engineer, and W. R. Ware, architect, see the Boston City Directory for 1862, pp. 325 and 417. Before her marriage to fellow Brookline resident Edward Philbrick, Helen Winsor was listed with her Winsor family in the 1850 U.S. Census for Massachusetts, roll M432_331, p. 78, image 109, available at Ancestry.com. By 1860, Helen W. and Edward S. Philbrick were married. See the 1860 U.S. Census for Massachusetts, roll M653_514, p. 822, image 738, at Ancestry.com.

7. Edward S. Philbrick to [unnamed correspondent], February 19, 1862, in *Letters from Port Royal Written at the Time of the Civil War,* ed. Elizabeth Ware Pearson (Boston: W. B. Clarke, 1906), p. 2.

8. E. S. Philbrick to Mrs. [Helen] Philbrick, March 2, 1862, *Letters from Port Royal,* ed. Pearson, pp. 4–5.

9. Philbrick to Helen Philbrick, March 17, 1862, *Letters from Port Royal,* ed. Pearson, p. 11.

10. William R. Ware to Harriet Ware, April 7, 1862, Annie Ware Winsor Allen Papers, Schlesinger Library.

11. Entries of June 20, July 1, 1862, in Journal of William R. Ware, William Robert Ware Papers, Massachusetts Institute of Technology, Archives and Special Collections, Cambridge, Massachusetts.

12. Ann Ware Winsor and Frederick Winsor to Harriet Ware, May 13, 1862, Annie Ware Winsor Allen Papers, Schlesinger Library.

13. Harriet Ware to [Family Members], May 3, May 8, 1862, in *Letters from Port Royal,* ed. Pearson, pp. 31, 36.

14. Harriet Ware to [Family Members], May 13, 1862, *Letters from Port Royal,* ed. Pearson, p. 43.

15. Charles P. Ware to [Mary Elizabeth Ware], July 6, 1862, in Charles Pickard Ware Papers, Moorland-Spingarn Research Center, Howard University, Washington, D.C. (hereafter Ware Papers, Howard University); Ware to [Family Members], July 20, August 14, 1862, *Letters from Port Royal,* ed. Pearson, pp. 75, 82.

16. Charles P. Ware to [Mary Elizabeth Ware], December 26, 1862, in Ware Papers, Howard University.

17. Harriet Ware to [Mary Elizabeth Ware], February 6, 1864, Annie Ware Winsor Allen Papers, Schlesinger Library.

18. Ibid.

19. Ibid.

20. Entries for [March 17, April 11], 1864, Journal of Catherine Robbins, AFC.

21. Entry for [May 18, 1863], Journal of Catherine Robbins, AFC.

22. Diary entry for July 4, 1863, *Letters and Diary of Laura M. Towne: Written from the Sea Islands of South Carolina, 1862–1884,* ed. Rupert Sargent Holland (Cambridge, Mass.: Riverside Press, 1912), pp. 113–114.

23. Edward S. Philbrick to William Gannett, March 24, 1864, William C. Gannett Papers, Rush Rhees Library, University of Rochester (hereafter Gannett Papers, University of Rochester).

24. Arthur Sumner to Joseph [Clark], June 15, 1863, typed transcript, in Arthur Sumner Papers, Southern Historical Collection, University of North Carolina at Chapel Hill.

25. Arthur Sumner to "Periwinkle," December 13, 1864, typed transcript, Arthur Sumner Papers, Southern Historical Collection, University of North Carolina at Chapel Hill.

26. Charles P. Ware to [Family Members], October 24, 1863, in *Letters from Port Royal,* ed. Pearson, pp. 227–228.

27. William C. Gannett to [Ezra Stiles Gannett], February 22, 1864, in *Letters from Port Royal,* ed. Pearson, p. 254.

28. Charles P. Ware to Sister, December 20, 1863, in Ware Papers, Howard University. In February 1865, Ware reported that "I have got money enough to live

as I wish to." Ware to Sister, February 19, 1865, Ware Papers, Howard University. William Gannett, in a letter to his Sea Islands friend and teacher, Miss M. E. Rice, stated that he had received $4,000 for his work in 1864 as a plantation supervisor. William Gannett to Miss M. E. Rice, July 10, 1865, Gannett Papers, University of Rochester.

29. Reuben Tomlinson to James McKim, October 17, 1862, January 16, 1863, Samuel J. May Anti-Slavery Collection, Cornell University.

30. The whipping of a Coffin Point woman by Charles Ware was detailed in a petition of John H. Major and eighteen other South Carolina freedmen to President Abraham Lincoln, March 1, 1864. The petition was published as Document 47A in *Freedom: A Documentary History of Emancipation, 1861–1867,* ed. Ira Berlin et al., ser. 1, vol. 3, *The Wartime Genesis of Free Labor: The Lower South* (Cambridge: Cambridge University Press, 1990), pp. 298–299. "Charl's Ware an agent of Mr Philbrick's turn'd the cloths of a Colard Girl over her head turned her over a Barrel, & whipd her with a Leathern Strap." Though "the case was reported," the "Agent still retains his place, Thiss is shamefull."

31. From the highest officials in the Treasury Department to the bureaucrats, generals, and reformers on the ground, whites were divided over the best land policy. Edicts were issued, suspended, and reversed by the authorities, dashing expectations and sowing confusion and distrust. Fundamental differences among whites, and the struggles of black workers to possess the land of former owners and farm it in familiar and familial ways, are chronicled in several landmark books. See *Freedom,* ed. Berlin et al., ser. 1, vol. 3, pp. 13–19, 87–113, with documents from pp. 113–344; Julie Saville, *The Work of Reconstruction: From Slave to Wage Laborer in South Carolina, 1860–1870* (Cambridge: Cambridge University Press, 1994), ch. 2; and Akiko Ochiai, *Harvesting Freedom: African American Agrarianism in Civil War Era South Carolina* (Westport, Conn.: Praeger, 2004), pp. 37–39, 71, 92–101, chs. 5–6.

32. Edward S. Philbrick to [unnamed correspondent], January 20, 1864, in *Letters from Port Royal,* ed. Pearson, p. 244. Italics added. Philbrick was in attendance and confronted John Hunn afterward. Philbrick told Hunn that he paid an average of more than 50 cents a day. Privately, Philbrick added that "a much higher rate of pay . . . would tend to diminish the amount of industry rather than to stimulate it, by rendering it too easy for them to supply their simple wants."

33. Harriet Ware to [Family Members], February 9, February 14, 1864, in *Letters from Port Royal,* ed. Pearson, p. 250.

34. Entries for April 7, April 8, 1864, Diary of William Francis Allen, typescript copy, in William Francis Allen Papers, State Historical Society of Wisconsin, Madison (hereafter William Allen Papers, Wisconsin Historical Society).

35. Harriet Ware to [Family Members], April 15, 1862, in *Letters from Port Royal,* ed. Pearson, p. 16; William Allen's description of the Sea Islands vegetation in the spring of 1864 can be found throughout his diary entries for March and April, 1864, in the Diary of William Frances Allen, typescript, William Allen Papers, Wisconsin Historical Society.

36. Theodore Rosengarten, *Tombee: Portrait of a Cotton Planter* (New York: William Morrow, 1986), pp. 67, 292. On some maps and documents, Coffin Point is referred to as "Coffin Point," on others as "Coffin's Point." I have chosen to cite it as the former. See the map at the outset of *Letters from Port Royal,* ed. Pearson ("Coffin's Point") and the map on p. 86 of *Freedom,* ed. Berlin et al., ser. 1, vol. 3 ("Coffin Point").

37. Entry for March 14, 1863, in *The Journals of Charlotte Forten,* ed. Brenda Stevenson (New York: Oxford University Press, 1988), p. 463.

38. Entry for April 11, 1864, Diary of William Francis Allen, typescript, William Allen Papers, Wisconsin Historical Society.

39. Entry for May 7, 1864, Diary of Laura Towne, Laura Towne Papers, Southern Historical Collection, University of North Carolina at Chapel Hill. The description of Mary Walker is not included in the published *Letters and Diary of Laura M. Towne,* ed. Holland.

40. Harriet Ware to [Family Members], October 22, 1863, in *Letters from Port Royal,* ed. Pearson, p. 226.

41. *Journals of Charlotte Forten,* ed. Stevenson, p. 390; Harriet Ware to [Family Members], April 29, 1862, in *Letters from Port Royal,* ed. Pearson, p. 25; Rose, *Rehearsal for Reconstruction,* pp. 161–162.

42. Catherine Robbins to Susan Lesley, May 5, 1864, AFC.

43. Harriet Ware to [Family Members], April 18, 1864, p. 258.

44. Harriet Ware to [Family Members], April 18, April 21, 1864, in *Letters from Port Royal,* ed. Pearson, pp. 258–261.

45. Harriet Ware to [Family Members], April 21, 1864, in *Letters from Port Royal,* ed. Pearson; Journal of William Gannett, April 21, 1864, on microfilm at the Gannett Papers, University of Rochester.

46. "John H. Major et al. to his Exelency Abraham Lincoln, March 1, 1864,"

published as Document 47A: South Carolina Freedmen to the President, in *Freedom,* ed. Berlin et al., ser. 1, vol. 3, pp. 297–298.

47. Ibid., pp. 298–299.

48. Entry of April 21, 1864, Journal of William Gannett, microfilm copy in Gannett Papers, University of Rochester; Harriet Ware to [Family Members], April 21, 1864, in *Letters from Port Royal,* ed. Pearson, p. 260; Diary of William Allen, April 24, 1864, typed transcript, in William Allen Papers, Wisconsin Historical Society.

49. Ibid.

50. Report of Austin Smith to the Secretary of the Treasury, May 15, 1864, published as Document 47B, Treasury Department Special Agent to the Secretary of the Treasury, in *Freedom,* ed. Berlin et al., ser. 1, vol. 3, p. 302. "As to the charge of cruel whipping, Mr. Ware did whip a very immoral & bad girl in the manner charged, but not under the circumstances, nor with the severity stated. . . . It was very much regretted by the person who inflicted it, & I am satisfied it will not occur again." Harriet Ware stated that her brother "was not questioned at all" by the president's agent. Harriet Ware to [Family Members], April 21, 1864, in *Letters from Port Royal,* ed. Pearson, p. 259.

51. Harriet Ware to [Family Members], April 22, May 27, 1864, in *Letters from Port Royal,* ed. Pearson, pp. 262–263.

52. Neither was the president's agent. Despite giving the impression to white and black witnesses that he sided with the New Englanders, Austin Smith wrote a report highly critical of Edward Philbrick, and recommended the prompt sale of land to the freedmen at $1 an acre. "Justice & equity demand that the freedmen should be provided with homes." "If the law does not hold these men to the fulfillment of their promises, public opinion will." If they should decline to grant "homesteads to these people at a nominal price," I "hope the government will inquire into the validity of their titles." The freedmen's hopes should be "no longer deferred." Report of Austin Smith to the Secretary of the Treasury, May 15, 1864, in *Freedom,* ed. Berlin et al., ser. 1, vol. 3, p. 303. Austin Smith's recommendation was ignored.

53. Charles Ware to Sisters, July 17, 1864, Ware Papers, Howard University.

54. William Gannett to M. E. Rice, January 21, 1866, in Gannett Papers, University of Rochester. The reformers' households were full of "savage private talks." See Gannett's comment on an article in *The Nation* of December 1865, written by William Allen under the pseudonym "Marcel." The article

made "the nearest approach to our savage private talks that I have yet seen in print."

55. The conflict over the corn in the cotton rows unfolded in the Journal of William Gannett during the spring and summer of 1864. See the entries of April 29, April 30, May 2, May 5, May 7, May 23, May 25, May 31, June 5, June 16, in the microfilmed copy of the Journal, Gannett Papers, University of Rochester. See also Gannett to Philbrick, early May, 1864, and Philbrick to Gannett, May 18, 1864, in *Letters from Port Royal*, ed. Pearson, pp. 264, 266–267. Gannett realized that he was miscast as a plantation supervisor. "I am unfitted to govern people," he confessed to his father. "At first I got on very well, & the people liked me; gradually the feeling changed & finally some plantations hated me very badly. I'm too particular, notice too much, am too insisting" and "don't control my feelings enough." It "is very discouraging to be consciously losing influence & respect, when half one's success & all one's pleasure depend entirely on possessing popularity." William Gannett to Ezra Stiles Gannett, June 22, 1864, Gannett Papers, University of Rochester.

56. Entry for May 9, 1864, Diary of William Allen, typed transcription, William Allen Papers, Wisconsin Historical Society.

57. After writing to his sisters that "I cannot tell how much longer I shall be able to stand this country," Charles Ware added: "Do I sound very wretched? I hope not, for I am happy enough, though not satisfied with this life. Harriet will tell you that I am, on the whole, a contented individual, though much given to grumbling." Charles Ware to Sisters, June 28, 1864, Ware Papers, Howard University. When he saw his photograph, he could laugh that it was a "Pretty picture! Looks glum and sober enough, as if I had the case of the whole Island on my shoulders, and was intensely grieved at the . . . people in allowing their pigs to run wild." Charles Ware to Sisters, July 17, 1864, Ware Papers, Howard University.

58. Ware to Sisters, July 17, 1864, Ware Papers, Howard University.

59. Harriet Ware to Charles P. Ware, July 31, 1864, Ware Papers, Howard University.

60. Charles Ware to Sisters, July 17, 1864, Ware Papers, Howard University.

61. Charles Ware to Sisters, August 9, 1864, Ware Papers, Howard University.

62. Ibid. The other plantation supervisor who lived in the house, Richard Soule, received a letter from Mary Walker recalling "our pleasant talks a year ago in the evening on the piazza while watching Jupiter and Scorpion." Richard Soule, Jr., to Charles P. Ware, July 11, 1865, Ware Papers, Howard University.

63. Charles Ware to Sisters, July 17, 1864, Ware Papers, Howard University.

64. Catherine Robbins to Susan Lesley, November 13, 1864; Susan Lesley to Peter Lesley, August 3, 1865, AFC.

65. Catherine Robbins to Susan Lesley, December 12, 1864, January 4, 1865, AFC; M. E. Rice to William Gannett, March 18, 1865, Gannett Papers, University of Rochester.

66. Mary Lesley Ames, ed., *Life and Letters of Peter and Susan Lesley,* 2 vols. (New York: G. P. Putnam's Sons, 1909), vol. 1, pp. 252–253.

11. *"To Part No More"*

1. Entry for [July 3, 1865], Journal of Catherine Robbins, Ames Family Historical Collection, private collection (hereafter AFC).

2. Entry for [April 25, 1865], Journal of Catherine Robbins, AFC.

3. Entries for [April 20–25, 1865], Journal of Catherine Robbins, AFC.

4. Entry for [April 25, 1865], Journal of Catherine Robbins, AFC

5. Entry for [June 9, 1865], Journal of Catherine Robbins, AFC.

6. Entries for [June 4, June 7, 1865], Journal of Catherine Robbins, AFC.

7. *Unionist Standard* (Raleigh, N.C.), May 1, 1865.

8. *Unionist Standard* (Raleigh, N.C.), May 5, 1865.

9. *Unionist Standard* (Raleigh, N.C.), June 7, 1865.

10. Paul Cameron to Sisters, May 27, 1865, Cameron Family Papers, Southern Historical Collection, University of North Carolina at Chapel Hill (hereafter Cameron Papers, SHC).

11. Rebecca Cameron to Mildred Cameron, June 2, 1865; Paul Cameron to Sisters, October 9, 1865; Andrew Kevan to Paul Cameron, November 27, 1865; Paul Cameron to Sisters, December 22, 1865; George Mordecai to Paul Cameron, December 26, 1865; all letters in Cameron Papers, SHC.

12. Entry for [June 28, 1865], Journal of Catherine Robbins, AFC.

13. Entries for July 9, [1865], and [July 14, 1865], Journal of Catherine Robbins, AFC.

14. Entry for [July 14, 1865], Journal of Catherine Robbins, AFC.

15. Entry for [July 17, 1865], Journal of Catherine Robbins; entry for July 18, 1865, Journal of Peter Lesley, AFC.

16. Susan Lesley to Joseph Lyman, November 27, 1863, in *Life and Letters of Peter and Susan Lesley,* ed. Mary Lesley Ames, 2 vols. (New York: G. P. Putnam's Sons, 1909), vol. 2, pp. 478–479.

17. Entry for [July 17, 1865], Journal of Catherine Robbins, AFC.

18. Agnes Burgwyn to Margaret Cameron Mordecai, October 7, 1865, Cameron Papers, SHC.

19. Ibid.

20. Mary Stearns to Wendell Phillips, June 5, 1866, Wendell Phillips Papers, Houghton Library, Harvard University.

21. Mary Stearns to Wendell Phillips, undated [June 7, 1866?], Wendell Phillips Papers, Houghton Library, Harvard University.

22. Bryant Walker's occupation was listed as "Coachman" on his marriage certificate of July 23, 1866. See the Massachusetts Marriage Register for 1866, vol. 189, p. 232, on microfilm at the Massachusetts State Archives in Boston.

23. Ibid. The marriage certificate of July 23, 1866, gave no occupation for Bryant Walker's bride, "Annie Gorie." I have used the spelling of her name, "Gorey," that appeared on other records, including the 1860 U.S. Census, the baptismal records of her children, and her death certificate. For the listing of an "Ann Gorey" as a textile worker in Lowell, see the 1860 U.S. Census for Lowell, Massachusetts, roll M653_507, p. 229, image 230. For the listing of "Ann Gorey" as a servant, see the U.S. Census of 1860 for Massachusetts, roll M653_521, p. 390, image 391, both records available at Ancestry.com. The Walkers' first child, Edward Walker, was born on February 22, 1867. See the Massachusetts Birth Register for 1867, vol. 197, p. 116, Massachusetts State Archives, Boston.

24. Noel Ignatiev, *How the Irish Became White* (New York: Routledge, 1995); Mark R. Schneider, *Boston Confronts Jim Crow, 1890–1920* (Boston: Northeastern University Press, 1997), pp. 162–166.

25. Elizabeth Halkin Pleck, *Black Migration and Poverty, Boston, 1865–1900* (New York: Academic Press, 1979), p. 114 (note 76).

26. Catherine Robbins to Susan Lesley, May 7, 1867, AFC.

27. Catherine Robbins to Susan Lesley, October 12, 1866, AFC.

28. John Owen's obituary in the Cambridge *Press* of March 29, 1882, noted that "He had a quite large estate" on Mt. Auburn Street, "was particularly fond of cultivating fruit and flowers," and "had at one time sixty varieties of roses growing in his yard."

29. *The Letters of Henry Wadsworth Longfellow,* ed. Andrew Hilen, 6 vols. (Cambridge, Mass.: Harvard University Press, 1967–1982), vol. 2, p. 183. For John Owen's devotion to Charles Sumner and equal rights, see *Letters of Longfellow,* vol. 2, p. 234; vol. 5, pp. 28–29. When Owen read Sumner's Senate speech entitled "The Equal Rights of All" in February 1866, he exclaimed to Longfellow, "Admirable! Admirable!"

30. The first and middle names of all the Walker children were listed in a Middlesex County Probate Court petition of July 1879. The petition named a new Howe family member as trustee to oversee the will of Mary Walker, on behalf of her grandchildren. See the Petition of July 1, 1879, to the Probate Court, found in Probate Court File 11280 for Mary E. Walker, Middlesex County, Cambridge, Massachusetts.

31. Entry for May 18, 1863, *The Journals of Charlotte Forten,* ed. Brenda Stevenson (New York: Oxford University Press, 1988), p. 485.

32. Forten noted her initial attraction to "Mr. W." in April 1863. "Mr. W." is misidentified as "[Charles P.] W.[are]" by the editor. For Charlotte Forten's growing interest in Charles Williams, see *Journals of Charlotte Forten,* ed. Stevenson, pp. 480–481, 499, and 509. The account of the engagement and its disruption by Charles Williams's parents is found in letters of a former Sea Islands schoolteacher to a fellow reformer. Mary E. Rice to William Gannett, March 28 and April 20, 1866, William C. Gannett Papers, Rush Rhees Library, University of Rochester.

33. Carolyn L. Karcher, *The First Woman in the Republic: A Cultural Biography of Lydia Maria Child* (Durham, N.C.: Duke University Press, 1994), pp. 191, 522–531; Cassandra Jackson, *Barriers between Us: Interracial Sex in Nineteenth-Century American Literature* (Bloomington: Indiana University Press, 2004), ch. 3.

34. Lydia Maria Child to Louisa Loring, January 1, 1868, Lydia Maria Child Papers, Schlesinger Library, Harvard University. Child had dedicated the book to the memory of Robert Gould Shaw.

35. The baptismal and marriage records for all the Walker children are found in the Archives of the Archdiocese of Boston. The baptismal records list the church, name of the baptized child, parents, date of birth, date of baptism, the officiating priest, and sponsors of the child. My thanks to Robert Johnson-Lally, Archivist and Records Manager of the Archdiocese, for locating the information on the Walker family. The Cambridge City Directory of 1874 provides the addresses of the city's Catholic churches and a map that shows their distances from the Walker residence.

36. Annie Gorey's birthplace in "Kildare, Hibernia" was noted in the baptismal record for her daughter Hannah Frances Walker on March 15, 1874.

37. James M. O'Toole, *Passing for White: Race, Religion, and the Healy Family, 1820–1920* (Amherst: University of Massachusetts Press, 2002), chs. 4, 6–8. For more on the relationship of African Americans and Catholics in America, see M. Shawn Copeland, ed., *Uncommon Faithfulness: The Black Catholic Experience* (Mary-

knoll, N.Y.: Orbis Books, 2009), especially the chapter by Albert J. Raboteau, "Relating Race and Religion: Four Historical Models."

38. George Mordecai noted the arrival in Raleigh of "The Burgwyns father & son" in October 1863. George Mordecai to Margaret Cameron Mordecai, October 9, 1863, Cameron Papers, SHC.

39. See the entry for John Fanning Burgwyn in William S. Powell, ed., *Dictionary of North Carolina Biography* (Chapel Hill: University of North Carolina Press, 1979), vol. 1, pp. 277–278. For information on the senior Burgwyn's illness prior to the family's move to Raleigh, see the diary entry of his grandson William, in Herbert Schiller, ed., *A Captain's War: The Letters and Diaries of William Burgwyn* (Shippensburg, Pa.: White Mane Publisher, 1994), p. 38, note 9. John Burgwyn's grandson William had a "faithful servant" named Pompey, whom he described as his "valet de chambers and man of all work and deeds." My conjecture is that the enslaved carpenter James Burgwyn served his owner in the same capacity in Raleigh after the move there in 1863.

40. See the 1880 U.S. Federal Census for Cambridge, Massachusetts, roll T9_543, Family History Film 1254543, p. 207.1000, enumeration district 427, image 0054, available at Ancestry.com. The 1880 Census gives James Burgwyn's age as thirty-seven, making 1843 his year of birth. The 1900 Census dated his birth as 1841 and the 1910 Federal Censuses placed his year of birth as 1840. In the 1910 Census, Burgwyn again gave England as his father's birthplace. See the 1910 U.S. Federal Census for Cambridge, roll T624_596, p. 14B, enumeration district 778, image 754, accessed through Ancestry.com.

41. The photograph of "Jim Burgwyn" is found in the folder of Harvard University Photographs entitled "Characters about Harvard," Harvard University Archives, Pusey Library, Harvard University.

42. Records of the Parish Committee, May 15, 1869, First Parish in Cambridge, Massachusetts. Records located in the Andover-Harvard Theological Library, Harvard Divinity School. My thanks to Gloria Korsman, Senior Reference Librarian at the Andover-Harvard Theological Library, for searching the Parish Records and finding the reference to Bryant Walker's appointment as sexton in May 1869, retroactive to January 1st of that year. The Cambridge City Directory listed Tracy Howe as the First Parish Church Treasurer in the late 1860s. The First Parish Church of Cambridge became Unitarian in 1829. Its more conservative members left and founded the Shepard Congregational Society, which in 1899 took the name First Church (Congregational) and is now part of the United Church of Christ. The current Meeting House of First Parish Church

(Unitarian Universalist) was built in 1833, and is located at 3 Church Street, Harvard Square. It was here that Bryant Walker became sexton in 1869.

43. *Letters of Longfellow,* ed. Hilen, vol. 5, p. 422.

44. The purchase of the Brattle Street house by James Murray Howe is recorded in the Book of Deeds, Middlesex County (South District), Massachusetts. George H. Smith and Annie Louise H. Smith to James Murray Howe, June 1, 1870, book 1120, pp. 540–545. The next day, Howe deeded the house to Mary Walker. James Murray Howe to Mary Walker, June 2, 1870, Book of Deeds, Middlesex County (Cambridge), Massachusetts, book 1120, p. 546. I have modernized the archaic term *Libro* to "book," and *Folio* to "page."

45. James Murray Howe to Mary Walker, June 2, 1870, Book of Deeds, Middlesex County (Cambridge), Massachusetts, book 1120, p. 546.

46. Baptismal record for Mary Agnes Walker, born August 6 and baptized August 15, 1870, Archdiocese of Boston Archives.

47. Dexter Pratt had bought the house in 1827 from fellow blacksmith Torrey Hancock, who had built the dwelling and shop in 1808. Pratt worked there until his death in 1847, and his widow, Rowena, remained in the home until her death in 1858, when it became the property of the Pratt's married daughter, Annie Louise Pratt Smith. The history of the house and Dexter Pratt, "the Village Blacksmith," is distilled in Sarah Zimmerman's "Landmark Designation Study Report" on the "Dexter Pratt House," October 21, 1988, and in the nomination of the dwelling for the National Register of Historic Places, both found in the files of the Cambridge Historical Commission. My thanks to Kathleen L. Rawlins of the commission for helping me locate these files. Neither of the reports and none of the researchers were aware of the Walker family's forty-two-year-long ownership and occupancy of the house.

48. Entry for January 1, 1872, Journal of Catherine Robbins, AFC.

49. Catherine Robbins to Susan Lesley, February 5, 1871, AFC.

50. *Cambridge Chronicle,* May 20, 1865.

51. *Cambridge Chronicle,* June 2, 1865.

52. Catherine Robbins to Susan Lesley, January 14, 1872, AFC.

53. Ibid.

54. Peter Lesley to Susan Lesley, February 26, 1871, *Life and Letters,* ed. Ames, vol. 2, p. 89.

55. Catherine Robbins to Susan Lesley, September 5, 1871; entry for [January 18, 1873], Journal of Catherine Robbins, AFC.

56. Almost legendary was the Raleigh house-servant named Abner, who tended

the plants and flowers of the mansion's greenhouse. It was understood that from time to time a few plants disappeared. If asked, Abner explained that the rats got them, much to the amusement of his owners. They knew he'd bartered the plants for a few drams at a Raleigh grog shop. When Abner actually stayed sober one entire Christmas, it was a matter of remark. Anne Cameron to Paul Cameron, January 8, 1848, Cameron Papers, SHC.

57. Bryant Walker had become a gardening apprentice to Abner in 1855. In 1861, while the owners were away from the Raleigh household, there was a break-in. On his return, George Mordecai investigated and reported to his wife, Margaret Cameron Mordecai, that the theft was an inside job. Neither silver nor money was taken; liquor was. Those suspected were sent away to Cameron plantations in the country. Bryant Walker was cleared. See Paul Cameron to [Margaret Cameron Mordecai], October 25, 1855, Cameron Papers, SHC; and George Mordecai to Margaret Cameron Mordecai, November 7, 1861, Cameron Papers, SHC.

58. Leo Spitzer, *Lives In Between: Assimilation and Marginality in Austria, Brazil, West Africa, 1780–1945* (Cambridge: Cambridge University Press, 1989).

59. Will of Mary E. Walker, July 4, 1872, found in the Probate Court Records, Middlesex County Courthouse, Cambridge, Massachusetts. The witnesses were Harvard Latin professor James B. Greenough and his wife, Mary Greenough.

60. Catherine Robbins to Susan Lesley, June 30, 1872, AFC. Mary Cashman—the fellow caretaker of Anne Jean Lyman throughout the 1850s—took Mary Walker on a trip to her native Nova Scotia. Mary Walker's physician advised that it was "quite important for her to get away from home & all care for some time."

61. Ephraim Gurney to Susan Lesley, November 16, 1872, J. Peter Lesley Papers, American Philosophical Society, Philadelphia (hereafter APS).

62. Entries for November 1, [November 5, November 7], 1872, Journal of Catherine Robbins; Catherine Robbins to Susan Lesley, November 7, 1872, AFC.

63. Entries for [November 8], November 10, [November 11 and November 12], 1872, AFC.

64. Susan Lesley to Chauncey Wright, November 14, 1872, Chauncey Wright Papers, APS.

65. Entry for [November 13, 1872], Journal of Catherine Robbins, AFC.

66. *Letters of Longfellow*, ed. Hilen, vol. 5, p. 615.

67. Susan Lesley to Chauncey Wright, November 14, 1872, Chauncey Wright Papers, APS. My thanks to Valerie Lutz of the American Philosophical Society Library for finding the misplaced last page of this letter.

68. Ephraim Gurney to Susan Lesley, November 16, 1872, Lesley Papers, APS.

69. Entry for [November 12, 1872], Journal of Catherine Robbins, AFC.

70. Entry for [December 21, 1872], Journal of Catherine Robbins, AFC.

71. Entry for January 1, 1873, Journal of Catherine Robbins, AFC.

72. Susan Lesley to Margaret Lesley, September 28, 1873, in *Life and Letters,* ed. Ames, vol. 2, pp. 113–114.

Epilogue

1. The Walker plot at Mount Auburn Cemetery is located on Kalmia Path, Lot No. 4312. Mary Walker and several grandchildren were buried there in the 1870s; Bryant Walker was interred in the plot in 1894. I have concluded that the obelisk was erected in 1895. There are two reasons for my inference. One is that the marker includes an inscription for Bryant Walker as well as one for his mother. The second is an 1895 letter from Agnes Walker Burgwyn to the superintendent of Mount Auburn asking about the cost of "raising the grave I spoke of without sodding or plants." I concluded that "raising the grave" was necessary for the proper placement of the marker at the cemetery plot. For the letter, see Agnes P. Burgwyn to Mr. J. L. Attwood, May 13, 1895, Walker/Burgwyn File, Mount Auburn Cemetery Archives, Cambridge, Massachusetts (hereafter Walker/Burgwyn File, Mount Auburn Cemetery). My thanks to Mount Auburn Cemetery Curator and Archivist Meg Winslow, and to Research Assistant Caroline Loughlin, for their assistance.

2. James Charles Burgwyn was born in April 1876 but died three and a half months later. He was buried at Mount Auburn Cemetery. See the Interment Record for the Cemetery Plot of Agnes P. Burgwyn, Plot 4312, Mount Auburn Cemetery Archives.

3. For the listings, occupations, and ascents of each of the Walker sons, see the Cambridge City Directories for 1894, 1898, 1901, 1904, and 1910.

4. For the marriage of Mary Agnes Walker to Emile Dubé at St. Paul's Church on July 20, 1890, see their Marriage Record in the Archdiocese of Boston Archives. Four years later, Frederick Walker became the first of the Walker sons to marry. For the marriage of Frederick Walker to Edith Ham by a Boston justice of the peace, see the Massachusetts Marriage Register, vol. 442, p. 112,

case 1467, on microfilm at the Massachusetts State Archives, Boston. Edith Ham's date of birth, and her occupation of dressmaker, were given in the 1900 U.S. Federal Census for Cambridge.

5. Bryant Walker's death on November 4, 1894, was recorded in the Massachusetts Death Register, vol. 158, p. 166; the cause given was "Accidental Poisoning." The more detailed coroner's report is in the Massachusetts Medical Examiner Returns for 1894, case no. 55, pp. 406–407. A Massachusetts law, passed after I saw the coroner's report in the early 1990s, has closed those records to all but members of the family of the deceased.

6. Mary Agnes Dubé gave her occupation as dressmaker when she was married in 1890. Hannah F. Walker, misnamed as Anna F. Walker in the 1900 U.S. Federal Census for Cambridge, also listed her occupation as dressmaker.

7. Agnes P. Burgwyn to Mr. J. L. Attwood, May 13, 1895, Walker/Burgwyn File, Mount Auburn Cemetery.

8. For Agnes Burgwyn's handwriting in 1895, see the letter to Mr. J. L. Attwood, Walker/Burgwyn File, Mount Auburn Cemetery. For Agnes Burgwyn's handwriting of the 1870s, see her signature on documents acknowledging the appointment of a new Howe family trustee to execute Mary Walker's will. Her signature can be found on documents of July 1 and July 2, 1879. Both documents are included in Probate Court Record 11280 for Mary E. Walker, Middlesex County Courthouse, Cambridge, Massachusetts.

9. "The Cantabrigian," *Cambridge Tribune,* December 14, 1907.

10. Obituary notice for Frederick Walker, *Cambridge Tribune,* July 10, 1926; obituary notice for Frederick Walker, *Cambridge Chronicle,* July 16, 1926.

11. For the quitclaims of all concerned and the sale of 54 Brattle Street to neighbor Marianne Batchelder on November 12, 1912, see the Book of Deeds, Middlesex County (South District), Massachusetts, book 3743, pp. 131–137. For Frederick Walker's purchase of a dwelling a block away at 14 and 16 Farwell Place, see the deed from Mary Stearns to Frederick J. Walker, November 19, 1912, Book of Deeds, Middlesex County (South District), book 3743, p. 358.

12. Will of James C. Burgwyn, August 4, 1916, in the Probate Court Record No. 109352 for James C. Burgwyn of Cambridge, Massachusetts, in the Middlesex County Courthouse. On James's bequest to his nephew Frederick, see the Executor's Inventory of Burgwyn's Personal Estate, November 15, 1916, ibid.

13. Will of Frederick J. Walker, April 5, 1917, probated on September 15, 1926. See the Probate Court Record No. 158400 for Frederick J. Walker. The total value of the bequest, as of April 1932, amounted to $9,519.51.

14. Interview with Ilse F. Heyman, refugee from war-torn Europe and employee of the Window Shop, copy in the Window Shop files of the Cambridge Historical Commission; Eleanor Roosevelt, "A Visit to the Window Shop . . . ," May 30, 1950, United Features Syndicate, copy in Window Shop Files. My thanks to Kathleen L. Rawlins and Sarah Burks of the Cambridge Historical Commission for providing me with copies of these documents.

Acknowledgments

Long in the making, *To Free a Family* has many forebears. Inspiration for this book came from Herbert Gutman, who found and published Peter Lesley's 1859 letter on behalf of Mary Walker in his landmark work, *The Black Family in Slavery and Freedom.* I was able to pursue Mary Walker's story thanks to the extraordinary generosity and labors of Mary Wolff and Ed Wolff of Boulder, Colorado. They first opened their home and their archives to me in 1993, when the letters and journals of their ancestors Susan and Peter Lesley were fresh out of attic trunks. In the years since, Mary Wolff and her daughter Linda Cowan have made the Ames Family Historical Collection—the largest known cache of American family papers still in private hands—into a superbly organized manuscript collection, the best I've consulted in fifty years of archival research. Knowing Mary and Ed and Linda, as well as their nineteenth-century kindred, has been a blessing in every way.

My journey as a historian began at Rice University, where two new faculty members—Francis Loewenheim and Louis Galambos—were my guides and teachers, the first a model of passion for history, the second a champion of its discipline. Rice, which had no summer session, sent me and classmate James Robert Doty to the Harvard Summer School to study with David Donald, a gift which opened the way to lifelong learning from a demanding, creative, and devoted teacher, writer, scholar, and friend, who became my dissertation advisor at the Johns Hopkins University in 1962, and twenty-five years later invited me to teach with him as a visiting professor at Harvard.

Duke University proved to be an extraordinary place to teach and learn for forty years. For a new faculty member, department chairs Richard Watson and Joel Colton were mentors and *Menschen* beyond compare. Anne Scott let a greenhorn instructor come to her classes and watch a teaching wizard at work; her enthusiasm has inspired me for decades. My expansion beyond political history and Jacksonian America to African-American and social history was galvanized by Duke colleagues, as well as by broader changes in the profession. Carol Stack riveted me with her work and our many talks about the African-American family. William Chafe and Lawrence Goodwyn brought home the excitement and possibilities of a more encompassing American history when they created the Duke Oral History Program, and subsequently the Duke Center for the Study of Civil Rights. With his vision, courage, and generosity, Peter Wood has sustained, challenged, and fostered me, as I ventured into a field that he helped to transform. Raymond Gavins and I logged years together as colleagues and miles together as joggers, and in both roles he set the pace and made sure I kept up. John Cell and Charles Bergquist, both superbly analytical historians, urged me to play to my strengths as a storyteller. No one could have asked for better students than the ones I had at Duke. In my senior honors thesis seminars, in my courses "The Southern Plantation: Odyssey in Black and White" and "The Experience of Emancipation," I learned every year from Duke undergraduates, from graduate students, and from enriching members of the Duke Liberal Studies Program. Dorothy Sapp, Vivian Jackson, Thelma Kithcart, Grace Guyer, and Vanessa Jackson kept me and our rambunctious History faculty in good humor and good order over the years.

My road to Mary Walker began down a far-flung path. Following a different lead suggested by Herbert Gutman, who wondered what had happened to a group of 114 enslaved persons sent in 1844 from North Carolina to a cotton plantation in western Alabama, I thought to test whether I could use oral history—pioneered by colleagues at Duke, by Jacquelyn Hall and comrades at the University of North Carolina, and most famously by Alex Haley—to recover a story of the great forced migration of the nineteenth century. Friends at the North Carolina Department of Archives and History in Raleigh, with whom I was working on a series of books that became *The Way We Lived in North Carolina*, encouraged me to give the Alabama project a try. With nurturance from Larry Misenheimer and future directors William Price and Jeffrey Crow, and support from then-director Larry Tise, I ventured west, armed with a new tape recorder, a borrowed Nikon camera (and a crash course in documentary photography from Alex Harris), and a list of 114 names—all of them first names, save one. The small project exploded into a huge one, and a fool's errand into a providential gift, when a phone call turned up the person in the Greensboro, Alabama, directory with the list's sole last name. Mrs. Alice Sledge Hargress knew the story of the coming out in the 1840s—and all that had happened since. Alice Hargress invited me to her home, opened the gates of others to me, and introduced me to Louie Rainey, the oral historian of the Alabama community, with whom I was to spend hundreds of hours in the years ahead. My welcome extended to the Cassimore A.M.E. Zion Church and to Hargress and Sledge family reunions, which I have attended ever since as an adopted family member.

Back in North Carolina, crucial encouragement came from George McDaniel, then a graduate student at Duke but already in the forefront of earning the trust and recollections of North Carolina plantation descendants for his luminous work on African-American material culture. His labors coincided with the creation of the Stagville Center for Historic Preservation, which evolved under the direction of Kenneth McFarland and Jennifer Farley into a protean state historic site that sponsored programs, field trips, and research into the black and white families that lived there. Jean Bradley Anderson wrote a richly detailed and discerning book—*Piedmont Plantation*—about the buildings and people of the Cameron plantation, and Alice Eley Jones added extensive new interviews with descendants of the black community. George McDaniel introduced me to the Cameron Grove Missionary Baptist Church of Durham, where the fellowship of members—including Addie Whitted, Janie Cameron Riley, Dorothy Peaks Johnson and her sisters Hattie and Luna and Gertrude, Bertha Hart, Lonnie Lloyd, and Pastor and Mrs. Jesse Alston—has graced my life over the years. Building on these foundations, I devised a large project, one that combined archival research with oral history, and won generous backing from the Rockefeller and Guggenheim foundations.

Ten years into the mission, I received an invitation from David Donald and the Harvard History Department to teach there in the fall of 1988 and from Bernard Bailyn and the Charles Warren Center to be a fellow for the academic year. The obligatory talk at year's end provided the incentive to pull together strands of a project that, by then, had become overwhelming in its scope and bounty. David and Aida Donald, Bernard Bailyn, Warren Center administrator Susan Hunt, my Currier House resident faculty comrade Jerrold Hirsch, Louis Ferleger, and Warren Center and younger Harvard colleagues made the year a wonderful experience. The opportunity also put me on site in Cambridge, where Mary Walker had lived the last two decades of her life. I spent the final month of my Warren Center term in the Middlesex Courthouse and in Cambridge city records, researching what happened to her and her family. What I learned made Mary Walker's story one that I couldn't put aside. I also thought it might become a short project which, when completed, would boost momentum for concluding the larger one. In decades to come, I redefined "short."

New England and Mary Walker beckoned again when historians James Wright and Mary Kelly invited me to teach at Dartmouth in the winter and spring of 1990. Leo Spitzer and Marianne Hirsch, Bruce and Donna Nelson, Margaret Darrow, Mary Kelly, and Jim and Susan Wright made me one of their own. In a memorable seminar where I presented findings about Mary Walker for the first time, Dartmouth colleagues asked challenging questions which both affirmed and changed the course of my project. Leo Spitzer's wonderful small book, *Lives In Between,* offered a framework for my work on Mary Walker, and his oral history project, *Hotel Bolivia,* modeled what I might do when I returned to the Alabama story.

The one constant in all of my peregrinations has been the support of archivists and librarians. Over the course of thirty-five years, I have returned again and again to the Cameron Family Papers housed at the Southern Historical Collection in the University of North Carolina's Wilson Library. Archivists at the Southern proved unfailing helpful; I am grateful to Carolyn Wallace, Richard Shrader, John White, Tim West, and staff assistants for their aid and patience over the decades. At Duke's Special Collections, Mattie Russell helped me first as a graduate student and then as a young faculty member. Dr. Russell and her successor, Robert Byrd, encouraged the involvement of Duke undergraduates in manuscript research; and at their invitation and with the guidance of William Erwin, Ellen Gartrell, Nelda Webb, and especially Linda McCurdy, generations of my students learned the challenge and joys of original inquiry. Duke's reference librarians—Florence Blakely, Kenneth Berger, Eric Smith, and Margaret Brill—answered countless appeals for help with alacrity, precision, and good cheer. Research on Mary Walker took me to numerous manuscript collections. I am especially thankful for the help of Valerie Lutz at the American Philosophical Society, which houses the scientific and a small portion of the personal correspondence of J. Peter Lesley; to Kathleen Rawlins of the Cambridge Historical Commission; and to Joellen El Bashir of the Moorland-Spingarn Collection at Howard University, where I found the rich correspondence of Charles and Harriet Ware, Mary

Walker's hosts on the South Carolina Sea Islands. Cecily McMillan allowed me to use a remarkable nineteenth-century photograph of the Coffin Point Plantation, where she lives now and where Mary Walker and the Wares lived in 1864. Margaret Howe Ewing, a descendant of the Cambridge family that became close to Mary Walker in the 1860s and 1870s, graciously invited me to view the Howe Family Collection at her home in Philadelphia, where I discovered valuable letters and wonderful photographs of persons central to Mary Walker's Northern life.

Bountiful support has come from friends, counselors, and family members who have listened with equal patience to my anecdotes about Mary Walker and to my silence about when her full story might see the light of day. In North Carolina, David Paletz and Marianna Torgovnick, Steve Channing and Nancy Clapp-Channing, Peter Burian and Maura High, Walter Bennett and Bill Thorp and Stan Chojnacki allowed me to make Mary Walker a part of their lives as well as my own. Martin Groder and Jean McLendon, lifesavers both, helped me again and again to find my way when I'd lost it. In Colorado, Peter and Deedee Decker and John and Jill Stevenson have made the move to a new home a joyous one; William Adler took time from his writing on Joe Hill to help me with my work; Laura Dodson encouraged me to make the most of the place I'd moved to, and Wendell Pryor and Margaret Coval of Colorado Humanities proved her right. Mary Hicks and Brenda and Alec Nesbitt, cousins and also transplants from Back East, added to the welcome of the West and were the first to detect my use of a word they'd not heard before: "finish." My blood-kin back east includes a good many writers, whose counsel proved wise and helpful: Leah Nathans, Ilene Raymond, and Jeffrey Rush encouraged me to think boldly about the audience for the story. Benjamin Nathans and Nancy Silverman hosted me repeatedly on my forays to Philadelphia, a special treat because I got to hear about Ben's pathbreaking historical work. Ben followed in the footsteps of his parents, Daniel and Joanne

Nathans, who hosted and elevated me a generation before when I was a Hopkins graduate student. Most other members of my extended family showed their affection, and earned my gratitude, by ceasing to ask about "the book." The exception was my uncle Robert Nathans, who reminded me that "a project is a good thing to have" and saw disciplined persistence where I saw protracted delay.

New persons in my life moved Mary Walker's story closer to a conclusion. I found descendants of Mary Walker, who, though they didn't know her story, were eager to learn it. The warmth, openness, and accomplishments of Donna Dubé Hryb, Clare Dubé Kenney, Dorothy O'Shaughnessy, and their nieces and daughters, along with photographs and stories of Mary Walker's offspring, allowed me to imagine Mary Walker's joy at what her strivings had wrought. Louis Galambos advanced me nearer to closure when he introduced me to Madeleine B. Adams, a developmental editor, who read my first complete draft and advised me astutely where to cut. Paul and Mary Liz Stewart of Albany, founders of the Underground Railroad History Project of the Capital Region, invited me to give a talk at its 2007 conference, where I had the good fortune to meet Fergus Bordewich. His subsequent criticism of early chapters sent me back to the archives and produced a better book. My Duke history colleague Claudia Koonz never read a word I wrote about Mary Walker, but she did me the great favor years ago of introducing me to editor Joyce Seltzer of Harvard University Press, who asked crucial questions about what this story had to say to a wider audience. I didn't have good answers then, but the questions stayed with me, and I hoped I'd answered them when I finally sent her a completed manuscript. She found two splendid readers, and they and she made excellent editorial suggestions, for which I am deeply grateful. Jeannette Estruth handled my many procedural questions with speed, skill, and good humor, making the whole process a pleasure. She urged me to seek out Philip Schwartzberg of Meridian Mapping to prepare the maps for the book, which he did beautifully. Shannon

Martin-Roebuck magically reformatted fonts and endnotes so that everything came out right. Maria Ascher—meticulous in her scrutiny and pitch-perfect in her suggestions—was a splendid copyeditor.

Those who traveled with me the longest somehow kept faith that I would complete this odyssey. My daughter Heather Nathans and son Stephen Nathans-Kelly pegged me early and got me right when as children they gave me a poster which read, "Relax? Don't tell me to relax. It's only my tension that's holding me together." Their laughter, creativity as writers and editors, gifts for nurturing others, and fulfillment in wonderful families of their own have modeled what matters most. Loving and beloved by friends and family on two continents, my sister and brother-in-law, Judy and Arnold Carmel, have enriched my life—and my understanding of life—with their joy, depth, devotion, and resilience. Cherished friends William and Lorna Chafe have been comrades at Duke, neighbors in Chapel Hill, hosts in Maine, visitors in Venice, and sources of wisdom, affection, and camaraderie for forty years. Bill read the earliest drafts of my writing on Mary Walker, deployed his genius as editor and writer to separate the dross from the gold, and from the first has understood and shared my passion for her story. As much as anyone, he helped to bring this book to fruition.

Judith White has lived with Mary Walker and her story as long as I have. Early on, a friend took Judith aside and alerted her that for historians, "Where there's life, there's research." My wonderful Judith has ever since taken my disappearances—sometimes physical, sometimes mental—in stride. "He's in the archives." When words finally came, Judith read every sentence of the manuscript, and at least as many more that wound up on the cutting-room floor. Her sensibility, her judgment and human understanding, and her passion for justice infuse every page and my very being. *To Free a Family* is as much her book as mine. Judith's vision and love have brought us to this happy hour, and have brought me joy beyond measure. Indebted as I am to so many, I am grateful above all for our journey together.

Index